DRIVING BACK THE NAZIS

DRIVING BACK THE NAZIS

THE ALLIED LIBERATION OF WESTERN EUROPE, AUTUMN 1944

MARTIN KING

This edition published in 2021 by Arcturus Publishing Limited
26/27 Bickels Yard, 151–153 Bermondsey Street,
London SE1 3HA

AD007756UK

Printed in the UK

And let us not grow weary of doing good, for in due season we will reap, if we do not give up.

Galatians 6:9

CONTENTS

PREFACE 9

INTRODUCTION 11

CHAPTER ONE
ONE SEMINAL SEPTEMBER 13

CHAPTER TWO
OCCUPATION AND LIBERATION................................ 23

CHAPTER THREE
AFTER PARIS.. 39

CHAPTER FOUR
WHOSE SIDE WERE YOU ON?................................... 53

CHAPTER FIVE
TOUCHING THE REICH.. 73

CHAPTER SIX
THE BRIDGES... 85

CHAPTER SEVEN
LUXEMBOURG IS HAUNTED 109

CHAPTER EIGHT
AACHEN HAS FALLEN... 117

CHAPTER NINE
MEANWHILE AT FORTRESS METZ............................ 139

CHAPTER TEN
IF YOU GO DOWN TO THE WOODS...........................147

CHAPTER ELEVEN
A PATH TO THE SEA.. 175

CHAPTER TWELVE
FIGHTING FOR YOUR COUNTRY 193

CHAPTER THIRTEEN
ACCORDING TO MY INFORMATION 203

CHAPTER FOURTEEN
WHAT MAY COME.. 211

CHAPTER FIFTEEN
DOWN TIME 227

CHAPTER SIXTEEN
THOSE WE KNEW.. 243

NOTES AND REFERENCES.......................................247

INDEX.. 251

PICTURE CREDITS.. 256

PREFACE

FOR MANY EUROPEANS, THE MONTHS of September, October and November 1944 were a time of liberation and jubilation, but it was simultaneously a time of anarchy and retribution for others. Historians often neglect what transpired between the close of the Normandy campaign and the start of the Battle of the Bulge, but it would define the eventual duration and direction of World War II in the European Theatre. In many respects those three seminal months marked the lowest ebb in Allied fortunes since D-Day.

Eisenhower's decision to attack everywhere at once wasn't proving particularly advantageous, and for the time being only served to show precisely why the war would most definitely not be over by Christmas. Nevertheless, the generals at SHAEF (Supreme Headquarters Allied Expeditionary Force, Eisenhower's command centre) initially concurred that victory was in sight, and there was a pervasive, almost palpable feeling disseminating throughout the ranks of 'we've got them on the run'. As enemy resistance declined and Allied momentum increased, it appeared that parts of Europe were finally beginning to emerge from four long years of punitive Nazi subjugation.

Despite having sustained more damage than originally anticipated, the Allied armies began to race across France toward the Belgian and Luxembourg borders after D-Day. Enthused by recent successes, General George S. Patton's Third Army had stretched its supply lines to breaking point. Looming confrontation and a disturbing lack of cohesion at SHAEF had resulted in widespread confusion and almost insurmountable logistical problems. That initial tidal wave of triumphalist euphoria quickly dissipated during the autumn fighting, as did confidence in Allied military acumen.

As swarming olive drab and khaki Allied columns spread their tentacles and bonhomie into French towns and villages, most of those being liberated were irrepressibly ecstatic. They shed tears of happiness, lined the streets with bunting, waved flags and cheered heartily. The all-conquering heroes were welcomed with '*Vive les Allies*', hugs, kisses and copious bottles of booze. For some it was a great time to be alive, a great time to live in the moment. The excitement was all-consuming, the victors had finally arrived, to hell with the evil Nazis; now was the time to dispel the past and absorb the heady, celebratory atmosphere. Well, it was for most, but there were marked exceptions.

If you or your family had actively, or even passively, collaborated with the Nazis things were about to turn very ugly indeed. If you didn't escape before the Allies arrived, the glorious liberation had the potential to devolve into castigatory retribution. And what about the defeated German soldiers? A vanquished grey-green mass of dejected, weather-beaten faces both young and old, laboriously marching and traipsing forward in ragged uniforms with expressionless eyes glazed in fixed stares, barely acknowledging the taunts and insults from passing Allied vehicles, or the spitting and punching of recently emboldened civilians. There was absolutely no pity for the seemingly endless procession as it moved toward a very uncertain future. The general consensus was that the Nazis were vanquished. The media was unambiguous. These insidious sentinels that had inflicted years of misery and terror on Europe neither merited nor deserved compassion. They were the epitome of evil, and for the moment at least good had triumphed.

While the Allies advanced, suffering prisoners in Nazi labour and concentration camps had other pressing concerns. Would they even survive the liberation? Then there were the thousands of captives languishing in the Stalags. What would become of them?

For many it was a time of great uncertainty. The liberation would mean vastly different things to different people. In this volume I will attempt to encapsulate and relate the experiences of some of those who were there at the time, based on one-to-one interviews with the main protagonists and previously unpublished accounts.

INTRODUCTION

THESE HUMAN STORIES APTLY DEMONSTRATE what it was really like to be in Europe during that tumultuous autumn of 1944. These are not the inane ramblings of generals harrumphing through self-aggrandizing autobiographies. These are real people who were emotionally engaged, who experienced the ultimate polemics of hope and despair, love and loathing, and some of the accounts are derived from immediate family members, most of whom are now sadly deceased.

The word 'liberation' is derived from the Latin word *liberates*, which means, 'to set free'. This equally infers 'to free an occupied territory from the enemy', but the Allies demonstrated that the word 'liberation' had many connotations. It's too easy to employ the passionate approach when describing the events of World War II. It is equally difficult to make sense of those who remained morally equivocal when confronted with the shocking realities of precisely what subscribing to Nazi ideology entailed. Decades after the fact, owing to the unprecedented situational and emotional extremes experienced by the protagonists, the subject of World War II remains influential to this day.

This is the history of a certain time during World War II, when the world was recovering from a massive nervous breakdown, and remedial therapies may have been available but were not always correctly applied. The cure for those long years of occupation didn't always alleviate the condition or the symptoms, because for some the affliction was irrevocable, and for some it was terminal.

CHAPTER ONE

ONE SEMINAL SEPTEMBER

IN 1944, AS DECIDUOUS TREES began to erupt in glorious shades of gold and scarlet and the sun cast long shadows, from the Pacific to the Atlantic and from the Baltic to the Mediterranean and beyond the war was still reaping a lethal harvest of fear and destruction. Was it possible, or even remotely conceivable, that Axis hegemony was finally beginning to crumble and dissipate? It was indeed, but not before the world had reluctantly been compelled to confront a fundamental reality. What the Western press had described as 'inhuman behaviour' was in fact very human; the basest manifestation of the true soul of humanity, and this war had proved beyond any reasonable doubt that people, normal, average people were indeed capable of enacting deeds of petrifying evil. But now the Allies had gained the upper hand. There were clear indications that this ostensibly indestructible veil of hate and subjugation, which had devastated so many lives, was finally beginning to lift. It would all depend on that one tumultuous season of mists and mellow fruitfulness, a time that would pivot precariously between decision and indecision, action and inertia, and ultimately determine the eventual outcome of the war in Europe.

The pervading opinion among the Allied armies in September 1944 was that after four arduous years, final victory over Nazi Germany was now within reach. On 1 September 1944 the Canadian First Army captured Dieppe, the French port that had been the site of the abortive commando raid in 1942, and were hammering a path along the northern French coast toward Belgium. A few days later the British Second Army had captured Brussels, while the US First Army entered the Belgian town of Tournai.

There were changes afoot. Freshly appointed German commander of the western theatre (*Oberbefehlshaber West*), Field Marshal Gerd von Rundstedt, who had a habit of falling out of favour with Adolf Hitler, had replaced Walter Model. The new appointment would do little to prevent or stem the Allied tsunami currently heading from the east and west toward the German heartland.

In late August the US First Army chief of intelligence magnanimously declared, 'it is unlikely that organized German resistance would continue beyond December 1st, 1944'. There were, however, some who didn't agree with his optimistic prediction. Patton's Third Army intelligence officer Colonel Oscar W. Koch remained convinced that the German army was just 'playing for time' and preparing for a 'last-ditch struggle in the field at all costs'. Ever hungry for battle, General Patton echoed his opinion: 'There are still six million krauts that can pick up a rifle. They're not done yet.' SHAEF could justifiably have been accused of over-confidence, brushing aside Patton and Koch's warnings, but it would soon transpire that it was indeed making far too many assumptions. Victory was not a foregone conclusion and the German army was not a spent force. British Prime Minister Winston Churchill suffered no such triumphalist delusions. He didn't believe for a moment that victory over the Third Reich was imminent. 'If you're going through hell,' he said, 'keep going. Success is not final, failure is not fatal: it is the courage to continue that counts.' All well and good, but knowing precisely how to continue was correspondingly important.

As the Allies haggled and argued about the next moves, the Third Reich rigidly prepared to contest the Allied advance and, under the direction of the Todt Organization, the German military's engineering and construction arm, 200,000 forced labourers were set to work around the clock fortifying the Siegfried Line.

Elsewhere in the world the tide was unquestionably turning in favour of the Allies. In Italy, Axis forces were in full retreat by September 1944 and the Todt Organization was hard at work yet again, herding approximately 15,000 Italian farmers and workers into labour camps where they were forced to dig antitank ditches, gun emplacements and machine gun and rifle pits for an intended 'Gothic Line' (*Goten Stellung*). As the Allied armies circumnavigated Rome and approached northern Italy they encountered stiff resistance, which was in part due to enemy efforts to complete defences before falling back to the mountains. Meanwhile, Italian Fascists continued the war against the Allies while maintaining their alliance with the Germans, participating in deportations and executing suspected partisans.

As German defences in Italy collapsed and the Allies advanced northward, Italian Communists of the partisan leadership decided to execute Mussolini. It took a few months, but they finally got their man as he attempted to cross the Italian–Austrian frontier disguised as a German soldier in a convoy of trucks retreating toward Innsbruck. Together with his mistress, Claretta Petacci, Mussolini was killed on 28 April 1945, their broken bodies publicly hung upside down in Milan's Piazzale Loreto.

TROUBLE ON THE EASTERN FRONT

While the Allies were advancing across Western Europe, on the Eastern Front the Red Army was moving obdurately toward the German border, where fighting continued to be an erosive, no-holds-barred slogging match, which the German forces, defending a 2,250 km (1,400 mile) front against an army of 2.4 million could not possibly hope to sustain.

After achieving victories in Belorussia and western Ukraine, Stalin, the eternal opportunist, had been informed that most of the German army's armoured units had abandoned Axis ally Romania, or were in the process of leaving the region. On the basis of this information and on the advice of his generals he determined that the time was ripe for a fresh offensive. On 20 August the *Stavka* (the Red Army's high command) launched the Iasi–Kishinev Offensive, which was designed to envelop and annihilate all remaining German and Romanian forces. It would inevitably succeed in all its objectives. The other focus for Red Army operations during the autumn of 1944 was centred on the Baltic region.

Casualties incurred by these armies in the east made the western theatre pale by comparison. The Russians were conceding roughly 20 casualties for every German killed, and despite this disproportionate balance and glaring lack of any significant military strategy except force of numbers, the Red Army was maintaining the momentum. Naturally, Stalin wanted all the credit. He was in essence little more than a semi-literate thug, a murdering paranoid despot with no military acumen whatsoever.

The Red Army was comprised of men and women who had survived two decades of turmoil at the hands of a Soviet state that had inflicted collectivization and purges against both the peasantry and the military, leading to millions of deaths and deportations. Every soldier had to comply with Stalin's Order No. 227 'Not a step back!', and blocking units were assigned to guard the rear and kill anyone who lagged behind or attempted to escape the battlefield. But while some Allied commanders still had faith in these dubious allies, others justifiably regarded 'Uncle Joe' Stalin with deep suspicion.

Despite repeated offensives Hitler had failed thus far to decisively defeat the Red Army and his policy of *Lebensraum* ('room to live') in the east had been an unmitigated disaster. The Nazi programme of eradicating Jewish populations and removing indigenous peoples from German-occupied territories and German-speaking areas such as Sudetenland in Czechoslovakia and Silesia in Poland had proved incredibly detrimental to agricultural communities there. The farmers had not benefitted in the slightest from this intended Nazi 'master and servant' pseudo-feudality. Moreover, they would become victims of terrible retribution when the Red Army arrived.

Frau Reitner was a German-speaking farmer's daughter. 'After the Nazis had been, there was nobody left to work my father's fields,' she remembered. 'We always harvested but in time there was hardly anyone left and in some cases whole crops were left to rot. Then the Russians came. I can't, don't want to remember how many times I was raped. Those fucking animals raped everyone in the house. When they were finished with me they started on my mother, and then my 88-year-old grandmother and my 6-year-old sister. I even saw them fucking sheep and cows, they were worse than animals, because at least stupid animals only mate with their own species.

'They murdered my whole family using farm shovels, the whole courtyard was covered in their blood and brains, but I escaped and managed to reach Prague. I spoke quite good Czech back then and managed to pass myself off as a former partisan. Sometime later I moved to Döbeln in Saxony and began a new life, but I will never forgive those Russian bastards. When I travelled from Prague to Döbeln I remember seeing whole former German-speaking communities reduced to ashes. Half incinerated, mutilated bodies that could have been men or women it was difficult to say, they were just hanging from trees. Just left there to decompose and stink, and this time this wasn't the work of the Russians, it was the Czechs that did this, but what had the Germans done?'

Later on, Frau Reitner overheard young German soldiers talking in a café in Döbeln about the depravity they had witnessed while serving on the Eastern Front. One soldier laughingly said, 'Once we caught this female partisan who had been charging around in the neighbourhood. First we smacked her in the tits with a stick and then we beat her bare ass with a bayonet. Then we all fucked her, before we threw her outside and shot at her. While she was lying there on her back, we threw grenades at her. Every time one of them landed near her body, she screamed. Eventually one just blew her head clean off. The body was lying there jerking just like a chicken.' At this point Frau Reitner was beginning to retch. She abruptly got to her feet and gave the German soldiers a long, cold stare before turning to the group and saying, 'Well maybe we're getting what we deserve.' Then, wiping tears from her eyes with a table napkin, she stormed out.

World War II witnessed some terrible punitive acts against civilians, which were not entirely the preserve of the Axis forces. German civilians suffered greatly from the devastating sorties conducted by Allied air power. By autumn 1944 many German cities and towns had already been decimated. On 27 August 1944, the RAF resumed daylight bombing raids over Germany, commencing with an attack on the Homberg Fischer-Tropsch plant in Hamburg.

More than 50 per cent of all active Bomber Command crews became casualties during World War II. They suffered an extremely high death rate, and it's estimated that out of 125,000 active aircrew, 55,573 were killed while a further 8,403 were wounded in action and 9,838 became prisoners of war. There were not many dissenters among the Allied aircrews, but those who refused to fly had their records ominously marked with the letters LMF ('Low Moral Fibre'). Consequently, these unfortunate individuals would be stripped of rank and allocated to the most menial and distasteful tasks. As with the land-based forces, little or no consideration was given to the psychological consequences of enduring sustained combat.

THE NORMANDY CAMPAIGN

During the preceding months in Normandy in 1944, the days had been long and daylight had come early. By late July almost every morning would be greeted by hesitant rays of light, which often revealed a horizon punctuated by vertical columns of acrid black smoke that on closer inspection became a harvest of smouldering, incinerated hulks of tanks, half-tracks and various other skeletal vestiges of German army vehicles. On some tanks, the charred remnants of former occupants jutted at oblique angles from half open turrets, or lay in close proximity, contorted in grotesque ballet positions. This was the seasonal harvest of Allied Typhoons and P-47s demonstrating the effectiveness of air superiority.

The attack on Caen had been supported by 7,700 tons of bombs. In the days leading up to the D-Day landings and the subsequent campaign to liberate Normandy the Allies dropped over 590,000 tons of bombs on France, which was equal to almost half the amount of bombs dropped on Germany during the course of the entire war. Air Chief Marshal Leigh-Mallory in his survey of the major air attacks in Normandy declared that the bombing offensive at Caen was 'the heaviest and most concentrated air attack in support of ground troops ever attempted'. It cost the lives of around 3.5 per cent of the city's population. It was a pyrrhic victory because the once beautiful city had been completely reduced to rubble and ash.

The ruins of Caen after the bombings.

As the Normandy campaign began to wind down the Germans were haemorrhaging men and machines, and two of their armies had, according to the Allies, been practically annihilated. In the ensuing rapid advance that followed, the Allies moved faster than the Germans had done when they stormed across France in the opposite direction four years earlier.

Normandy left the German soldiers demoralized and deflated, but contrary to popular myth they were not completely destroyed. Their commanders had indeed demonstrated rigidly predictable intransigence, which had rendered their forces in the field vulnerable and ill supplied, but despite this they still managed to extricate 240,000 men and get them back across the River Seine. One young German soldier who experienced the campaign first-hand was Rudolf von Ribbentrop, of 1st SS-Panzer Division *Leibstandarte SS Adolf Hitler* and 12th SS-Panzer Division *Hitlerjugend*. The son of Hitler's foreign minister Joachim von Ribbentrop, he was suffused with Nazi hubris. He later remembered: 'One day I was in a VW *Kubelwagen* exploring the area where we had our accommodation on the Seine estuary between Bernay and Honfleur, when we were attacked by a low-flying Allied warplane. It was already night-time when I heard its engine. Suddenly machine-gun bullets began impacting the road in front of us. I put my head between my knees in customary fashion to avoid being hit when I felt a powerful blow between my shoulder blades that temporarily paralyzed me. Bleeding profusely, I instructed the driver to get me to a nearby ditch as quickly as he could because the Allied warplane was swooping low over us repeatedly firing his machine guns. I wasn't in shock though, but this was probably because I had already been wounded several times before.

'The driver somehow managed to drag my limp body to the ditch. As the driver applied a useless wound compress I began to lose consciousness and felt as if this was the one that would kill me. Then I decided that it wasn't my time to die yet. I felt a tingling sensation in my toes that reassured me that my spinal cord was undamaged. Within a few short moments my ability to move was restored sufficiently enough that I could raise myself out of the ditch and return to the car. I was taken to the Air Force hospital at Bernay where the surgeon told me that if the machine-gun bullet had hit one millimetre to the left it would have completely severed the carotid artery and shattered my spine. If that had been the case, he added, then an operation would have been a waste of time. I had trained my company from day one and I wanted to remain with them more than anything. Many of us had been hardened on the Eastern Front. The 12th SS-Panzer Division fought hard against the Allies and held them back for weeks.'[1]

The campaign in Normandy had been a hard fought, uncompromising feat of attrition that had cost the lives of 36,976 Allied ground forces and a further 16,714 from the Allied air forces. The German tally had been even more devastating; spurred by the debilitating expedients of fanaticism, fear of retribution and bitter hatred, losses incurred by their divisions in Normandy actually exceeded those of the Eastern Front at the time. The exact number isn't known but it is estimated that they sustained around 200,000 casualties. Armies in the 77-day Normandy campaign suffered front-line casualties that were proportionally worse than some of the major battles that had been fought along the Western Front during World War I.

CHAPTER TWO

OCCUPATION AND LIBERATION

PRESIDENT FRANKLIN D. ROOSEVELT SAID of Allied troops, 'they fight not for the lust of conquest. They fight to end conquest.'[2] By August 1944 the Allies had landed over two million men on the Normandy beaches, and on 25 August the Germans surrendered Paris.

Fighting through the Normandy hedgerows, the field-to-field fighting the troops called '*le bocage*' had been unrelenting and deeply demoralizing for both Allied and Axis forces. The incessant August rain inundated fields and having to endure almost constant combat took its toll on all combatants. In June alone, in Normandy, 10,000 Allied soldiers were incapacitated and treated for battle fatigue. Between June and November 1944 this constituted a staggering 26 per cent of Allied casualties. Psychiatric services were available and deployed to Normandy to maximize the return of front-line troops to duty, but some Allied military commanders doubted their efficacy and believed that their mere presence undermined the fighting spirit of their men. It is estimated that around 36 per cent of admissions returned to combatant duty, while 53 per cent were evacuated to the UK. The scale of psychiatric casualties incurred by the Allies during the Normandy campaign was unprecedented.

Then there was the serious collateral damage inflicted on French towns such as St. Lo and Caen that had been almost 95 per cent destroyed. During the campaign they were reduced to skeletal remnants of their former glory and the inhabitants had suffered depravations that defied description. Around 35,000 French civilians had died as a result of the campaign. For many this was most definitely not the liberation that they had envisioned. One French farmer remarked, 'in the morning we were liberated and sometimes by the evening we were occupied again, sometimes this went on for days. Most of my livestock was bloated and rotting in the pastures where they had been decimated by bombs and bullets. When I close my eyes I still recall that insidious stench.' The subsequent interaction between Allied forces and French inhabitants often resulted in a visceral distrust that didn't particularly advance the Allied cause.

The difference in perspective between town and city was quite stark, particularly in Paris where some French citizens were characteristically nonplussed and almost completely oblivious to the liberation. In one Paris suburb at 122 Rue de Provence, the former home of Napoleon's favourite cavalryman, the flamboyant Joachim Murat, Fabienne Jamet, an eminent Paris Madame who ran the famous Le One-Two-Two club, didn't even raise her pencilled eyebrows when she heard about the Allied successes. She just took a long draw on her Gitane and, through the exhaled smoke, quipped, 'German, French, British, Americans, they all have le zizi, no difference'.

Fabienne was a dusky, young, no-nonsense businesswoman who didn't particularly care where the money came from as long as the clients were entertained. Her slim, somewhat angular visage could have been painted by Toulouse-Lautrec. She always had a smoking cigarette protruding from the side of her heavily rouged mouth, and a champagne glass was never far from her grasp. She hadn't experienced any particular problems during the occupation: 'I remember those SS men all in black, so young, so beautiful, so intelligent, they spoke perfect French and English, and were all well-educated. They all adored my ladies and me and appreciated the delicacies I provided.'[3]

A few short weeks before the Allied landings, Jamet had entertained the corpulent, debauched Luftwaffe commander Hermann Goering,

The building that housed the infamous 'One-Two-Two' club in Paris.
The brothel was run by Fabienne and Marcel Jamet, who were happy to take
money from both sides.

who, being a fervent lover of the high life, never failed to visit the brothel when he was in Paris. German officers and French collaborators had all frequented the place and business was booming. During its 20-year history the *One-Two-Two* hosted Belgium's King Leopold III and the British statesman Randolph Churchill, along with such illustrious names as Charlie Chaplin, Cary Grant, Humphrey Bogart, Mae West and Marlene Dietrich. The *One-Two-Two* claimed that it could cater for every fantasy and perversion. During a post-war interview Madame Jamet said that she had despised the Germans, but later amended her stance and contradicted this by saying that she had experienced some of the best nights of her life during the occupation.

Fabienne did not suspect that her life would be any different after the liberation, and even though suspicions had been aroused about the level of her involvement with the Nazis she continued to do a roaring trade with the Allies while successfully managing to deflect attention. But the damage had been done and in 1946 the *One-Two-Two* was forced to close its doors for good. It was just one of a number of famous French brothels that fell victim to an uncharacteristic paroxysm of public morality organized by the newly appointed French authorities. This wasn't received well by the French public. Fabienne Jamet and her infamous *femmes de la nuit* were later heavily criticized and accused of having collaborated with both the Germans and the Vichy regime, but no charges were ever brought against them. Fabienne died penniless but remained defiant to the end. 'Fuck the liberation,' she said, 'if the Germans had won the war, the brothels would still be open.'

If Hitler had his way Paris would have been decimated, especially if the German governor of Paris, General Dietrich von Choltitz, had acted on the orders he received from the Führer on 24 August 1944: 'Paris must not fall into the hands of the enemy or only as a pile of rubble'.[4] The day that Choltitz surrendered to the French it is alleged that Hitler phoned him, incandescent with rage, and asked whether Paris was burning? For many, Dietrich von Choltitz is regarded as the 'saviour' of Paris. Thanks to his refusal to execute Hitler's orders the city was left relatively intact, its citizens waiting eagerly for their liberators to arrive.

General von Choltitz was described by some as the 'Saviour of Paris' for disobeying Hitler's order to destroy the city. He later claimed that he did this because he loved the city and had decided that Hitler was no longer compos mentis.

THE FRUITS OF LIBERATION

At the SHAEF HQ, Supreme Allied Commander Dwight D. Eisenhower had other pressing problems to attend to. Some of his subordinates disagreed vociferously on the way forward. General Bernard Law Montgomery, awaiting his promotion to field marshal, was an implacable advocate of the 'concentrated, single axis thrust on a narrow front', but his popularity rating among some American generals wasn't particularly favourable at that time. Some had openly accused him of having been over-cautious and timid, particularly regarding the capture of Caen, which was originally earmarked as a D-Day objective, but which eventually took almost seven punishing weeks to liberate.

Due to the ferocity of the fighting, Caen was largely destroyed. But even though Operation Goodwood had failed to achieve its initial objective, it engaged significant German forces to allow the launch and execution of Operation Cobra, the next phase of the Normandy offensive. It didn't, however, leave the population of Caen feeling particularly 'liberated'. In his defence, Montgomery maintained that the reason he had made slow progress during the Normandy campaign was his reluctance to squander lives the same way that his commanders had done in World War I. He was a capable strategist, but on most occasions he insisted on numerical superiority before engaging the enemy. The most notable occasion when he did not adopt this policy was, notoriously, Operation Market Garden (see chapter six).

Eisenhower was indisputably an expert communicator and consummate diplomat, but his occasionally incoherent style of command often incited criticism and even derision from his detractors. But his method was undeniably all-inclusive because his 'broad front' strategy required American, British, Canadian and Polish forces to advance in concert, to avoid creating any dangerous salients. In the process, these forces would simultaneously apply constant pressure to the German front lines. Well, that was the theory at least.

After the closing of the Argentan-Falaise Gap, Monty began developing plans for his advance to the Rhine. He maintained, to the point of distraction, that the best way forward was a strong, concentrated narrow advance using coordinated armour and infantry while providing appropriate flank protection. Once Monty had determined that this was a winning plan he could not be persuaded otherwise, a factor which inevitably caused friction between him and Eisenhower.

While Monty wasn't entirely flavour of the month in some departments, the leader of the Free French forces, General De Gaulle, didn't fare particularly well in the popularity stakes at SHAEF either. Nevertheless, Allied command had complied with his request to lead the French 2nd Division into Paris on point. Churchill made his feelings abundantly clear when he dispatched an apologetic cable to Montgomery one week after the 1944 D-Day landings concerning the impending visit by the French leader. 'I must inflict upon you a visit from General de Gaulle tomorrow. This is, on no account, to be a burden to you in any duties you have to discharge.'5

The heavy fighting in Normandy had given the Allied soldiers all the reasons they needed to cut loose. They were the victors, the current *force majeure*, and now, in time honoured fashion, they demanded the spoils of war. Paris soon became the target of unfettered lust, as testosterone-fuelled young men charged around the city's narrow streets, started drunken brawls and stormed into the brothels. One GI recalled, 'I popped my cherry in Paris along with two other buddies. Those French ladies didn't smell too great, but they looked absolutely gorgeous so we didn't care. We were fucking everything that moved, and in between we was brawling and drinking like there was no tomorrow. Man oh man, I think that it was possibly the best time of my life.'6 *Life* magazine, one of the prominent publications of the day, even went as far as printing that 'France is a tremendous brothel inhabited by 40,000,000 hedonists who spend all their time eating, drinking and making love.'

Naturally, there were also some chaste souls among the Allies, such as those who hailed from devoutly religious communities and who had no intention of compromising their honour with foreign Jezebels. According to one British veteran, 'You could easily recognize the Bible thumpers. While the rest of us were fucking like rabbits, they walked bent double most of the time to conceal their erections.'

But while many Allied troops enjoyed the sexual opportunities that liberation offered, not all of the women they encountered were willing partners. 'With the Germans, the men had to camouflage themselves; when the Americans arrived, we had to camouflage the women,' ran one ironic joke circulating in Normandy not long after D-Day. Rape and sexual assault did take place, as did other crimes. After the liberation of Bayeux and Caen British troops ignored the Hague Conventions and rampantly indulged in small-scale plunder. They were also accused of looting, rape, and prisoner execution.

One report estimates that between 1942 and 1945 American GIs in Western Europe raped around 14,000 women. In France alone, 152 American soldiers were accused of committing rape and 29 were hanged. The true number of attacks is surely higher, the morality of the day and France's conservative Catholic culture ensuring that many assaults went unreported by victims keen to avoid the social stigma attributed to rape. The situation may not have been helped by the US media especially portraying the war to conscripted soldiers as an opportunity for them to meet attractive French women and, to put it crudely, get laid.

Of course, the vast majority of Allied troops happily abided by the laws and culture of the countries they liberated and treated the women in particular with courtesy and respect. Liberated populations, in return, appreciated the heroism and sacrifice of the Allied soldiers who had come to their aid. But it's also the case that the behaviour of the small minority of Allied soldiers who indulged in rape, theft, beatings, murders or other crimes undoubtedly contributed to the marked ambiguity and deep ambivalence felt by some of the liberated. It should be remembered that the abolition of Nazi rule was not a completely joyful experience for everyone the Allies encountered on their journey from the beaches of Normandy to the boulevards of Paris.

Yet, for the majority of people, the Allies when they came were welcomed with open arms. 'The men, women, and children surged against our trucks on all sides, making a four-mile travel to our positions hours long,' wrote Carlton Stauffer, Company G, 2nd Battalion, 12th Infantry Regiment, 4th Infantry Division, recalling his entry into Paris. 'There were cries of, "*Merci! Merci!* S'ank you, No Boche in the building! S'ank you *Vive la Amerique!*" Hands reached out just to touch the hands of an American soldier. Babies were held up to be kissed. Young girls were everywhere, hugging and kissing the GIs. Old French men saluted. Young men vigorously shook hands and patted the GIs on the back.

'Finally, late in the afternoon, we took up our position for the night. I had the good fortune to be assigned to a chemistry building at a university on the west side of the Seine. We walked into the building and were met by a lady who was determined to make life just wonderful for us.

'Captain Tallie Crocker, who was our company commander at that time, spread his blanket on the floor. Being an infantryman, he was always getting as close to the ground as possible. The lady immediately took his blankets and spread them out on a sort of couch that looked like an operating table. It was easier to let her do that than to explain anything. When she left, Captain Crocker put his blanket on the floor. At about this same time, we all heard loud machine-gun fire outside the building. I went out with the captain to see what all of the noise was about. In the courtyard outside our building, a Frenchman of their 2nd Armoured Division was in a jeep with a .50 caliber machine gun firing away at the corner of a building in the court. Captain Crocker approached the Frenchman and asked what he was firing at. The Frenchman told him there were Boche in the building. Captain Crocker tried to convince him there were no Boche in the building. There was no meeting of minds. Finally, the Captain took the Frenchman on a Boche hunt through the building, proving once and for all—no Boche. Situation resolved! The girls came back to the jeep and we did more wild riding around Paris. When we went back into the chemistry building, Captain Crocker's blanket was back on the table. That evening some of us went for a walk around town, hitting a few places for a celebration drink. The best part of the evening was to return to our chemistry building with its indoor plumbing.

'At 09:30 hours on the morning of August 26, Father Fries, our regimental chaplain, held Mass in the famous Notre Dame Cathedral, the first mass said after the liberation. Joe Dailey and I attended. It was a strange sight for Notre Dame to see us doughboys sitting at Mass with our rifles and battle gear. The problem confronting us at Mass and afterwards was to keep civilians away. There were ten civilians to one soldier. At last, the company commanders told the crowds that the soldiers were tired and needed sleep. Immediately, and with apologies, the civilians left our positions. That evening we were abruptly brought back to the reality of war when, at 23:30 hours, the Germans launched a heavy aerial bombing. Fortunately, all we encountered were the flashes

American troops parade in front of the Arc de Triomphe in front of crowds of French civilians after the Liberation of Paris.

and the booms, someone else at the distant part of Paris took it all.'[7]

John MacVane, a young correspondent working for NBC radio, vividly recalled 'the bells of Notre Dame were ringing out as they had done for hundreds of years, but this time it was to announce the joyous liberation of the city'. Two men wearing Paris firemen uniforms approached MacVane. They asked him if he was American and MacVane confirmed that he was before asking why they were dressed as firemen. He discovered that they had been in Paris for over a month. They were a pilot and a navigator from the 8th Air Force that had been shot down. The French underground had taken care of them and they had experienced a hell of a time at night, fighting fires and killing Germans when they got the chance. When they left, the pilot said that neither of them spoke a word of French, adding, 'Hell of a thing to have to go back to flying after all this fun.'

Not all USAAF crew were as fortunate. Captain Clark R. Amen, 367th Squadron, 306th Bomb Group, 8th Air Force, like many other Allied airmen ended his war in captivity. 'By the time we flew our 5th mission I was one of the most experienced navigators in the squadron. On this mission I had the opportunity to fly in the lead plane of our group, which was leading the wing of 60 planes on a raid to Wilhelmshaven. This plane had all kinds of extra navigation equipment. The other navigator (they used 2 in lead planes) was on his 24th mission and was so nervous he was airsick the whole trip.

'Since I got shot down on the next mission, I never did find out if he made it through his 25th and got to go back to the States. On the raid that we were shot down we bombed the railroad terminal at Frankfurt. Our plane got shot up pretty good going in over the Ruhr Valley and then again over the target. On our way back to England we were struggling along on two engines when we took a direct hit in one of the good engines. This was as [we] were nearing the coast of Belgium. The explosion made a large hole in the nose of the plane and flying metal hit me in the head and leg, making me eligible for a purple heart. There was a fire in the wing so the pilot gave the order to bail out. I had some problems as my parachute was in a corner out of the way so I had to get it, put it on and get to the escape hatch. It was panic time but I did everything in record time. The escape hatch didn't fall free as it was supposed to after pulling the release so I jumped on it and went out of the plane along with the door. When I tried to pull the ripcord on the parachute nothing happened. I was pulling on the carrying handle. In the rush the parachute had been clamped on upside down. The ripcord was finally located and pulled with my left hand, the chute opened, and suddenly everything seemed temporarily peaceful and quiet.

'Because of my problems in locating the ripcord, there was a delay in opening my chute and I did not land in the same neighbourhood as the rest of the crew. When I hit the ground there was a brisk wind and the parachute acted as a sail, dragging me through the mud of a ploughed field. A group of German soldiers ran alongside pointing a Luger pistol at my head, commanding me to raise my hands. This did not help to get things under control since raising my hands allowed the parachute to keep dragging me through the mud. Finally, one of the soldiers jumped in front of the chute and collapsed it. The German with the gun then said, "For you the war is over" in very clear English. I had landed near where the Germans were building launching pads for buzz bombs. This was the reason I had such a large reception party.'

THE ADVANCE INTO BELGIUM

American troops crossed into Belgium on 2 September at 11.07 am. This reconnaissance group were the first Allied soldiers to actually begin the liberation of another European country. As soon as they made contact with members of the local population in the village of Plomion, a peaceful farming community of 800 inhabitants 13 km (8 miles) southwest of the border, they began hearing stories of atrocities. According to some locals 14 men, ranging in age from 70 to 17, were massacred there. One news correspondent claimed to have seen the bodies and questioned surviving inhabitants, and though some details were vague he had no doubt that a crime had been committed. It transpired that a German force of around 60 SS men had been quartered in Plomion for six days before the recon group arrived.

The cause of the attack was uncertain. Some villagers claimed that a member of the French resistance had fired a shot from a window into a truck and killed a German. Others denied this but they were unanimous when describing how enraged Germans leaped from their trucks and randomly rounded up 14 men. Entering one house, they took a 70-year-old grandfather, his three sons and one grandson, aged 18, while they were eating supper together.

Accompanied by the derisive screams and wails from local women, the Germans dragged their captives along the street and into a meadow at the edge of the town. Then they rounded up nine more men, kicking and beating them into the meadow and dispatching all 14 of their victims with automatic weapons. As the remaining villagers fled into the surrounding fields the SS lobbed incendiary grenades into their houses. It was only the arrival of the US recon team that caused the SS to mount their vehicles and get away. The bodies of the 14 dead men were recovered the following morning. Some had been savagely mutilated beyond recognition. Is this the shape of things to come, the villagers asked? They weren't even close.

THE LAST DAYS IN OCCUPIED ANTWERP

In 1944 François Schaerlaecken was 11 years old. He lived in a small village in the Dutch Flemish-speaking province of Antwerp and he remembered the occupation very well indeed. 'Life with the Germans wasn't all that bad from what I recall. The guards from the Nazi Labour camp Breendonck used to visit my mother's café quite regularly and they were always polite and smartly dressed.' His opinions would change in time but as the Allies closed on the province of Antwerp there remained a notable affinity between the German occupying forces and some Dutch-speaking Belgians. German attitudes toward them were on the whole quite amicable right up until their hasty departure.

A few days previously in Antwerp the German authorities began arresting all suspected Allied sympathizers and establishing command bunkers in the city's parks. They also started laying mines in the River Scheldt. Some months before the Allied advance all radios had been confiscated and barbed wire blockades set up on the city's approach roads. By 1 September 1944, almost all senior German officials had gone back east, leaving the city's defence in the hands of *Platzkommandant* (regional commander) Count Stolberg, who was enthusiastically assisted by Flemish-Nazi soldiers. As the Allies drew closer the feverish atmosphere reached a hiatus. In a hurry to evacuate Antwerp, a small exodus of German soldiers and collaborators forcibly requisitioned all possible means of vehicular transportation and destroyed as many potentially incriminating documents as possible. On 3 September the duplicitous mayor, Leo Delwaide, went to ground along with his fellow council members.

In the Netherlands, on 4 September the final transport of 2,087 Dutch Jews left the internment camp at Westerbork for Auschwitz. Anne Frank and her family were on that train. She and her family would spend tortuous days in a cattle car with around 40 other men, women, the elderly and children. They were hermetically sealed, with hardly any air, no lights, no water and no food, suffocating in a tiny space saturated with pungent human detritus and ravaged by thirst. The following day became known as 'Mad Tuesday' when, in a fit of guilt and cowardice, 65,000 Dutch Nazi collaborators absconded and wormed their way to Germany.

CHAPTER THREE

AFTER PARIS

THE LIBERATION OF PARIS HAD done little to assuage Eisenhower's four-packs-a-day smoking habit. In the autumn of 1944 he was a slave to the nicotine, at odds with Monty, and deep in the process of working out a plan to move forward.

Pugnacious General Patton and his Third Army had arrived in Normandy in late July. After Operation Cobra they raced across France looking for the next battle. They wouldn't have to look far and would soon encounter a determined German defence at Metz that would severely test the general's ability. To some, Patton had earned the ignominious title 'the best traffic cop in the history of the US Army'. This opinion didn't extend to the armoured units, who held an entirely different view. They were quick to point out his tactical innovations and intuitive feel for the battlefield. There's no doubt that Patton understood tanks. In the final months of World War I he had driven a French FT Renault, and among his adversaries there was only one German general who possessed the same depth of knowledge of armoured warfare: Heinz Guderian.

There is no doubt, however, that Patton's taste for publicity and his one-sided rivalry with Montgomery often exacerbated Eisenhower's difficulties. Patton was no easy subordinate. When he was assigned as commander of the Third Army, charged with leading the push out from Normandy towards Paris, Eisenhower's old West Point buddy, the high-ranking general Omar Bradley, complained that Patton should never have been allowed anywhere near such a key military position. Nevertheless, like Montgomery, Patton inspired tremendous loyalty from most of the soldiers under his command.

On 23 August 1944 Eisenhower tentatively approved Monty's single thrust concept, allowing him to conduct the main effort while Bradley supported the attack with all nine divisions of his First Army. At the same time, Patton's Third Army would advance along the southern axis, but would not have priority on supplies.

The speed with which the Allied advance had developed from the beginning of August to the middle of September caused many senior officers and staff planners to become mired in complacency, convinced that the German army was on the verge of collapse. It was widely acknowledged at SHAEF that there had been an attempted coup against Hitler in July 1944, and this, combined with rapid retreats, the apparently uncoordinated shuffling of German units, little or no air cover from the Luftwaffe and the scarcity of fuel for Panzers were all regarded as strong evidence that the Germans were a spent force.

THE COSTS OF COLLABORATION

Meanwhile, on the streets of Paris and other French towns, the days and weeks following liberation incited heinous acts of revenge and retribution among the civilians. Mob rule supervened, as many French women accused of *collaboration horizontale* were frogmarched into public places and humiliated by having their heads shaved. The practice of head shaving became ubiquitous during the liberation rapture in France in 1944. During the ensuing months the trend would extend to Belgium, Luxembourg and the Netherlands. Men who collaborated were often summarily executed without trial.

It didn't appear to matter that many of the head-shaving perpetrators were not and had never been members of the resistance. It was suspected that several of them had been petty collaborators themselves, who sought to divert attention from their own lack of resistance credentials. A strong element of exhibitionism and vicarious eroticism evolved among the *tondeurs* ('head-shavers') and their enthusiastic crowd, even though the punishment in fact symbolized if anything the de-sexualization of their victims. It was a public display to appease the masses not unlike those gatherings before the guillotine 150 years earlier.

The initial moral outrage quickly subsided when French authorities began to examine individual cases. Although some accusations were defensible, many weren't. A significant number of the head-shaving victims were simply prostitutes who had plied their trade with Germans as well as Frenchmen. Others were just errant teenagers who had associated with German soldiers in an attempt to remedy that centuries' old teenage affliction, boredom. There were also a number of cases that involved single female schoolteachers who unwittingly became the focus of mob derision, because German soldiers had forcibly requisitioned their homes for the duration. Many victims were just desperate young mothers, whose husbands were in German prisoner of war camps. During the war, they often had no means of support, and their only hope of obtaining food for themselves and their children was to reluctantly begin a liaison with a German soldier.

The lines were often blurred and it was conveniently forgotten that most French citizens placed their emphasis on self-preservation above any national considerations. It later emerged that the majority of the French population had collaborated with the Nazi authorities in one form or another.

OPERATION DRAGOON

The Allies had now entered Belgium and were heading north. Monty's Twenty-First Army Group, supported by the First Army, was given the objective of taking Antwerp, to open up the harbour to Allied shipping. This was a purely logistical consideration. Taking this important harbour town, the second largest in Europe, would relieve pressure on the Normandy harbours and shorten the supply lines for the eventual Allied push north and east. Taking it intact wouldn't be easy but initial British reconnaissance units dispatched north met with little or no enemy resistance.

A few weeks earlier, on 15 August 1944, Operation Dragoon had been launched when the US Seventh Army and the French First Army landed

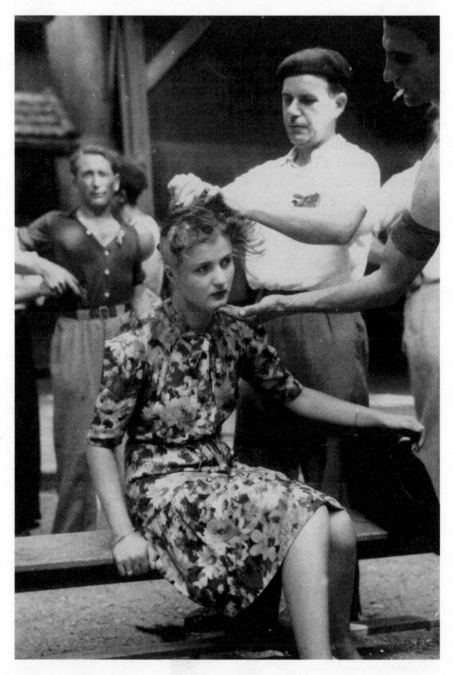

Shaving the heads of suspected and confirmed collaborators was common practice in all countries that were liberated in autumn 1944.

on the sun-baked French Riviera, where there were only four poorly equipped German divisions to oppose them. While US forces drove to the Alps to take Grenoble, the French took Marseille on 23 August and then advanced eastward up the Rhône Valley through France, to be re-joined by the Americans north of Lyon early in September. Both armies then moved swiftly north-eastward into Alsace, where Patton had established Third Army positions. Owing to the enthusiastic welcome the Allies received from the French and the initially weak German resistance to the invasion, the operation became known somewhat derisively as the Champagne Campaign.

'So in August it was like 15th or 17th, I don't exactly remember the date, we made the invasion. I was on the second wave. The front wave was the little boats that they took us in on. The first wave hit the beach first, and then three minutes later, I hit the beach. And then we went through a seawall. Got through that. There were only a few Germans there,' said Richard Francis Adams, C Company, 1st Battalion, 157th Regiment, US 45th Division. 'Then we marched up, I didn't get wounded. Of all that period, three or four months I spent on Anzio, the metal flew around me, but nothing hit me. I landed in the middle of August, and on September 25th, in the morning, about 10:00 one morning, I was lying behind this tree, and a shell hit the tree, and the tree blew all apart.

'All I got was shrapnel in my hand. I got six or seven pieces of shrapnel in my hand. So the sergeant said, "You'd better go back," because it was bleeding a little bit. I would say profusely. It was bleeding in one spot here, and one spot here was pretty bloody. The medic said "Well, there's a couple pieces in here ought to be taken out." And he said, "I really don't know how to do that." So I walked back and caught a Jeep, and it took me back to the aid station. And there, they took a couple pieces of shrapnel out of my hand. And they sifted sulpha powder in it. And they wrapped me up and said, "Well, your trigger finger can still work. Hit the ration truck. You can go back up tonight." So the night of September the 25th, I went back up. We fought continuously every day. And one time in October, I got two days off to go back and get a shower and some clean clothes. This wasn't like any other branch of the service. You didn't know when you was going to get a new change of underwear or anything.'

Things began to change at Montelimar. From 24–27 August, the US 36th Division faced concerted resistance from the Germans. Early on 25 August, the 3rd Infantry Division advanced northward to Avignon. This was when the Germans really began to feel the pressure being applied from behind. The 3rd Division advance would gather momentum by the time it reached the Vosges area of France. This would be where reputations would be written in blood and legends would be made, and where a young sergeant called Audie Murphy from Texas would become the most highly decorated US soldier of World War II. At the end of August, the US Seventh Army had completed the liberation of southern France. The next step was to link up with Patton's Third Army.

Winston Churchill had vociferously opposed Operation Dragoon and some high-ranking ETO (European Theatre of Operations) staff supported his stance. When plans for Operation Dragoon (originally called Operation Anvil) were tabled and approved, Churchill immediately dispatched a letter to Roosevelt to express his concerns about dividing the Mediterranean forces. He wrote: 'The splitting up of the campaign in the Mediterranean into two operations, neither of which can do anything decisive, is, in my humble and respectful opinion, the first major strategic and political error, for which we two have to be responsible.' However, it's unquestionable that Churchill's personal political and empirical considerations, rather than strategic ones, motivated his disapproval of Operation Dragoon. Moreover, at that juncture he was already becoming suspicious of Stalin's ambitions, and he hoped that a successful invasion of Italy would keep Eastern Europe out of Soviet control.

President Roosevelt, ever the pragmatist but also suffering from ill health, attempted to placate Churchill's reservations: 'I honestly believe that God will be with us as he was in OVERLORD and in Italy and in North Africa. I always think of my early Geometry: "A straight line is the shortest distance between two points".'[8]

ENTRY INTO BRUSSELS

On 2 September 1944 an armoured division of the British Guards Regiment was near Douai in northern France when Lieutenant General Brian Horrocks, commander of the 30th British Army Corps, gave the order to his men to 'go and liberate the city of Brussels'. By the evening

Audie Leon Murphy was one of the most decorated American combat soldiers of World War II. He received every military combat award for valour available from the US Army, as well as French and Belgian awards for heroism.

of 3 September, after covering over 160 km (100 miles) in one day, Horrocks and his men arrived at the city limits. The following morning, the German authorities responded by setting the Palace of Justice on fire in an attempt to destroy any potentially incriminating documents.

One day later, the 1st Infantry Brigade of the Free Belgian Armed Forces, accompanied by British soldiers, made a glorious entrance into Brussels. Within a few short hours Brussels had been transformed from a city under Nazi occupation to a liberated city of delirious pandemonium. The scenes were reminiscent of the many other cities that had already been liberated, as a multitudinous crowd of shouting, laughing, cheering people jammed the streets, waving flags and throwing kisses and flowers at the column of British army vehicles driving through the centre. The city's streets were bedecked with Belgian, American, British and French flags and street vendors, mysteriously stocked with *boutonnieres* of the Allies' colours, did a roaring trade. At every street junction and places where the vehicles slowed down people clambered aboard, enthusiastically kissing their liberators and shaking hands.

'I recall September 2, it was a strange day. On the one hand, everything was so quiet,' said Albert Guyaux, who was a nine-year-old French-speaking Belgian. At the time of the liberation he was living in Ixelles, a suburb of Brussels. 'I saw the Germans hurrying to leave the city. They used every possible kind of transport including horses and carts. There were no more patrols; some people already hung out their Belgian flags. But the Gestapo was still there, and even on that day resistance fighters were executed. The Allies were still more than 100 kilometres from Brussels, and we didn't know what was going to happen. There was a train carrying wounded German soldiers scheduled to return to Germany under the supervision of the Red Cross, but that train never left. It got looted.'[9]

On 7 September an official meeting was convened at Brussels Town Hall between the Mayor of Brussels and General Montgomery. A few days later Belgium's government in exile returned to Brussels to restore legal authority, which, in classic Belgian fashion, would take a while. Belgium's was the first normally constituted government to return to the Continent from London. It was immediately confronted by a technical difficulty. Belgium had been a constitutional monarchy since its conception in 1831, but in September 1944 there was no king in residence. The nominal ruler, King Leopold III, was in Germany. Moreover, the controversy over his surrender in the field at the head of his army in preference to exile remained extremely contentious. His reign would end in ignominy, when, a few years later, he would become the first Belgian monarch to forcibly abdicate his throne in favour of his son, Baudouin.

The Dutch monarch Queen Wilhelmina had no such problems. The House of Orange retained both the respect and affection of most of their subjects. Her son Prince Bernhard acted as her official representative when he joined the British armies heading towards the Netherlands.

THE NEW FRENCH REGIME

Liberation had arrived sooner for French towns and cities in the north of the country. After the Allied landing in Provence on 15 August 1944, it gathered momentum in the south. The Allied forces, assisted by the French resistance, gradually forced the Germans to retreat. The Provisional Government of the French Republic (GPRF) was officially installed on 3 June 1944, and it eventually replaced Marshal Pétain's obsequious, Nazi-sympathizing Vichy regime – the supposedly independent government that ostensibly controlled much of central and southern France after Germany occupied the north of the country.

Following the retreat from Dunkirk in 1940 there had been growing anti-British sentiment in France. The general consensus was that the British had failed the French miserably, when in fact nothing could have been further from the truth. The commander of the French forces at Dunkirk had been Maurice Gamelin, the incompetent, egregious Marshal of France. Despite having better tanks than the Germans, Gamelin, an old-school strategic thinker, did not know how to deploy them effectively and had little knowledge of more modern military concepts such as mobile war, favouring the outdated tactics of the Great War such as static defence, and infantry-led attacks. It was his intransigent attitude exacerbated by innovative German strategic thinking that ultimately cost the Allies dearly and culminated in the fall of France. Unbowed by this failure, Gamelin went on to become one of Marshal Pétain and the Vichy regime's most vociferous supporters.

But Gamelin was not alone. It's an irrefutable fact that, shortly after Dunkirk, Marshal Pétain and Vichy France enjoyed the support of most of the French population. Although this support declined over the course of the war, it's still the case that, statistically, more Frenchmen took up arms for the Axis than for the Allies during World War II.

The country's future leader, General Charles de Gaulle, had escaped France following the Nazi occupation and spent the rest of the war languishing in exile in London. In response, the Vichy government branded him a traitor and sentenced him to death *in absentia*. The Vichy government was not an out and out fascist regime and Pétain refuted the accusation that he was a puppet of the Nazis. He even tried to claim that his government was neutral, supporting neither side in the world conflict raging around him. 'We are not in the war,' he claimed, and even made desultory and unsuccessful attempts to establish contacts with both the Allies and, as the writing on the wall became clearer towards the end of the war, De Gaulle. But despite his protestations of independence, Pétain and his government almost always acted in the interests of France's German occupiers.

The Vichy government's main means of control was through its secret police service, the *Milice* (militia), which was created largely by the SS and which was tasked with carrying out the racist policies the Nazis expected of this faux France. Within six months of assuming office the Vichy regime had incarcerated around 60,000 non-French citizens in 30 camps. Pétain authorized and sanctioned an active campaign against the French resistance, and implemented numerous anti-Jewish laws, which resulted in the deportation of tens of thousands of Jews to the Nazi death camps. The paradox was that Hitler had little regard for Pétain or the Vichy regime, and often imposed indirect sanctions against his client state, such as maintaining an artificially high exchange rate for the Reichsmark against the French Franc.

By September 1944 Pétain, along with his most steadfast sycophants and Nazi sympathizers, had been forced into exile at Sigmaringen in southwest Germany, where he would remain a virtual prisoner of the Germans until the end of the war. Meanwhile, back in the state that Pétain had once ruled with so much public support, it seemed that every Frenchman and Frenchwoman was now claiming to have been an active

After France was defeated in June 1940, Pétain was appointed Prime Minister, after which time the Cabinet resolved to make peace with Germany. The entire government moved to the spa town of Vichy in central France.

and long-standing member of the resistance all along. This was in part because, along with Pétain and his supporters, most of the Germans in occupied France had also fled the country by the autumn of 1944. The departure of Pétain on 20 August, followed by the liberation of Paris five days later, effectively saw France returned to independence. The Americans wanted to put the country under military administration, but De Gaulle, as convincing as ever, managed to dissuade them from this course of action. The Allies officially and collectively recognized De Gaulle's provisional government on 23 October 1944, after which the country resumed its place in the Allied camp.

By this time, acts of retribution against Vichy and its supporters had already begun. On 18 September 1944, *The New York Times* published a two-page article accompanied by a photograph showing a baying crowd witnessing the public execution of former *Milice* men. During the summer and autumn of 1944 recently established French authorities executed nearly 10,000 suspected collaborators, sometimes without trial. On 15 August 1945 Pétain himself was tried and convicted for his collaboration with the Nazis. The 89-year-old was initially sentenced to death by firing squad, but De Gaulle intervened and commuted his sentence to life imprisonment. For the remaining years of his life Pétain was imprisoned, albeit in relative luxury, on the island of Île d'Yeu, off the Atlantic coast of France. He died on 23 July 1951, aged 95.

THE CHERBOURG BOTTLENECK

As the autumn of 1944 progressed German forces under the command of *Oberbefelshaber West* withdrew in disarray. The Allies pursued them closely, preventing the enemy from establishing a new front line that may have inhibited their advance. By the beginning of September most of France and Belgium had been liberated, following a spectacular advance that saw Allied forces move forward more than 320 km (200 miles) in a single week.

Yet despite the vast amount of territory the Allies had gained, the majority of the French ports in the English Channel remained in the hands of the German Fifteenth Army. This meant the Allies could only land their supplies at Cherbourg and on two temporary Mulberry Harbours off the Normandy beaches. Although air drops were a daily occurrence most supplies were still delivered by truck, the railway system having previously been destroyed by Allied air power and rendered useless. At such a distance from the front line and proceeding along congested roads through heavily bombed towns, not enough supplies could be produced to maintain the advance at its current pace.

At 2.50 pm on 7 September 1944, after a punishing 95 km (59 mile) route march, elements of the US 30th Infantry Division arrived at their assembly area near the famous battlefield of Waterloo. One young GI asked his commanding officer what was so special about Waterloo. The officer told him that the whole future of Europe had been decided by one magnificent battle in one day, to which the GI replied with a lazy southern drawl, 'Well boss, I guess they musta had better tanks than us.'

CHAPTER FOUR

WHOSE SIDE WERE YOU ON?

SEPTEMBER INEVITABLY BROUGHT AUTUMN RAINS. Most days were framed with heavy, dark blue-grey clouds that unleashed an almost incessant deluge soaking everything and everyone to the skin. For the poor footslogging Allied soldiers everything was damp, dank and rather miserable. This feeling didn't extend to the command though, who were still in a rather exuberant mood. Following the liberation of Paris, they were all liberally imbibed with heady elation. The mighty Red Army was sweeping into the Balkans and closing in on East Prussia and the British were racing across Belgium towards Holland. Patton's Third Army had already reached the River Moselle, and in the centre other American forces had crossed the Luxembourg border and would soon be in Germany.

Ernie Jelinek was with the 5th Armored Division, 10th Tank Battalion. Its M4 Sherman tanks were lightly armoured and were no match for heavy German tanks equipped with 88 mm guns. He said, 'My battalion entered the battle with 54 tanks but, in 5½ days, we were down to just five tanks.' Ernie ended up sleeping rough with his crew after various encounters with German Tiger and Panther tanks. 'We were sleeping in foxholes and anything we could find. The weather was cold and we were sleeping in sleeping bags. Then, I was 24 and an Army captain when I was involved in the liberation of Luxembourg from the Germans.'[10]

Ernie Jelinek helped liberate Luxembourg during World War II. He recalled: 'It was four years since they had their own rule. When they saw the American tanks rolling into the capital city, they were as happy as they could be. They were handing us bottles of wine as we were coming through town and some of them were holding American flags. It was just a grand finale. It was indescribable.

'Sixty years after the liberation, I was invited back to Luxembourg for the anniversary of the end of the Nazi occupation on Sept. 10, 1944. The nation of Luxembourg paid for my airfare and expenses for five days. A ceremony took place on a parade ground and there were half a dozen bands there. I spoke in front of about 5,000 people.'

TENSIONS AT HQ

Back at SHAEF HQ, Montgomery was becoming increasingly exasperated. He was compelled to cooperate with Eisenhower, even if he harboured some disdain for Ike's lack of battlefield experience. Ike often exclaimed, 'Damn it, Montgomery's the only man in either army I can't get along with.' Eisenhower wasn't entirely ignorant on the subject of strategy and tactics, and he found that continually having to deal with Monty's frequently patronizing, superior attitude tested his patience, to say the least. There's no doubt that Monty could be self-aggrandizing, intransigent and very opinionated. He was by nature a loner, not known for reserving his opinions, and although in most cases he was well liked by the troops, he didn't always endear himself to his peers and superiors.

While Monty headed north with his Twenty-First Army Group, Patton had commenced his assault on the city of Metz. But his supply problems were mounting. His vehicles were consuming an average of 1.6 million litres (350,000 gallons) of gasoline per day and the supply route was becoming desperately overextended.

By 11 September Allied troops had physically crossed the German border, which only served to strengthen the errant optimism at SHAEF. The 1st British Corps, Canadian First Army, was attacking the French port of Le Havre. The British Second Army had captured Antwerp with its extensive deep-water port facilities largely intact but which was, for the time being, unusable. The US First Army commanded by General Courtney Hodges had taken the Belgian city of Liege on the country's eastern border with Germany and the city of Luxembourg. Patton's Third Army was in northeastern France, consolidating positions along Moselle and establishing a viable bridgehead near the fortified Alsatian city of Metz.

Much has been made about the alleged rivalry between Monty and Patton, but the hard truth of the matter is that there was no rivalry between them. Rivalry is only possible between equals. Montgomery was so much higher up the food chain than Patton that he was largely oblivious of or disinterested in Patton's opinions. Nevertheless, 'Old Blood and Guts' Patton made no bones about the fact that he despised Monty with a passion, referring to him on one occasion as a 'tired little fart'. The one thing that they did share was an avid love of self-publicity, but even here Monty frequently outshone Patton, who wasn't always the darling of the media.

In the remaining Nazi-occupied areas, spurred on by Allied progress, European resistance movements were gathering momentum. One young Belgian girl codenamed 'Vera' joined a Belgian resistance movement, falsifying documents to disguise the fact she was only 15 years old. Before long she had become a seasoned resistance fighter who participated in destroying bridges, ambushing troops and repatriating Allied airmen. She even experienced direct combat, and helped destroy a railway station in Brussels when it was congested with German soldiers returning home for Christmas.

In the autumn of 1944 she was arrested while working as a courier and handed over to the Gestapo at whose hands she endured intense questioning and horrendous torture. She was left in her freezing cell in waist-high water for days on end, and even had her fingernails torn out with pliers. She was eventually transferred to a labour camp near the Dutch border in Germany and put to work in a factory making munitions. Starving and malnourished, she was shot in the arm while attempting to escape. German doctors treated her wound and she recovered sufficiently to make a second and successful escape attempt: while being transported from the munitions factory back to the camp she jumped from the back of the lorry and disappeared into the nearby woods. She evaded capture for almost six weeks, walking only at night and sleeping rough during the day. For sustenance she ate stolen raw eggs and vegetables. When she eventually reached the Netherlands she managed to contact the Dutch resistance, who aided her repatriation to Belgium, where her commander hid her while she recovered. She was so emaciated when she arrived home that her father decided to wait until her health had improved considerably before telling her mother that she was still alive.

Malnourishment due to the harsh conditions at the camp had caused all her teeth to fall out and her fingernails never grew back. When Belgium was liberated Vera climbed on to an Allied tank and directed the troops to their rendezvous. The tank was commanded by a Welsh Guards officer that she later married. This young girl was one of many who fought courageously in the Belgian resistance in World War II.

VEKEMANS' INITIATIVE

British progress towards Antwerp had been relatively straightforward. During their approach, on 3 September 1944, at 9 am, a Flemish-Belgian resistance operative and former soldier, Robert Vekemans, tuned in to the BBC. He had been an engineer in the Belgian army in 1940, and had endured a few months in captivity as a POW. He hadn't been a member of any particular resistance movement and enjoyed his full-time job working for the Antwerp Waterways department. Standing only 1.6 m (5ft 3in), he was myopic and wore thick-rimmed bifocals that accentuated his dark, narrow facial features. That morning he listened attentively as the broadcast announced that British troops had reached the city of Tournai in the south of Belgium. It was too late to contact the resistance so Vekemans decided to use his initiative. He noticed that the main bridges over the River Rupel in the direction of Antwerp were heavily defended by German troops and mines had been laid beneath them. He surmised that the best alternative road to Antwerp ran parallel to the Brussels–Charleroi canal. There was a bridge there in the village of Klein Willebroek that appeared to be undefended.

The following day Vekemans waited for the British army at the intersection of the main Brussels–Antwerp highway, a few miles south of the town of Boom. Early that morning he saw the leading Sherman tank of a British 3rd Battalion Royal Tank Regiment column arriving from the direction of Brussels. Vekemans broke his cover behind a nearby hedgerow and ran into the middle of the road, waving his arms frantically. The lead tanks probably assumed that Vekemans was just another enthusiastic admirer so they ignored him and drove on. But a Major Dunlop, who was in the fourth tank, raised his arm to draw the column to a creaking, shuddering halt. Vekemans garbled something and appeared incoherent at first, but the stoic major calmly lit a cigarette and smilingly passed it to him. Within a few moments Vekemans was able to relay his vital information. He was just in time, because at that moment Germans began to appear on the northern horizon about half a mile ahead. Dunlop immediately recalled the other tanks and approached his commanding officer, Colonel Silvertop. After digesting Vekemans' information, Silvertop gave permission to Dunlop to reconnoitre the route suggested by the informer. There was some initial suspicion, but the recce turned out to be good and Silvertop gave the go-ahead to change track. A cool, calm tank commander from the northeast of England who had fought across north Africa with Montgomery's Desert Rats, Silvertop had been awarded the Military Cross after sustaining injuries at the crucial battle of Medenine in Tunisia in March 1943.[11]

After the D-Day landings Silvertop participated in the July 1944 operation near Caen and was then in on the subsequent breakout and overnight advance to Amiens, catching the Germans by surprise at dawn and liberating the French city. Another rapid advance into Belgium took him to Antwerp, covering over 600 km (370 miles) in eight days. When the parachute landings failed at Arnhem, Silvertop was ordered to cross into the Netherlands and help relieve the trapped troops.

After the capture of the village of Sint Anthonis in the Netherlands province of North Brabant, Silvertop was standing beside his tanks and talking to some other officers. Suddenly, a soldier in a column of SS prisoners being walked through the streets threw a grenade that instantly killed David Silvertop and two of his colleagues.

Crossing the bridge suggested by Vekemans allowed a few British tanks and troops to outflank the German defenders who were waiting expectantly at the main bridge just a few hundred yards north. The Germans were completely taken by surprise and surrendered almost immediately. The British column then headed towards Antwerp roughly

Colonel David Silvertop, commander of the 3rd Tank Regiment, 20th King's Hussars, is a hero to the Flemish-Belgian people of Boom. He fought with Montgomery's Desert Rats. Courtesy of Boom Town Hall culture secretary Alex Ramael.

WHOSE SIDE WERE YOU ON?

13 km (8 miles) north. There are still some Flemish people living in the area that dispute Vekemans' story, and claim that he was not the first to make contact with the advancing British troops – even though the story was corroborated by both David Silvertop and Major Dunlop.

THE FLEMISH RESISTANCE

Although there were innumerable collaborators in the Antwerp province, there was also an active underground resistance. Enraged by certain Flemish parties in the municipal administration that openly collaborated with the Nazis, a young Flemish man named Marcel De Mol established the resistance group that became known as the 'Black Hand' (*Zwarte Hand*). Marcel wanted to expose and execute all collaborators. He also published pamphlets condemning members of the VNV (the *Vlaams Nationaal Verbond,* Flemish National Union, the leading collaborationist party in Flanders). Authoritarian by inclination, the party advocated the creation of a Greater Netherlands called *Dietsland,* which would effectively combine Flanders and the Netherlands.

One of the most incompetent and tragic Belgian resistance groups of World War II, De Mol's Black Hand, recruited members throughout Belgium's central Flanders region. Although its intentions were solid, the Black Hand's methods were often considerably less so. In some villages it defiantly chalked the 'V' for Victory sign on gable ends and encouraged the locals to identify VNV (*Vlaams Nationaal Verbond* – Flemish National Union) members. It attempted to establish contact with SOE (Social Operations Executive) in the United Kingdom via a secret channel with the purpose of forwarding information regarding German military activities. In one Flemish town that had a military airfield it blew up a kerosene boiler. On 21 July, the Belgian national holiday, Marcel De Mol repeatedly played the Belgian national anthem on a piano with great defiance. This was broadcast on the radio by the group's secret channel. The clandestine broadcast culminated with a vain rallying cry to the Belgian population to resist the German occupation. The fact that the transmitter probably didn't reach more than a few miles wasn't considered particularly detrimental to the cause.

Soon after, things began to go badly for the organization and what transpired was a comedy of errors of Shakespearian dimensions. A member of the Black Hand who wasn't renowned for his clear thinking had somewhat unwisely card indexed the names and addresses of all of the group's members. When he was captured, the Germans easily discovered the list, which resulted in the arrest of the entire organization. Almost all of the members ended up in concentration camps, where many succumbed to illness and torture. Twelve of the leaders of the Black Hand who were rounded up were executed by firing squad at a shooting range in the German town of Lingen. Marcel de Mol was among them. A courageous man indeed.

After liberating the bridges, the British tank column, supported by a brigade of infantry, advanced almost unimpeded to Antwerp's city park. At this juncture they met with some German resistance that took several hours to neutralize. By the evening a local resistance leader convinced the German commander General Stolberg to surrender. Antwerp was liberated! Stolberg demanded that he and his troops be treated as prisoners of war. He feared being handed over to the baying mob of Antwerp citizens who were out for blood. Among this mob were, presumably, many of the same citizens of the city who just a few years earlier had actively supported the Nazi occupiers and who had viciously attacked residents and property in the city's Jewish quarter, an event that became known as the Antwerp Pogrom. With the assistance of German forces the crowd, encouraged by Flemish Nationalists and Flemish SS, flagrantly looted the city's synagogues. Many Jewish-owned shops and businesses were incinerated. No individual was ever indicted for this crime.

After the city was liberated some of the captured German soldiers recognized and pointed out Flemish collaborators who were furtively attempting to switch sides and mix in among the mob. It later transpired that most of Antwerp's adults had collaborated with the Germans on some level or another during the occupation. But the recriminations would come later; the primary objective of freeing Antwerp in order to save its port from destruction had been achieved. Even so, this did not immediately solve the Allies' supply issues. The battle for the Scheldt estuary would continue for almost another two long, gruelling months. As long as the Scheldt estuary remained in enemy hands no ships could enter the city's harbour.

Antwerp was liberated on 4 September 1944. The capture of Antwerp was integral to the Allied plan but failing to clear the estuary of Nazis prevented Allied shipping getting through. The harbour wasn't fully operational until 28 November 1944.

George Schneider, 120th Regiment, 30th Infantry Division, wrote: 'There was very little resistance across the rest of Belgium as we advanced faster than the Germans realized. On the southern outskirts of Brussels in the town of La Hulpe we spent the night in a castle on the edge of town. Just as we had experienced in Gaurain, the civilian activity was fairly normal. A friend and I decided to explore the town in the early evening. We stopped off at the first bar we saw and had a drink with some of the locals. We then moved on and came across a hospital that we entered and found a large ward. We were invited to inspect the facilities and found a wounded German soldier the Belgians were treating. We gave him a few cigarettes and went back on the street. The next stop was to talk to a Belgian standing in front of his butcher shop. He invited us in for a drink, showed us his hiding place for his illegal radio, and made conversation. He invited us to return the next day for a steak dinner and we accepted. We didn't know where he planned to get the

Personal friend of the author, George Schneider, is still proud to wear his 'Old Hickory' 30th US Infantry Division badge.

steak since there wasn't a piece of meat in the shop. Many of the German artillery were horse drawn and when these animals were killed the civilians would carve a nice piece of meat out of the horse's rump. I suspect our steak was to be a horse. We pulled out early the next morning and we never got our horse steak!'[12]

THE BREENDONCK PRISON CAMP

Some weeks before the British liberated Antwerp, in the Flemish-Belgian village of Willebroek young François Schaerlaecken was sat quietly reading a comic book in the corner of his mother's café when he heard the familiar sound of heavy boots outside. He looked up as a tall, impeccably attired German officer entered with his dog and two soldiers. The officer, Phillip Schmitt, was a wiry man of about 1.82 m (6 ft). He had thick eyebrows and a sallow complexion, which in François' opinion gave the man an uncanny resemblance to Boris Karloff. Schmitt winked at the boy as he settled at the bar and delved into his tunic pocket. Then he produced a bar of chocolate and waved it ever so slightly. 'Have you been a good boy?' he asked François, who answered the question by nodding vigorously. The officer then turned to François' mother behind the bar, her thin lips piercing a forced smile on her round face above an ample double chin. These Germans were regular visitors to the café and she was on first name terms with most of them. Wearing a flowered pinafore around her bulbous waist, and with her short hair pinned back, she didn't particularly like these impromptu visits from the Germans. They disturbed her regular customers. But, in contrast to the regulars, the Germans always paid before they left and always brought nice things to eat.

François later heard how the local Nazi authorities had on one occasion staged a mock execution down beside the canal. They had rounded up a group of 20 men of all ages and lined them up in front of a firing squad. He didn't know the reason for this action, but he knew that his grandfather was one of the unfortunates randomly chosen that fateful Sunday afternoon. The Germans cocked their rifles and aimed at the row of terrified men. The officer in charge checked his watch, removed his Luger from its holster and shouted 'fire'. The shots rang out but all the Mauser rifles were loaded with blanks. Suddenly, one of the prisoners

Breendonck commander SS Sturmbannführer *Phillip Schmitt playing with his German shepherd dog, 1943.*

creased and tumbled forward on to his knees. It was François' grandfather. The shock had caused a massive coronary that terminated his life as effectively as any bullet would have done.

In the café Commandant Schmitt asked, 'Have you earned this bar of chocolate?' before playfully concealing the item behind his back. 'Heil Hitler' shouted François before standing bolt upright and giving the Nazi salute, followed by a military one just to make sure he'd covered all the bases. 'Well in that case,' laughed the officer as he handed the chocolate over to the boy. It was a deep, throaty, closed-mouth laugh that didn't register in the officer's eyes, or change the position of those thick, bushy arched eyebrows. '*Danke schon,*' said François as he tore away the wrapper, breaking off a sizeable block that he ravenously stuffed into his mouth before returning to his comic book. The commandant was always friendly, even if he did work at the local *arbeitslager* (prison camp).

François later recalled a peculiar culinary event that occurred about a week after he'd seen Schmitt for the last time. He was standing outside the café when he heard the sound of an approaching engine. It didn't sound like anything he'd ever heard before. He narrowed his eyes and looked up the road to see an approaching Mk II British Universal Carrier. It was carrying five or six soldiers and it drew to a halt right in front of him. All the soldiers looked cheerful and they were all smoking cigarettes. One of them said something to François but he didn't understand the language. The soldier handed him what looked like a sandwich. The angular square bread was cut about an inch thick and there was some kind of strange meat in it that François had never tasted before. It wasn't bad but he would have preferred a bar of chocolate. Corned beef hadn't been seen in Belgium since World War I.

François only discovered later what some of his mother's regular Nazi customers had done. One of them, Antwerp-born Fernand Wyss, had failed as an amateur boxer and had quite a serious reputation. One former prisoner of Breendonck remembered how 'Wyss impatiently tapped the side of his polished jackboot with the handle of his horsewhip. He was proud of his SS uniform, and the unbridled power it gave him over us. His whole demeanour exuded that arrogance, that seething hatred and contempt reminiscent of many SS camp guards as he strutted among us inciting unrestrained dread and terror.'

Another former prisoner recalled of the camp guard how 'Wyss screamed at one of the prisoners, "Who am I?" The man froze and a pool of urine welled at his bare feet. "You dirty, stinking, disgusting bastard. I am Napoleon," scowled Wyss. "You didn't know I was Napoleon, did you?" The terrified prisoner just looked forward, his eyes fixed in an expressionless gaze. "Away with you, get on with your work." The prisoner turned around and began to move indolently back toward the rock pile he was clearing with his fellow prisoners. "I won't ask you again vile bastard who am I," sneered Wyss as he raised his horsewhip, and before the prisoner had time to respond he landed a powerful blow between the man's shoulder blades, causing him to slump to the ground. Then, unable to supress his volcanic temper, red-faced Wyss erupted in a fit of rage, dropped his horsewhip and aimed repeated withering punches at the man's head and shoulders until the unfortunate recipient of this fury stopped moving. "Now look what you have made Napoleon do." Still fuming, Wyss rose to his feet and attempted to regain his composure as he wiped the blood from his hands on the dead prisoner's ragged clothes.'

This was just another day, no different from any other in the Breendonck *arbeitslager*, where Flemish SS guards were mainly responsible for committing most of the atrocities against their own people. After his shift Fernand Wyss usually called into the café where François lived for a few glasses of beer before returning home to his loving wife. They had heard the news that the Allies were approaching and were preparing to do something about it.

One former inmate of Breendonck, Petrus Joannes de Schutter, made a statement to the Belgian police in the autumn of 1944. He said, 'Of the Flemish SS men Wyss was the worst of all, followed by De Bodt. They went about always whip in hand, and struck in all circumstances and without the slightest reason. Wyss was particularly barbarous; I have seen him strike a man on top of the head so that the blood flowed. I know that he sometimes threw a shovel into the water from the fort and made a Jew go in and fetch the shovel out. Many were said to have been drowned in this way. It was generally thought in the fort that Wyss was certainly responsible for the deaths of about 20 people. It was also said that Wyss and De Bodt had a bet as to who should be the first to

*Fernand Wyss (left) earned a fearsome reputation as a guard at the infamous Fort Breendonck labour camp (*arbeitslager*).*

kill a Jew.'[13] Both men took extreme pleasure in inflicting the most terrible punishments on the prisoners. They frequently tortured and murdered at will for their own entertainment. On one occasion they beat a man to death simply for a bet. The prize was a bottle of cognac.

Commandant Schmitt and his staff had already fled before the British arrived on the scene, and the former inmates had been transferred to the Dutch camp Vught a few days earlier. Some terrible atrocities had occurred at Breendonck. It had been used as both a labour camp for political prisoners and a transit camp for Jews. Detainees were frequently tortured, executed and worked to death in the most horrific circumstances. The main perpetrators of these crimes had been Flemish SS guards such as Wyss. Commandant Phillip Schmitt, along with a number of the guards, was later apprehended and tried in a Belgian court. Most of them were sentenced to death.

When the British liberated Breendonck the Belgian government was still in transition, and what followed was a tirade of recrimination and accusation. With no assertive legal authorities to control the situation anarchy soon ensued. The facility was used again as a prison camp by the Belgian resistance. Between 4 September and 11 October 1944, around 750 suspected collaborators and remaining Germans were incarcerated there without trial. These prisoners were at the total mercy of a vindictive and hateful resistance, which proved to be just as evil and despotic as the former guards. They manically beat, raped and humiliated their prisoners with total impunity. These atrocities were discreetly hidden from the public for decades.

Before World War I Breendonck was used as one of Antwerp's ring of fortifications. When the Germans occupied the fort on 20 September 1940, newly appointed *Sturmbannführer* Phillip Schmitt introduced his first victims to the camp. The fort simultaneously became a transit camp for Jews and the local hub of the *Sicherheitspolizei-Sicherheitsdienst* (SIPO/SD), the German political police.

During the first year of occupation, Jews constituted around half of the camp's population, the other half being mainly political prisoners. From 1942 a new transit camp was established for the Jews at an old army barracks in the nearby Flemish-Belgian city of Mechelen. Jews were assembled there before being transported east to their deaths in Nazi

Some prisoners at the Fort of Breendonck, which was used as a Nazi labour camp in World War II.

extermination camps. On 22 September 1941, the first convoy of Belgian political prisoners was transferred from Breendonck to the Neuengamme concentration camp close to Hamburg. On average, prisoners were incarcerated for three months at Breendonck before being deported to concentration camps in Germany, Austria and Poland.

The regime established in Breendonck operated along the same lines as any other official concentration camp. The guards used systematic inhumane torture, deprivation and murder to wear down the prisoners. Initially, the camp was garrisoned by a few German SS troops and a detachment of *Wehrmacht*. From September 1941 Flemish-Belgian camp guards actively assisted them.

One particularly sadistic monster who moved into Breendonck after the liberation was a French-speaking Belgian by the name of Pharailde Jeanne Hoekmans, also known as 'Auntie Jeanne'. Two days after the

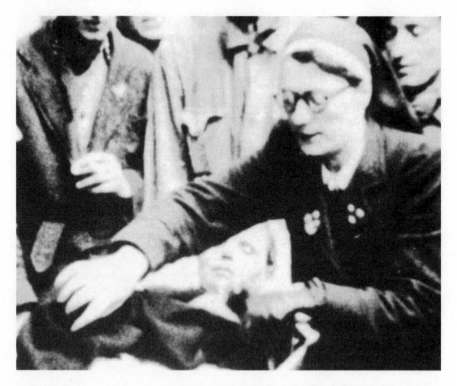

Jeanne Hoekmans shaving the head of a collaborator, who she later forced to lie in a coffin. Hoekmans was later found guilty of collaboration herself and sentenced to three years in prison.

liberation, she appeared at Breendonck, surrounded by a host of obsequious young so-called former resistance operatives. Dressed in a nurse's Red Cross uniform embellished with three captain's stars and armed with a pistol, she set to work. She was immediately put in charge of all the female prisoners. From that point on she could flagrantly inflict her sado-masochistic perversions on them. These women first had their heads shaved. Then they were stripped naked and their breasts, genitals and buttocks were daubed with swastikas. Then they were slowly paraded before the baying mobs that gathered daily at Breendonck to enjoy the spectacle. Many of these victims were systematically raped and sexually abused.

At the request of this maniacally disturbed pseudo-nurse, everything was carefully filmed. One particular woman who was subjected to many degrading sexual assaults was later discovered to be innocent, a case of mistaken identity. A former prisoner of Breendonck visited the place during the liberation and remarked that, 'They were treating the collaborators just like the Nazis treated us. It made me very sad to see this.' In a startling revelation it was later revealed that Hoekmans had actually been an active black marketeer who had frequently collaborated with the Germans during the occupation. She was eventually tried, found guilty on all counts and sentenced to three and a half years in prison. It was far less than she deserved.

On 11 October 1944, British soldiers, having promptly reclaimed the fort, heard about these shocking excesses. The remaining prisoners were transferred to Kazerne Dossin in Mechelen, which had been used as a transit camp for Jews during the occupation. On 29 October 1944, a Belgian newspaper reported that a group of around 300 former Breendonck prisoners had gathered in an old music hall in Brussels to form a philanthropic survivors' society designed to care for the families of those who had died in the camp. Discussing their plans for the society in hushed, reverential tones, there was little talk of retribution. One speaker raised the painful subject of Belgian collaborators, arguing that 'the conscience of Belgium is stained. In the name of the martyrs of Breendonck, if Belgium is to escape becoming once again a victim of Germany, we must act against those threatening our country. It is necessary to punish not just to make an example, but also simply to purge the nation. It is one sure condition for the security, peace and prosperity of Belgium.' Members of the new society then laid a wreath at the tomb of the Unknown Soldier.[14]

At the end of December 1944, due to the lack of space in Belgian prisons, Breendonck was used again as an internment camp. Around 800 prisoners were brought there under the supervision of the Belgian National Guard and the Belgian army. In 1947 the Fort of Breendonck was inaugurated as a national monument and it is still open to the public today.

REACHING GERMANY

On 2 September 1944 a meeting took place at Versailles between generals Eisenhower, Bradley, Patton and Hodges, along with 9th Air Force commander Hoyt Vandenberg. Eisenhower told them that the First Army was moving to the north to support the Twenty-First Army Group. He then outlined his plans for the near future, saying that once the First Army had completed its move to the north, both the First and Third Armies would remain 'generally static' until sufficient supplies could be accumulated to allow the Army Group to move toward the Siegfried Line and seize it. Following the meeting, Bradley briefly outlined a plan that designated Patton to lead the future axis of advance calculated to cross the Rhine in the Mannheim-Frankfurt sector, once permission was received to advance again. Patton immediately phoned his headquarters to give instructions that the Third Army was not to advance beyond the Meuse bridge line. He did, however, authorize recon elements to probe forward, just in case.

At the end of August 1944, when the German First Army made its ignominious retreat across that same River Meuse, it consisted of only nine battalions of infantry, two batteries of field guns, ten tanks, three flak batteries, and ten 7.5 mm guns. Although it did not pose a particularly formidable threat at the time, the Allies' stagnation in early September allowed that force to refit and rebuild its strength substantially.

On 9 September 1944 the first American troops crossed into Luxembourg from France and Belgium, facing little enemy resistance and liberating the entire country within five days. In the sleepy little village of Pétange villagers came out to greet Lt. Hyman Josefson of 85th Cav Recon. Squadron, 5th Armored Division. He was driving his M-8 Greyhound scout car along the cobbled road and waving at the locals when a German antitank shell impacted his vehicle and killed him immediately. He was the first American soldier to be killed on Luxembourg soil and his death is commemorated annually to this day.

Two days later, an American patrol from the US 5th Infantry Division crossed the border into Nazi Germany. But, for all its symbolism, this was a strangely anti-climactic event. This is where the difference between liberation and occupation would be emphasized. Most Germans didn't want liberating. What they wanted was decent food and an end to the seemingly relentless Allied bombing.

CHAPTER FIVE

TOUCHING THE REICH

WHILE MONTY PUSHED NORTH TOWARDS the Dutch border, US troops set about liberating the French-speaking south of Belgium. On 9 September 1944 a group of resistance operatives contacted American troops and provided them with all the necessary information they needed to move on Bastogne. On the same date, the US 9th Infantry Division crossed the River Meuse at Dinant in Belgium. What then transpired was a brief period of apparent inertia while commanders at SHAEF argued on the way forward.

Fierce competition existed between Allied infantry and armoured divisions. During planning for offensives there were often heated exchanges between armoured and infantry commanders as to who should be on point during an attack. 'Hey, why is it always our asses on the line?' asked an irate 'tankie' from the 4th Armored. 'You sons of bitches can run under trees or get behind rocks when the heinies are letting us have it, while we're stuck in them goddam metal coffins.'

The biggest fear among the Allied tankies was a condition that became known as 'Tigerphobia'. This came to light during the Normandy campaign. The condition, if it was a condition at all, was exacerbated by Panzer aces such as German tank commander Michael Wittmann, who eliminated an entire British armoured battle group with his lone Tiger I near Villers-Bocage just seven days after D-Day. It was alleged at the time that Tigerphobia was prolific among Allied tank crews in Shermans and Churchills, and that they would go to great lengths to avoid combat with German Panzers. To some observers, the Tiger tanks may have appeared invincible, but this wasn't the case. One crew in an M8 Greyhound disabled a Tiger I with just three rounds from its meagre 37 mm cannon, fired straight into the rear engine compartment. In general, this was the tactic adopted by Allied tank crews, who used superior speed and manoeuvrability to flank an attacking Tiger and get behind it. The 17-pounder gun housed on a Sherman Firefly was even capable of piercing the frontal armour of a Tiger I. From D-Day until the fall of the Reich in 1945 US tank crews allegedly only experienced three recorded encounters with Tiger tanks.

THE BATTLE OF BASTOGNE

The war was far from over in the autumn of 1944 and there was still a lot of liberating to do. In the town of Bastogne the Belgian resistance sent in forward patrols during the night of 9–10 September to disrupt the few remaining Germans. On the morning of 10 September, General Norman 'Dutch' Cota, commander of the 28th US Division, ordered the 110th Infantry to attack the town. At 11 am the advance guard of the 2nd Battalion arrived at the perimeter of the tiny hamlet of Marvie, roughly 3 km (2 miles) east of Bastogne along the main Bastogne–Wiltz highway. After a short skirmish the Germans made a hasty retreat. While the 3rd Battalion went into action west of Bastogne, the resistance fighters, many of whom were Belgian veterans of the 2nd *Chasseurs Ardennais*, donned their 1940s uniforms. By noon they were marching through the town followed by vehicles of the 28th Division. Bastogne had been liberated. Two days later, on 12 September, Patton's Third Army met forward elements of the US Seventh Army. Most of France had been liberated but there were still concerted pockets of resistance and some would prove more difficult to dislodge than others.

To the men doing the fighting the machinations of generals and commanders were just aspects of life on the front lines in autumn 1944.

There were other considerations, too. Warm food, dry clothes and good company usually outweighed all other concerns. It was a dank, rain sodden morning in early September 1944 when American lieutenant Ernest Gessener of the 110th Infantry Regiment, 28th Division, tenuously peered out of the ditch at the side of the road and zeroed in on his intended target. The *Panzerkampfwagen IV* couldn't have been more than 10 m (30 ft) away, and while it lumbered slowly forwards, preoccupied with the machine gun fire directed at it that caused bullets to clatter and bounce off its front panel, Ernest deduced that this was the perfect opportunity to pop a shell into its right flank. While his friend Donald Riesman loaded the M1 bazooka Ernest carefully levelled the weapon, aimed it at the tank and gently squeezed the release mechanism. He scored a perfect hit. The shell exploded on impact at the part of the tank where the turret was joined to the hull, unleashing a stream of molten copper into the vehicle cabin that would have incinerated most of the crew. The only problem with this bazooka was the thunder flash that came from the muzzle when it fired that immediately gave away its position, concealed or otherwise.

As the smoke dissipated Ernest timorously raised his head above the side of the ditch to survey the damage. 'I think we got him good,' he said, and Donald remained crouched low in the ditch and replied: 'Yep, you got him now get down you idiot, the Krauts will be able to see where we are.' Suddenly, while Ernest was admiring the result of his effort, he felt a powerful blow to his sternum that completely knocked him off his feet, but strangely enough he couldn't feel any pain. As the GI lay there helpless, he could feel warm blood seeping down the inside of his tunic and he looked down to observe the expanding dark stain below where the bullet had impacted. Then he slumped down like a felled pine, his eyes began to roll back into his head and he groaned. Donald edged toward his friend and cradled his head in his arm as he looked at his wristwatch. It was 11.45 am, 10 September 1944, and Ernest Gessener had died in his arms. He was officially the first American to be killed in Bastogne. He wouldn't be the last.

Pfc. Benjamin Elisberg, 3rd Battalion, 110th Infantry Regiment, 28th Infantry Division, was also there. 'There was a German in this foxhole and I jumped into the thing, and here we are facing each other,' he remembered. 'We each had a rifle in our hands and what I did, I chased the guy out, out of the foxhole and he jumped out. We didn't shoot at each other – it was a crazy thing and he jumped out of the foxhole and he started running. I don't remember what became of him but that was really close contact with a German. And, there were some crazy incidences we had. I remember a couple of Germans. I remember we had a couple of German prisoners and this one had some black bread and he had this big knife and he's cutting this bread, feeding himself and I didn't think anything of it. It looked so darn normal and everything. I didn't say anything. I didn't do anything. But later I said oh my God, this guy is going back, he's carrying a knife and I didn't think anything of it. Someone said to me "Oh don't worry about it, they'll get the knife from him." You know there aren't any – it's no fun – you don't remember anything funny in combat. Maybe years later you look back at it and laugh at it but not at the time.

'In Germany. And I remember that city being levelled. Nothing stacked. One incident, now that I really think about it is that they had a section that they called Dragon's Teeth, it was reinforced concrete. And in order for the American tanks to get through, they had to bomb them, bomb the Dragon's Teeth. And where you had Dragon's Teeth you had German replacements, underground bunkers, whatever they called it. And what they had was like, if I remember right, metal doors with slits in them. And I remember one time an American tank, positioning itself by one of these replacements and firing a flamethrower through the slits. And I remember a guy screaming and crying, coming out, and his whole face – the skin was burned off and you could see the skeleton, the bones. And I remember we, we killed him right there because the condition the guy was in, the pain he was in, there was absolutely nothing, there was nothing we could do for him.'[15]

A few days earlier, on 7 September, the US 4th and 28th Infantry Divisions had crossed the Belgian–French border relatively unopposed and advanced to the town of Bouillon. By the following evening they had liberated Jemelle, Saint Hubert and Jamoigne. On 9 September the 5th US Armored Division executed a pincer action at the town of Arlon where, a few days earlier, the Gestapo had executed 20 suspected resistance fighters.

In the west, three Allied army groups extending from the North Sea to Switzerland thought that they were poised to deliver the *coup de grâce* against the Nazi Homeland, but the consensus on precisely how they were going to achieve this was another matter entirely.

THE SIEGFRIED LINE

After the liberation of Bastogne US army progress continued to accelerate. The town of Arlon on the Belgian–Luxembourg border was liberated on the morning of 10 September, and by the evening Vielsalm, Clervaux, Esch-Sur-Sure, Ettelbruck and Luxembourg had been taken. Here the soldiers were greeted with the classic scenes of jubilant civilians waving homemade American flags while plying the men with wine and beer. By 11 September, US army columns had reached the Luxembourg–German border in several locations. Some troops tenuously set foot on German soil for the first time and some even advanced to the notorious Siegfried Line. Then, for no apparent reason as far as the civilians could see, the Allied advance appeared to grind to a stuttering halt.

The 28th Infantry Division Pennsylvania National Guard was one of the divisions attached to the US V Corps. By the end of August and into the beginning of September it was struggling to keep up with the pace of the pursuit. The 28th had advanced using a combination of vehicle and foot marches. During the first ten days of September the division moved from Paris, through Luxembourg and part of Belgium to a place in proximity to the German border. Resistance was generally light, but for the infantrymen moving on foot the pace was exhausting. Finally, on 11 September, the division halted along the German border near the northern tip of Luxembourg. Ahead of the 28th lay the River Our, swollen by autumn rains and, beyond that, the Siegfried Line. Known to Germans as the 'West Wall', it was in fact an incomplete structure – and by the time of the German retreat in the west it had fallen into terrible disrepair.

Pfc. Claude W. Hoke, Company C, 109th Infantry Regiment, 28th Infantry Division, said: 'I was about to get captured. There was a friend of mine from Aiken, South Carolina, got captured. There was one German. We was in Belgium. And there was a German boy or French ... We went down there. And they had us cornered down in there where we couldn't get out. I was the only one that escaped that evening. I came back the

American infantry make their way through the dragon's teeth of the Siegfried Line in autumn 1944.

way we went. The rest of them was involved the other way. There was a railroad track. And I stayed there firing back and forth, like it was several of us. And they was getting pretty close to me, and I had to move. And one fellow started coming up from the railroad track, which I throwed a grenade, and I had taken care of him. I decided it was time for me to move out. And it's hard telling how many thousands of bullets went over me. I'd hit the ground and crawl while it was potato patches. I bet they was about that high, Irish potatoes. I was in them rows. And I would crawl as long as I could, and then I would get up and run as low as I could. When I would get up and run as low as I could, them machine-gun bullets were going all over me. I could just feel them going across me.

'I got to a wire fence, a barbed-wire fence there. I said, "Well, I will crawl under that thing." And I got my hand on that thing, and it was hot. And I didn't know what I was going to do. I never could jump. But I said that's the only thing I got to do is get back and jump over that fence. That's the only thing I could see. And I got back and jumped over that fence. And after I got down, I was going downhill. So I went into this town, this Belgium town. And I passed out when I got in town. They was trying to revive me. When I got back with my outfit, I tried to get the captain to let me go get a group and go back and try to get those boys.'[16]

On 13 September 1944 the 28th Infantry Division became the first American division to cross the German border in force and initiate attacks on Germany's Siegfried Line, but they were already falling behind schedule. Two rifle battalions from the 109th and 110th regiments crossed the River Our just east of the Luxembourg village of Binsfeld under the cover of darkness. The patrols encountered virtually no resistance. Due to recently emerging logistical problems, the 28th, along with other US divisions, was critically low on ammunition and fuel. Because of this there was almost no artillery support for the foray into Germany. Specialized munitions required for clearing bunkers, such as pole charges, satchel charges and Bangalore torpedoes were simply unavailable. Even small arms' ammunition was in desperately short supply. Based on these shortages, General Cota restricted the attack and by the close of the first day the division had little to show for its efforts except a few casualties.

The attacks stalled well short of their initial objectives. Both rifle battalions dug in that night within sight of the first line of German pillboxes. On the following day, Cota decided to sanction a further attack in force. The attacking infantrymen were given permission to call on division artillery support but the shells fired had little effect on the massive reinforced concrete bunkers. The units met with some small successes, but fierce German counterattacks quickly eliminated any gains. During the night of 15 September a small German force of the 2nd SS Panzer Division *Das Reich*, armed with automatic weapons and flame-throwers and supported by tanks, almost completely annihilated F Company of the 110th Regiment.

The 28th now began to realize what it meant to make an incursion into Nazi territory. It became the unwilling subject of withering enemy enfilade machine gun fire emanating from well-positioned pillboxes. These actions pinned down whole units, while German mortar and artillery fire devastated the ranks of the assault forces. Advancing under such fire proved to be extremely detrimental to the 28th. NCOs attempting to move the men forward quickly became casualties. These initial encounters with fortified positions required greater skill and greater numbers than the 28th had access to. It discovered to its dismay that such operations were considerably more complex than expected. Other units assigned to V Corps were discovering the same thing. On 17 September, V Corps commander Major General Leonard Gerow carefully assessed the situation and ordered all offensive operations to cease. Within days, much of the corps had withdrawn back across the River Our.

In the north, GIs were already beginning to make incursions into German territory. The city of Aachen was close by and the liberation was about to turn into occupation as US forces closed in on the Siegfried Line.

THE SS AND THE SECRET ARMY

For the 17-year-old Flemish-Belgian Paul Baeten liberation couldn't come soon enough. He survived the horror of no less than four German concentration camps. While the Allies were planning D-Day he got himself into some serious trouble. Full of adolescent fervour, he had joined 'Fidelio', an active Belgian resistance group. He recalled his teachers at the school he attended turning up wearing the black uniforms of Flemish fascists. They stood at the front of the class and encouraged the pupils to join the Flemish SS fighting on the Eastern Front. That's what motivated Paul to join the resistance. The Fidelio Brigade in the town of Lier was as notorious to the authorities as the Independence Front and the Belgian Legion that later became known as the famed Secret Army.

Flemish SS men were reputedly worse than their German counterparts and began rounding up young Flemish males for the purpose of forced labour in German factories. They looted houses and used extreme methods to detain those they suspected of not supporting the Nazi cause. By the tender age of 17 Paul was already an experienced resistance fighter, though. His parents were largely oblivious to his nocturnal activities as he participated in the distribution and printing of illegal publications. He quickly learned how to keep off the SS radar and to avoid raids and roadblocks. But his luck eventually ran out when he was betrayed and arrested. Paul was interrogated and then sent to the labour camp at Esterwegen, then to Gross-Strelitz, Gross-Rosen, Buchenwald and finally Dora-Mittelbau, which manufactured the dreaded V-1 and V-2 rockets used in late-war bombing campaigns against the UK. At Dora-Mittelbau prisoners were kept mostly underground, deprived of daylight and fresh air, and enclosed in unstable tunnels. The mortality rate was higher than at most other concentration camps. Prisoners too weak or ill to work were sent to Auschwitz or Mauthausen for extermination. In 1944, a compound to house forced labourers was built above ground level south of the main factory area. Once full production of V-1 and V-2 missiles began from the autumn of 1944, Dora-Mittelbau had a standing prisoner population of at least 12,000. Paul didn't think that he would survive this one.

After he was liberated and until his death in 2017 Paul refused to be present at official ceremonies where the symbolic Flemish Lion was displayed. His reason was that Flemish SS had been allowed to wear the Flemish lion rampant insignia on their uniforms. Apart from that, they were the only non-native German SS contingent allowed to wear German insignia because Nazi historians claimed that they were Teutonic brothers.

This was of course 'fake' history, a subject the Nazi regime excelled in.

At this juncture the Allies had begun to prioritize their schedules. Opening Antwerp docks was of great importance to the Twenty-First Army Group, but the estuary was still not secured. Moreover, Monty had persistently argued for the introduction of an alternate strategy that would allow him to focus on other objectives. Eisenhower approved Monty's audacious idea to launch an Allied air assault deep into enemy territory – an operation that had to be planned and prepared in just seven days.

CHAPTER SIX

THE BRIDGES

THIS CHAPTER WON'T GO TOO deeply into the semantics of Operation Market Garden. It's already been done elsewhere, and done well. It is generally understood that Eisenhower would have preferred an Allied advance along a broad front, taking advantage of all lines of attack. The British, and Monty in particular, had derided this method of warfare as an unfocused, unimaginative approach that had the potential to unnecessarily increase Allied casualties and prolong the war. However, Eisenhower was a profoundly intelligent man and referring to his strategy a 'broad front' approach was a serious misnomer invented by his critics and purely intended as a condescending term of ridicule. He would eventually be proved right, but these were early days.

It has been established that Eisenhower's relationship with Monty was fraught and problematic at the best of times. They were frequently at odds, but that wasn't unusual for Monty, whose own subordinates had wanted him replaced on a number of occasions. Eisenhower had given his express permission to attach the newly formed Allied Airborne Army to Monty's Twenty-First Army Group as early as 4 September. This in effect paved the way for Operation Market Garden.

The announcement of Eisenhower's decision to support Montgomery's Market Garden plan evoked a whole host of emotional and professional derision throughout Allied command. Omar Bradley found the decision particularly nauseating to the point that he immediately phoned Patton and gave his personal assurance that he would re-direct half of any supplies available to his army group to the Third Army. Patton was largely oblivious of Monty's plans. He was too preoccupied with his unsuccessful attempts to reduce the forts around Metz and capture them from the Germans.

Meanwhile, Monty had to contend with discontent among his own staff. Brigadier Belcham, Chief of Operations, didn't like the plan at all, particularly the narrowness of the thrust along low ground. Brigadier Richardson, Chief of Plans, had no knowledge of the proposed drop until several days after the announcement.

As early as 4 September Eisenhower issued a directive that in effect defined what he expected of Monty's Northern Group of Armies. He emphasized the importance of securing Antwerp, which was in fact taken that same day. This in turn prompted a strongly worded telegram from Monty to the Supreme Commander: 'I consider we have now reached a stage where one really powerful and full-blooded thrust towards Berlin is likely to get there and thus end the German war.'

Monty was, as always, unequivocal in his demands and completely convinced that his plan to strike north via the Ruhr would obtain the most favourable results, even though it was highly unlikely a bridge over the Rhine in the northeast of the Netherlands could have affected a successful conclusion to the war before Christmas 1944 as Monty had predicted. Eisenhower replied the following day, agreeing with the concept of a powerful drive towards Berlin, but not at the exclusion of all other manoeuvres. He also insisted there would be no reallocation of existing resources. It was his opinion that the success so far gained should be exploited by crossing the Rhine on a wide front and seizing both the Saar and Ruhr.

In an effort to appease the situation Ike gave Montgomery temporary supply priority for fuel and ammunition, and realigned the US First Army under General Hodges on the British southern flank until the Allies secured Antwerp, despite his personal reservations. He firmly believed that opening the Scheldt estuary and the port at Le Havre was considerably more important to the Allied war effort. Monty, who when animated often sounded like a British Elmer Fudd, would get his way and the 'pawatwoopers' would be sent in. There were no aspersions cast regarding Monty's tactical acumen, only the means by which he achieved his purpose at the expense of other pressing concerns. He was so fixated with his plan that he completely neglected to clear the Scheldt estuary, or attempt to cut off Gustav-Adolf von Zangen's Fifteenth Army when it retreated unmolested across the Beveland Island in southern Netherlands towards Germany. Consequently, Zangen escaped with the bulk of his army intact and took the precaution of leaving behind enough troops and artillery to keep the Scheldt estuary blocked indefinitely.

Monty's erroneous new plan would entail one powerful, full-blooded thrust in the north. Eisenhower may have been covering his tracks a little when he later wrote: 'There was still a considerable reserve in the middle of the enemy country and I knew that any pencil-like thrust into the heart of Germany such as [Montgomery] proposed would meet nothing but certain destruction.' The fundamental disagreements between Monty and Eisenhower came to a head when the two met in Eisenhower's aircraft at Melsbroek airfield (some documents indicate it was Evere) near Brussels on 10 September. General Bedell Smith, Eisenhower's Chief of Staff, detested Montgomery and reportedly remarked that he 'Deserved the greatest censure for his intransigence and behind the scenes conniving to enhance his own prestige and to obtain a major measure of command.'

Monty was simply living up to his reputation for asserting his own point of view. Whereas his superior, Field Marshal Alan Brooke, 1st Viscount Alanbrooke, was a great supporter of Monty, Winston Churchill was less convinced; he despised Montgomery but respected his abilities. In the summer of 1940 Churchill had met Monty for dinner at a Brighton hotel. Churchill was aghast when Montgomery refused alcohol, 'Never touch the stuff. Don't drink, don't smoke, and I'm one hundred per cent fit!' Churchill stared at the general in disbelief and said, 'Well, I drink as much brandy as I can get and I smoke cigars and I'm two hundred per cent fit!' During a later meeting with King George Churchill said, 'I think that Monty is after my job.' The King's eyes softened and a wry smile appeared when he replied, 'Thank God for that Winston, I thought he was after mine.'

Monty prevailed on Ike to allow him to use the airborne force to seize the bridges over the Maas (Meuse), the Waal and the lower Rhine. In consenting to Monty's plan, however, Eisenhower wasn't being contradictory. Whereas Monty visualized the operation as a vital knockout punch, Ike merely saw it as an extension of his initial plan of using a two-pronged approach. The British 1st Airborne Division was given the furthest objective of taking the bridge at Arnhem. It transpired after the war that the 101st US Airborne Division had initially been allocated this task, but the British 1st Airborne Division requested a switch because of its familiarity with the terrain. It had planned but never executed an earlier operation in that area.

EVERY MAN FOR HIMSELF

Happily oblivious of the movements of the Allies, in the small village of Terhagen, one of the hubs of the lucrative Flemish brick-making industry 24 km (15 miles) south of Antwerp, Louis de Pauw, an accomplished marathon runner, went about his usual routines. Terhagen nestles at the confluence of three important rivers that provided both the rich clay soil that helped make the bricks and the barge transportation to move them to market. None of the inhabitants had been requisitioned for forced labour in Germany and, despite the German occupation, life had generally not been all that bad. The village priest enjoyed good relations with the Nazis and, although he was a menace to many of the younger male members of the parish, nobody seemed to mind too much.

In 1944 the Nazi-influenced administrations in Belgium still totally identified with the neo-paganism and Social Darwinist racism of the German Nazis. Despite Belgium being a devoutly Roman Catholic country, the German occupation forces remained well aware that the Catholic Church was a powerful player on the socio-political field. In Flanders as in Wallonia, thousands joined the SS under the banner of localized nationalist sentiment and the Germans had managed to raise two whole divisions from the Flemish- and French-speakers of Belgium. The extensive and antiquated organizational powers regarding congregations

Louis de Pauw took a bullet to the chest from a Canadian sentry who was manning a border control post. It nearly killed him and he spent months recuperating.

and Catholic education were the primary sources of this power in Belgium, hence the German authorities were wary of them. Initially, the Vatican influenced Nazi policy in Belgium, but since the Italians signed an armistice on 8 September 1943 the Catholics were no longer regarded as a protected authority. But they were still a force to be reckoned with.

These factors prevented the military administration from imposing uniform German cultural policy too stringently at an educational and social level. By mid-September 1944, the Germans had vacated Belgium and, until the Belgian government could reassert power, it was every man for himself. Food became exceptionally scarce, particularly in the north of the country, leading to the development of a rampant and dangerous black market.

The village priest had heard from some members of his congregation that Louis de Pauw was the man to see if supplies were needed. So, he approached Louis and complained bitterly about the lack of communion wine for his services. 'It's difficult to get your hands on these days,' he moaned. Louis, who wasn't devoutly religious and who was well aware of the priest's sexual peccadillos, replied: 'You don't seem to have any problem laying your hands on anything else, Father. I'll get you some wine but you have to solemnly promise never to lay a finger on my kids or I'll fucking choke you with that dog collar.' The priest acquiesced, and Louis told him it would take a few days to organize what he needed. That evening, Louis and his 15-year-old son Petrus got on their bicycles and pedalled all the way to the German border in Limburg, which was roughly 130 km (80 miles) away. After biking through the night they arrived just before noon the following day. Louis met his nefarious frontier contact and he and his son filled their bicycle saddlebags with 12 bottles of ill-gotten red wine. With no time for rest or recuperation, Louis and Petrus made their farewells and set off back to Terhagen.

They had only travelled about 50 km (30 miles) when they ran into an Allied roadblock. The soldier shouted something in English, but Louis and Petrus didn't understand. Louis stopped briefly, furrowed his brow, shrugged his shoulders and set off again. Seconds later he felt a searing pain on his solar plexus as if a heavyweight boxer had punched him full on. He looked down to see a dark red stain spreading across his chest. Petrus looked on with his mouth agape. 'Dad, are you alright?' he asked. 'I'm not sure,' Louis replied, before promptly slumping like a dead weight on to the cobbled road. His breathing accelerated and moments later he was unconscious.

When he was brought to a British military hospital surgeon discovered a Lee Enfield rifle bullet had pierced his chest just millimetres from his heart. It had deflected off his solar plexus and was wedged between his upper ribs. For the next few days it was touch and go as Louis maintained a tenuous grasp on life. On two occasions a priest was summoned to give him his last rites. His recovery would take two full years, and many years later whenever he was asked about the liberation he slowly and purposefully opened his shirt buttons and pointed at the jagged, circular scar. 'This was liberation for me,' he would say bitterly. 'I had no problem with the Krauts. It was an Allied soldier that did this.'[17]

THE BATTLE FOR THE BRIDGES

On the same day that Monty had met with Eisenhower he had presented his outline instructions to Lt. General Miles Dempsey, Commander of the British Second Army, and to Lt. General Brian Horrocks, Commander of 30 Corps, so that detailed planning could begin at army and corps levels. On 12 September formal orders were issued by HQ of the Twenty-First Army Group. The British Second Army, supported by the Allied Airborne Army, was to advance 160 km (100 miles) from the Meuse-Escaut canal, near Neerpelt in Belgium, straight north to the IJsselmeer, close by Zwolle, from where it would turn east into Germany.

Horrocks and his 30 Corps would lead the 'Garden' section of the operation. Once north of Arnhem, 30 Corps would force crossings over the IJssel at Zwolle and at Deventer, the bridge featured in the 1977 movie *A Bridge Too Far*.

The task allocated to the Airborne Corps as the 'Market' part of the operation was to seize and hold the primary canal and river crossings along the 30 Corps' route from the north of Eindhoven to Arnhem. The 'Garden' would be provided by the 30 Corps armoured spearhead, attacking a narrow axis seized in advance by the airborne formations. The 52nd (Lowland) Division would be flown in to an airfield near Arnhem to reinforce the position, and facilitate the crossing of the IJssel at Zutphen. It was estimated that the leading formation of 30 Corps, the

Guards Armoured Division, would reach Arnhem within two or three days at most. Once this force was established in the northeast of Holland, the British Second Army, led by 30 Corps, would then push into Germany, to encircle the Ruhr in conjunction with the First US Army. The Canadian First Army would continue to clear the approaches to Antwerp in order to gain access to a forward port for supplies, and to liberate the rest of northern Holland, including Amsterdam.

It was a daring, audacious plan quite uncharacteristic of Monty's normally conservative strategies. From the Battle of Normandy to the very end in Germany, the British army's performance was profoundly influenced by its inability to withstand heavy casualties. His superiors in London repeatedly warned Montgomery about the shortage of manpower. Within days of the landings in France, much to Montgomery's chagrin, British battalions were being requisitioned to provide replacements.

Monty liked to know that the odds were stacked in his favour before he launched any offensive, as was the case at El Alamein. Market Garden was the antithesis of this. Too many aspects depended on too many preconceived assumptions and not enough attention had been paid to potential logistical problems. The landscape of the Netherlands is latticed by rivers and canals, which had the potential to render any advancing Allied columns vulnerable and there was no plan B. Furthermore, negligible attention had been paid to recent intelligence provided by ULTRA, which had clearly revealed a disturbing reinforcement of troops and armour in the Arnhem area, in the Albert Canal area, and along the border with Luxembourg.

As commander of the British Second Army, Dempsey paid a visit to Monty to relay his deep concern over both the ULTRA information and Dutch resistance reports of an unknown number of tanks near Nijmegen and Arnhem. Moreover, Dempsey was far from convinced that his army had the ability to advance as quickly as the plan demanded and to join up with the airborne troops in accordance with the strategic requirements.

The Dutch intelligence reports were dismissed almost out of hand. This was in part due to what was known as 'The England Game' (*Das Englandspiel*), an intricate and well-devised counter intelligence operation launched by the German intelligence agency (*Abwehr*), during World

The British 1st Airborne lands in the fields of Arnhem on 17 September 1944.

War II. German forces had captured Allied resistance agents operating in the Netherlands and used their secret codes to mislead the Allies into continuing to provide the agents with information and supplies. It had resulted in the arrest and execution of around 50 Allied agents, and from that point on British intelligence decided that Dutch intelligence could not be trusted.

Even when Monty's own Chief of Staff, Major General Freddie De Guingand, called from his hospital bed to express his deep concerns about increasing enemy resistance and logistical dependence, Montgomery could not be dissuaded and persisted in his objective of plotting his

Allied tanks cross the bridge at Nijmegen, 21 September 1944.

course to the Rhine. The sheer magnitude of the operation was staggering. It included over 5,000 transport aircraft, 2,613 gliders, and almost 5,700 sorties of bombers, fighters and other close support aircraft.

On 17 September, one young Dutchman wrote: 'I saw an enormous number of English planes above our village. In the afternoon the radio reported the landing of parachutists in Breugel, Son, Cuyk, Arnhem, etc. In the vicinity of Eindhoven the Germans flee in the direction of the border. The traffic at Wanssum is getting busier. All returning soldiers requisition food, vehicles, horses and bicycles.'

On 18 September, 16-year-old Dutchman Roel Kerkhoff wrote: 'We drove to Son with father. According to the sources, the first tanks of the second British army of Dempsey had already arrived there, but I think we only found American soldiers who were consolidating their position. We saw two young German soldiers lying dead. They were on the south side of the canal, just to the west of the bridge on a small piece of arable land. A little further away was a barn. Years later whenever I passed through Son I always looked at that building.'

After the 82nd Airborne managed to complete most of its allotted tasks it was required to cross the River Waal at Nijmegen under fire in flimsy canvas boats. The Americans found it nothing short of inexplicable and exasperating that after they had secured the vital bridges that allowed British armour to tangentially proceed, British 30 Corps rested for 24 hours before moving on to Arnhem. Not that it would have made a great deal of difference; the battle for Arnhem had been irrevocably lost in the first few days.

THE MYTHS OF MARKET GARDEN

The movie *A Bridge Too Far*, based on Cornelius Ryan's excellent book of the same name, accurately depicted most of the events. Some even claim it was the most historically accurate war movie ever made, but it also perpetuated some myths. Ryan wasn't personally impressed with the result, but that had also been the case with the filming of his other book, *The Longest Day*. The official report on Operation Market Garden makes reference to the inadequacy of the radio equipment provided for the British Airborne. It states that, 'the No. 22 Set has not adequate range nor is its receiver sufficiently selective'; 'the No. 68 Set is quite inadequate'; 'the No. 22 Set has proved quite inadequate for its role'. Whereas some of this criticism is defensible, the radio modelling and first-hand accounts prove that the equipment, when correctly and skilfully operated, was adequate for the task, but only just. General Urquhart, who commanded the 1st Airborne Division at Arnhem and who later wrote a book about the operation, was also responsible for disseminating the story of faulty radio equipment.

It is possible, however, to corroborate most of Ryan's details, such as the famous crossing of the River Waal by the 82nd Airborne Division.

The 82nd's most decorated soldier to date is James 'Maggie' Megellas. In his book *All The Way To Berlin* he recounted the crossing: 'At 1500, when Major Cook blew the whistle to go, my men and I charged over the embankment toward the river's edge clutching the boat. Those of us without paddles used the butts of our guns to help keep the boat moving in a straight direction. I had a miserable time trying to paddle with my short-stocked Thompson submachine gun while keeping low in the boat. Private Simon Renner, seated in the middle of my boat, was holding guns so others could row. I was also concerned about my weapon. It had to be ready for business if we made it across the river.

'Fear gave way to hysteria. The fear of making it never entered my mind. I was one of about 250 fanatical men driven by rage to do what had been asked of us: capture the two bridges at Nijmegen, intact if possible. In the early going I was aware of Chaplain Kuehl, Major Cook, and Captain Shapiro in the boat next to me valiantly trying to hold a steady course. I could distinctly hear Major Cook, a devout Catholic, in a loud, quivering voice trying to recite the rosary, but "Hail Mary, full of grace", continuously repeated, was all he could utter. Then the "Hail Mary, full of grace" became just "Hail Mary", which he kept repeating as a sort of cadence for the rowers just as a coxswain would rhythmically beat on the side of a shell to synchronize the efforts of oarsmen. Chaplain Kuehl kept repeating, "Lord, Thy will be done": Undoubtedly, the Germans firing at us were praying to the same God: "Thy will be done" and "give us the strength and courage to defeat our enemies?" Whose prayers would be heeded? Whose cause would be deemed righteous and whose not? Which side would be favoured over the other, and who would live or die? I ask these questions, but I have no answers for them.

'I was only a combat platoon leader whose MOS was to kill Germans. I had been endowed with physical strength, courage, and an instinct for survival, as undoubtedly were our enemies. My creed was, God helps those who help themselves and does not take sides in human conflicts. Lead was flying at us from all directions. In other boats, bullets opened gaping holes in the canvas sides. The men were frantically trying to keep their boats afloat, bailing with their helmets. Some boats didn't make it. Others unable to navigate the strong current floated aimlessly down the river. Of the twenty-six boats that took off from the south bank, only thirteen made it across; eleven were able to return for the rest of the 3rd Battalion. The rest had been sunk in the crossing or their engineers killed, leaving the boats to float downstream carrying the dead and wounded with them.'[18]

Private First Class William Hannigan was also with the 82nd Airborne and was there when it crossed the River Waal. During a conversation with 'Maggie' he asked him, 'Was I in the same boat as you Maggie, I can't remember?' Maggie looked at him and said, 'Well I suppose that we were all in the same boat if you think about it Bill.' Then, smiling, he added: 'No, you were in the boat next to mine from what I recall.'

NIJMEGEN BRIDGE

One hero of Operation Market Garden who is often overlooked by historians was Captain Arie Dirk 'Harry' Bestebreurtje, who parachuted in with General 'Jumping Jim' Gavin of the 82nd Airborne. This Dutch captain activated elements of the Dutch underground and played a major role in the 82nd Airborne's operations in the battle to capture the Nijmegen Bridge intact. A few minutes after landing on his beloved Dutch soil the captain called up all of his partisan contacts that had been operating behind the German lines at Nijmegen. These partisans helped to prevent the Germans from blowing up the Nijmegen Bridge. The Dutch captain directed a veritable host of 2,000 well-organized resistance fighters, 400 of them formed into a combat unit that actively opposed the Germans. 'It is impossible to overemphasize the captain's help to us,' one American general said. 'I never saw a man with such guts. Arie had never used an American parachute before the landing and he jumped with one after only three minutes of instruction. I never saw such

Lt. James 'Maggie' Megellas, the most decorated airborne soldier in World War II. He commanded a platoon in Company 'H' of the 3rd Battalion, 504th Parachute Infantry Regiment, 82nd Airborne Division.

enthusiasm as these Dutch have. They really are people who deserve liberation.' As they came through the woods after landing the captain and the general personally shot several Germans and captured a few others.

Meanwhile, British paratroopers that had landed at Ginkel Heath were miles away from their intended objective and were becoming increasingly embroiled in a deadly confrontation with two German SS Panzer divisions. One of the SS division commanders was Kurt Student, who had himself been a paratrooper and understood the machinations of airborne units. Furthermore, the German commander Alfred Model had received a copy of the Allied plan, which had been obtained from the body of a dead American paratrooper. The 2nd Battalion, Parachute Regiment, had secured the northern side of the bridge at Arnhem, and was now faced with the task of holding it until the arrival of 30 Corps. From that point on, Lt. Col. Frost and his small force of around 550 men were subjected to almost continuous attack. They fought with every ounce of strength they could muster until they ran out of ammunition and food and were finally compelled to surrender. He wrote: 'I remember saying to Douglas, "Well, Doug, I'm afraid we haven't got away with it this time." "No, sir," he replied, "But we gave them a damn good run for their money." We still could not believe that [30 corps] would fail to come to our rescue. It was difficult to feel that there was enough genuine opposition to stop them. It was desperately disappointing that having done everything we had been asked to do we were now prisoners. It was shaming, like being a malefactor, no longer free. For the moment all this was alleviated by the sympathy and even admiration of our captors. I could remember saying to someone when it did seem inevitable that we would fall into the hands of Hitler's S.S., "I don't think that this is going to be much of a pleasure." We had all heard stories of them shooting their prisoners or herding them into burning buildings, but these men were kind, chivalrous and even comforting.'[19]

Major Charles Panter of 1st British Para wrote: 'During a lull I had a look outside and collected about twenty five more men, which included Sgt Jackman and some of the Mortar Platoon and some men from "A" and "B" Coys. We placed everyone under cover and it was decided that we should have to stay put until the Second Army relief force reached

Arnhem as the Boche were all round us. Captain Hoyer-Millar and myself holed up in a burnt-out cell or vault, there were four of them with steel doors and we chose the end one.

'After settling down we started to make plans for harassing the Germans when they started to withdraw, never doubting for a moment that we should be relieved during the morning. After a while we heard a lot of shouting in the main building. It proved to be the German S.S. troops who had captured our party including the C.O. and the Adjutant. Without food and water and practically no ammunition and in our exhausted condition capture or death must have been inevitable.'[20]

The after action report for Operation Market Garden stated that in attempting to summarize the main lessons of this operation, it is appropriate to realize that a deep thrust of some 96 km (60 miles) was made into country occupied and held by a stubborn enemy, that five major water crossings were successfully negotiated in the face of strong opposition, and that the plan as originally conceived was, according to Montgomery, 90 per cent successful.

In the circumstances, the enemy was found to be in considerably greater strength than had been anticipated; but for the weight of this support and for the magnificent fighting qualities of the breaking-out troops, the junction with the airborne troops might well have been delayed for a number of days.

Veteran Arthur Letchford was there with John Frost when they surrendered and he had another perspective on the proceedings. 'It was a bloody shambles,' he said. 'We lost some good men, I lost some very good friends and we all got shot to bits. When I heard about Monty claiming it was a 90 per cent success I said, 90 per cent success my arse. It was a 100 per cent disaster for me and my lot. We spent the rest of the war in German prisoner of war camps and didn't get liberated until 1945. What a bloody mess.'[21]

By 27 September around 800 men and women had been arrested in recently liberated Nijmegen, suspected of having collaborated with the Germans. They were locked up in the city jails pending trial before a specially convened Dutch court. Those convicted received severe sentences. The Netherlands abolished capital punishment in 1870 but the Netherlands government in exile in London had issued a decree on

*During the Battle of Arnhem, Arthur Letchford, Company C of the 2nd
Battalion Paratroops, fought alongside his twin brother at the road bridge.*

22 December 1943 restoring the death penalty for convicted Dutch
collaborators. The public humiliation of collaborators in the Netherlands
was just as harsh and punitive as it had been in France and Belgium,
where shaven-headed suspects were paraded through the streets in the
presence of jeering crowds demanding immediate retribution.

Per capita, the Netherlands produced a higher proportion of Nazi collaborators than any other German-occupied territory. The other parallel with Belgium in particular was the depleted Dutch police force calling on the assistance of so-called patriots for assistance. These chosen patriots even helped in directing traffic, along with reuniting separated families and assisting in the distribution of hot meals at the various public kitchens that were established by charitable and religious organizations, who received supplies of milk and vegetables from surrounding areas (but no meat, because most of the livestock had been requisitioned by the German army). Meanwhile, the Allies' civil affairs organization awaited the delivery of better food supplies from allocated ration depots in the southern Netherlands and in Belgium, deliveries that were contingent on the situation regarding military convoys. However, the Dutch authorities said there were no reported cases of starvation in the immediate weeks after liberation. It was generally accepted that the people didn't get as much nutrition as they needed but, thanks to the nuns and monks and the charitable organizations, nobody went hungry for the time being.

After Operation Market Garden, Nijmegen managed to maintain its electric power plant with the addendum that electricity was to be used sparingly and only for essential purposes. Nijmegen residents were allowed to have electric light in their homes for two or three hours each evening. There was even special Netherlands 'invasion' money printed for the Dutch people fortunate enough to live in liberated zones. These notes were printed by an American banknote company and were emblazoned with engravings of Queen Wilhelmina together with figures showing their denomination. Initially they weren't particularly well received by the frugal Dutch, who suspected they were fake, but the word soon got around that this was in fact legal tender. Nijmegen was one of the first liberated Dutch cities to have newspapers that weren't clandestinely printed and distributed by the underground movement. The first issues sold for six cents a copy and consisted of a single sheet printed on both sides carrying the latest news broadcasts by Allied radio stations.

Eisenhower later noted that he harboured no regrets concerning the decision to embark on Operation Market Garden. He believed it was a risk worth taking at that moment, and he would attempt it again if the same situations existed. 'I am certain that Field Marshal Montgomery, in the light of later events, would agree that this [operation] was a mistaken one,' wrote Eisenhower in his memoirs. 'But at the moment his enthusiasm was fired by the rapid advances of the preceding week and, since he was convinced that the enemy was completely demoralized, he vehemently declared that all he needed was adequate supply in order to go directly into Berlin.'

General Bittrich, commander of II SS Panzer Corps, said later that he 'had never seen men fight as hard as the British at Arnhem and Oosterbeek'.

Lt. Col. John Frost was liberated in March 1945. He had an ankle wound that had opened up again and he was transferred to the POW hospital at Obermassfeldt. He was there when the spearheads of General Patton's Third Army arrived, and he was freed and promptly returned home.

In Major General R. E. Urquhart's final report on Market Garden he wrote: 'The operation was not 100% successful and did not quite end as we had intended. The losses were heavy but all ranks appreciate that the risks involved were reasonable. There is no doubt that all would willingly undertake another operation under similar conditions in the future. We have no regrets.' Of the 8,969 men who landed at Arnhem only 3,910 escaped with their lives and their freedom intact. Urquhart was one of them. Before he left his HQ at Hartenstein he found the bottle of whisky that he had brought in his pack. He passed it around for everyone to have a sip before they left. Then he visited the wounded in the cellars to say goodbye. Shortly after that the survivors departed in single file, following the lengths of parachute tape down to the riverbank. The journey took an unusually long time because the Germans, in close proximity, continued to lob over volleys of mortar and small arms fire that forced the paratroopers to halt from time to time. All displayed incredible stoicism as they waited quietly and patiently for their turn to be ferried across the lower Rhine.

A FAILED ASSAULT

Operation Market Garden was an unequivocal military failure. The whole idea of taking and holding the bridges over the Rhine, Meuse (Maas), and Waal rivers was formulated within the larger framework of the Eisenhower goal of capturing the Ruhr Valley, the heartland of Germany's industrial production. Monty was on many levels a gifted tactician, but his lust for glory on this occasion superseded the practical realities. Historian Dr John Warren noted, 'All objectives save Arnhem had been won, but without Arnhem the rest were as nothing. In return for so much courage and sacrifice, the Allies had won a 50-mile salient leading nowhere'.[22]

The so-called 'salient' was actually nothing more than a tactically negligible cul-de-sac that the Allies would spend the ensuing months defending. They had gravely underestimated Hitler's resolve, General Alfred Model's tactical acumen and the German army's capacity to refit and re-equip when in retrospect it should all have been glaringly obvious. The German border is only a few miles from Arnhem and Nijmegen. ULTRA reports indicating that the Germans had rearmed along the Siegfried Line, the Albert Canal in Belgium, and in Arnhem were acknowledged but completely discounted even by Monty himself. Eisenhower was also reliably informed about the German reinforcement efforts, but due to his difficulty in communicating with Monty he didn't personally challenge the plan based on the intelligence reports. Nevertheless, it was ultimately Lieutenant General Frederick 'Boy' Browning who briefed Monty on the situation and repeatedly dismissed the available intelligence.

Browning landed near Nijmegen with a Tactical Headquarters unit but found it difficult to command the troops due to communications failures. His use of 36 aircraft to facilitate his Corps Headquarters deployment on the first lift has been criticized, because the number of combat troops on the first lift was already restricted due to a decision not to make two drops on the first day. The US General 'Jumping' James M. Gavin, commanding the US 82nd Airborne Division, noted in his diary on 6 September 1944 that, '[Browning] unquestionably lacks the standing, influence and judgment that comes from a proper troop experience, his staff was superficial. Why the British units fumble along becomes more and more apparent. Their tops lack the knowhow, never do they get down into the dirt and learn the hard way.'

After the battle, Browning's critical evaluation of the contribution of

Polish forces errantly led to the untimely removal of Polish Brigadier General Stanisław Sosabowski as the commanding officer of the Polish 1st Independent Parachute Brigade. Montgomery never attributed blame to Browning, who had deceitfully deflected responsibility for the failure of Operation Market Garden by using Sosabowski as his scapegoat. Browning received no further promotion and subsequently became Chief of Staff to Lord Mountbatten, Commander in Chief of the South East Asia Command. In fact, Browning should have received a dishonourable discharge for his obvious failings and glaring neglect.

Eisenhower had placed the whole Allied airborne army under Monty's command, along with sanctioning the operation and giving permission for it to go ahead, despite clamorous protests from other Allied commanders including General George S. Patton, who wanted additional supplies for his drive to the Rhine. It was ultimately Monty who had operational command of Market Garden but, as they say in the army, 'Shit never falls up'.

Following Operation Market Garden the men that had fought at Arnhem were hailed as heroes. Five Victoria Crosses were awarded for acts of outstanding bravery during the battle. Then, as with Dunkirk, the British press was ever so slightly diplomatic with the truth. This was probably due to government-imposed restrictions. In classic British style they attempted and largely succeeded in transforming a resounding defeat into a victory.

On Saturday, 23 September 1944, after the battle had ended, the German military authorities ordered the immediate evacuation of the whole population of Arnhem. The Red Cross was given just three days to complete the evacuation, after which time there would be systematic carpet-bombing of the entire city. 150,000 people were evacuated to what were considered safer areas. There were no exceptions; everybody had to go, young and old, women and children along with the sick and wounded. The problem was that evacuation was extremely precarious for many people who had been forced into hiding during the Nazi occupation. These included Jews, students, policemen, and even a significant number of escaped British soldiers and Dutch civilians who had assisted them and who now risked execution by the German military authorities.

The population fled to wherever it could reach. Some even ended up in places such as the Zoo and the Open Air Museum just north of the city, while others went to neighbouring villages and cities, with the expectation that they would be able to return home after a short while. Sadly, they would have to wait until well after liberation to go back. Many others were forced to travel much further afield, to places such as Friesland.

During and after the evacuation chaos ensued as the city fell prey to Nazi-commissioned widespread looting and destruction. Meanwhile, some managed to rescue vital food supplies at great personal risk, which they provided for the larger groups of evacuees. They also succeeded in rescuing many priceless art treasures. The punitive measures taken by the German military authorities against the population of Arnhem were among the harshest inflicted throughout the war.

All Dutch civilians were forcefully prohibited from going into the Arnhem zone for the duration on pain of deportation or death. General von Rundstedt personally sanctioned the German plunder crews and their ignominious Dutch helpers, who proceeded to ransack, loot and destroy Arnhem on a scale that afflicted all sectors of the society and the economy. They took everything they could get their hands on from the factories, shops, banks, offices, laboratories, stocks and supplies, raw materials, farms and livestock, along with Dutch cultural items such as paintings, complete library collections and antiques. They also requisitioned all private property, houses, furniture, clothing, valuables, pianos, beds, books, paintings and other household goods. Absolutely everything of value was taken and carried off, or thrown into the streets and burned. Arnhem was annihilated and plundered.

LUXEMBOURG IS HAUNTED

IN SEPTEMBER 1944 THE COUNTRY of Luxembourg was haunted. It unsuspectingly played host to an Allied tactical deception unit known as the Ghost Army. The 1,100 men of the 23rd Headquarters Special Troops were a strictly clandestine unit that operated with the utmost secrecy. Their activities remained classified for almost 36 years after the end of World War II. It was a unit unlike any other, a peculiar collective of highly skilled artists and craftsmen recruited mainly from northeastern art schools that had but one remit: to deceive the enemy.

Using inflatable tanks and other vehicles, it successfully tricked the Nazis into thinking that the June 1944 invasion would come from Dover. During the war the unit devised many ingenious means to fox the enemy, such as phony convoys, phantom divisions and even ersatz headquarters. In more than one instance, the Ghost Army successfully misled the German army into thinking certain US divisions were present when they were nowhere near.

The purpose of the Ghost Army was to sow the seeds of chaos and confusion among the Axis forces, and this it did incredibly well on many occasions. It used much more than simple visual props to achieve the deception. It also used something referred to as 'sonic deception'. Assisted by engineers at Bell Labs, a team from the unit's 3132nd Signal Service Company Special travelled to Fort Knox to record sounds of armoured and infantry units on to cutting-edge wire recorders (the predecessors to tape recorders). Then they created complex audio mixes compiled from sounds that matched the atmosphere they wanted to create. These sounds would be broadcast from powerful amplifiers and speakers that were mounted on halftracks. This combination proved to be so effective that the sounds could be heard up to 25 km (15 miles) away. It was in effect a forerunner of psychological warfare. The Ghost Army even orchestrated 'fake news' radio broadcasts, long before it became a popular contemporary expression.

These radio broadcasts were so convincing they even fooled Mildred Gillars, the pro-Nazi American broadcaster known to the Allies as 'Axis Sally', into thinking that certain Allied units were in certain areas. Some of her radio broadcasts were disconcerting, though. One GI said, 'While we were getting some downtime we used to listen to Axis Sally because she played great big band music. She would come on, though, and do things like tell us what our password for the night was, which was kind of a blow in the ass!'

While General Patton was massing his forces around the French town of Metz in preparation for an attack, the Ghost Army was donning the insignia and emblems of the 6th Armored Division. In his haste to reach Metz, Patton had erroneously allowed a potentially precarious gap of 113 km (70 miles) to develop in his line on his northeastern flank. At that time there was only a smattering of US troops belonging to the 3rd Cavalry Group covering the whole region.

When the call came though the 23rd Headquarters Special Troops raced 400 km (250 miles) across France in an attempt to remedy the situation. Aware that certain German units were in proximity, for four straight nights they deployed 'sonic' trucks to project the sound of a division assembling. The deception proved to be so convincing that a colonel from the 3rd Cavalry approached some of the Ghost Army men to ask what was going on. They explained that they were only broadcasting pre-recorded sounds of moving tanks but the colonel was difficult to assuage. He could hear tanks and that was good enough for him. It took a while to calm the man down and fully explain the situation. Meanwhile, some of the men wearing 6th Armored insignia began infiltrating nearby towns and villages to add more credence to the ruse.

The Ghost Army even went as far as dressing some of its soldiers in Military Police uniforms adorned with 6th Armored patches, placing them at intersections along the route. The whole escapade became known as Operation Bettembourg and proved to be another resounding success for the Ghost Army. It was originally planned to last just two days until the US 83rd Infantry Division arrived to plug the hole in the line. Unfortunately, the 83rd was experiencing some delays in getting to its destination, so the deception was compelled to carry on regardless. With each day that passed it became increasingly dangerous to maintain this facade. Local civilians relayed messages that German forces had been seen in nearby woods and shots had been heard. By this time some German units had managed to reorganize after the retreat from Normandy.

Grant Hess was with the 3132nd Signal Service, a key component of the Ghost Army. He later recalled: 'Four of us were broadcasting to the German positions. Our technical guys installed a speaker, amplifier, microphone and generator in the back of a three-quarter-ton truck. It was good for voice transmission over a distance. Because I was familiar with that type of equipment, we, the four of us, would drive up to the lines and park it on a hilltop facing the German line. We had a man— some loud military type who spoke German—and we would crank it up. He would try to talk to the German troops, telling them if they deserted to the American lines they would be treated well, and would be safe and well fed. Each time he would say we would be back tomorrow to talk some more. The first time, nothing happened. The next day the Eighty-third troops captured a German bazooka team in the woods of the edge of the place where we usually went. They were sent there to knock out our truck. We were lucky that they had been spotted and captured. On the third day, after we had the truck in position on the hill, the Germans fired two artillery shells at it. One hit behind, one hit in front, bracketing it. The third shell never came because one of our L4 artillery spotter planes came over and I guess the Germans didn't want to expose their gun location. I have to tell you, however, that, in

An inflatable Sherman tank, used by the Ghost Army to deceive the German forces in 1944.

a strange way, I would like to have seen that third shell just to see if they could hit our truck. We were some distance away, using a long cord. I can't tell you if we talked any Germans into surrendering. We were told that the Germans had men in uniform who weren't too keen about fighting for them. At any rate, just one man in the Eighty-third Division caught some shrapnel from the first shell, which we felt bad about because it had been very quiet there until we showed up with a loudspeaker.'[23]

As far as the Germans were concerned, Luxembourg was their territory. They claimed that the ancestry of its people was Teutonic and that the first German language had originated there. As technically gifted as the Nazis were, their so-called academics and pseudo historians often re-wrote history to suit their purposes.

Luxembourg resident and historian Christian Pettinger's father was a young boy at the time, but he vividly remembered the first US troops that he saw in Luxembourg. He said: 'I remember the Liberation of Glabach. I was seven years old in 1944. Glabach is a very small farming community in the centre of Luxembourg, 6km northeast of the town of Mersch. Glabach was liberated on 10th September 1944 by troops of CCR 5th Armored Division. The first American soldiers who came into town were black soldiers. Two or three of them were marching each side of the road in front of the first armoured vehicles that entered the town. These guys were a bit "trigger happy". They fired at everything that moved.

'Previous to the arrival of the American troops, tired and exhausted German soldiers, who were fleeing the Americans, were crossing the town. Some took a rest at my parents' farmhouse and asked for water and food, which my grandmother gave to them. At that time a German truck loaded with ammunition must have been parked in front of the farmhouse next to the entrance to the inner courtyard. During the German retreat American [P-47] planes circled in the sky. Some of the German soldiers were shooting with their rifles at them, which the P-47 riposted. Some bullets must have caught the truck that burst into flames. The flames spread to the farmhouse that began to burn down.

'My mother asked the Germans to help her save some of the farming implements from the flames and some Germans actually helped her.

When the Americans arrived they took a German soldier prisoner at the farmhouse. I watched as they escorted the German soldier away. Suddenly one of the Americans who was walking behind the soldier grabbed his pistol and shot German in the back.

'My parents had a dog that had caught fire as the house burned down. My mother saw the dog running away doused in flames and they never saw him again. This scene haunted my mother all her life. The farmhouse burned down to the ground and was never rebuilt. My parents and their three children were evacuated to Schrondweiler, near Glabach. A fourth child was born there.

'I recall seeing some Germans that had been killed by a P-47. They had rolled down a hill and were lying beside the road at the entrance to Glabach. I can never forget seeing the one that had his rifle still pressed against his chest. A little further outside of town I saw a German motorcycle and sidecar with the rider and passenger lying dead beside the vehicle. Looked like they had been hit by the P-47 too. American soldiers had searched their pockets, and their personal belongings were lying around on the ground.'[24]

With every hour that passed the situation of the Ghost Army was becoming increasingly dangerous. A major from the Special Plans branch visited the unit to inform it that enough reliable intelligence had been gathered to ascertain German divisions were regrouping for a possible offensive. Old Blood and Guts General Patton himself acknowledged that a potential problem was developing on his flank.

The following day, while the Ghost Army men were still wiping the sweat from their brows, the 83rd Infantry Division arrived on the scene. Its arrival was warmly welcomed and a possible disaster had been averted. Operation Bettembourg had been the longest deception orchestrated by the Ghost Army to date. Its men proved beyond any reasonable doubt that they were becoming masters of the art of deception. Shortly after that the Ghost Army relocated its HQ to the Limpertsberg campus of the University of Luxembourg. While there, its men attended a Marlene Dietrich concert, and in their spare time they sketched and painted.

While US forces were broaching Luxembourg and the German border, the capture of the French port of Le Havre had been assigned to the British 1 Corps under Canadian command. Prior to the actual attack the town was subjected to a massive coordinated bombardment by British naval guns and RAF bombers that decimated 80 per cent of the town. The attack on Le Havre cost the lives of 5,126 civilians, including 2,053 civilians killed during the bombardment. Despite a request by the German commander, Oberst Eberhard Wildermuth, to be given a two-day armistice to evacuate the residents from the besieged city, the attack went ahead despite his request. This was probably because Wildermuth had earlier rejected the British demand of unconditional surrender. The attack on Le Havre lasted 48 hours, during which 11,302 German soldiers were captured and around 600 killed. British losses were less than 500. Liberation didn't come cheap.

CHAPTER EIGHT

AACHEN HAS FALLEN

DURING THE MONTH OF SEPTEMBER, beset by increasingly debilitating supply problems, General Courtney Hodges' US First Army was stuttering forward. The First Army consisted of the 30th Infantry Division, the 1st Infantry Division, the 9th Infantry Division and the 2nd and 3rd Armored Divisions, along with air support by the Ninth Air Force. Collectively they were part of VII Corps under the command of General 'Lightning' Joe Collins. Opposing the US forces were remnants of various German divisions commanded by LXXIV Corps.

The weakest corps in the German Seventh Army, the LXXXI Corps, commanded by *Generalleutnant* Friedrich August Schack, was tasked with defending the Aachen Gap. While its four divisions were stronger than their counterparts to the south, they were also in a state of disrepair and Rundstedt requisitioned the 9th Panzer Division, the only reserve available, and dispatched it to assist LXXXI Corps. Only lead companies would arrive near Aachen by 11 September. Before they were deployed, a few battalions of 353th Infantry Division held West Wall positions south of Aachen.

Some 2,000 years ago the all-conquering Romans enjoyed the town's thermal springs; Charlemagne was crowned Emperor of the Holy Roman

Empire in its cathedral; and in the Middle Ages Frederick I, or Barbarossa, was crowned there. In 1801 Napoleon had annexed the place. Everyone knew and respected the German city of Aachen. Its place in history had long since been secured by great names and even greater deeds, but in the autumn of 1944 it awaited a considerably more ominous prospect. It was zeroed by the Allies and would be the first major German city to be attacked by ground forces. The propaganda value of such as attack was evident to both sides. Hitler was incandescent when he heard that an Allied army had had the temerity to encroach the borders of the Third Reich and, consequently, gave specific instructions that Aachen was to be held until the last man.

Josef Bieburger of Luftwaffe Ground Forces later recalled: 'After the training as Luftwaffe Ground Forces we were sent to the Westwall, the Siegfried Line, as a *Festung Sturmabteilung*. That was in the summer of 1944. We were in bunkers manning the Westwall near Zeebrucken, Belgium, as reserve. It was around this time I remember seeing V-1s launching at night. The flame from the tail lit up the night sky. Then, whoosh, off it went into the night. One right after the other. It was incredible. Then in the Fall we were moved further down into France. Then we were at the southern end of the Westwall.'[25]

In September 1944, the Germans claimed that 25 divisions collectively constituting around 230,000 men were defending the Siegfried Line. This was undiluted Nazi propaganda intended to deter the Allies. In reality, many of these divisions were hastily assembled '*Volkssturm*' units that had a reputation for fielding a high proportion of young, inexperienced boys and elderly men who were inadequately equipped, badly led and poorly trained. Just beyond the Siegfried Line was the city of Aachen that had a population of around 165,000 and was in retrospect of negligible military value, except as a prize propaganda trophy for the Allies. The city rests near the axis Germany, Holland and Belgium converge. The intended route to the industrial heart of Germany in the Ruhr region led directly through the 'Aachen Gap'. This terrain to the north of the city was potentially conducive to the movement of armoured units thanks to it being relatively flat, with few natural obstacles to impede progress. That wasn't the case in the densely forested south toward the Schnee Eifel region.

'From inside our tank we heard a sinister and deadly whistling and noise, and we pressed against the cold steel, as if it could save our lives. Then we saw the earth shoot up in fountains when the grenades exploded, the shrapnel whined over us,' said August Gövert, 116th Panzer Division *Windhund* (Greyhound) Division. 'Luckily we were not hit. After some time I noticed a bunker. I jumped down from the tank and ran inside the bunker. Then to my surprise I heard someone say something in English. "Come in my boy, and shut the door!" The Americans who had occupied the bunker accidentally captured me. The "Amis" were incredibly friendly, they offered me a space to sit down and dressed my wound on the right of my forehead, and gave me a cigarette to smoke with them. After months of smoking German camel shit it tasted glorious. Sometime later from inside the bunker we heard the sound of a tank, the hum of the engine, and the clanking of chains. I said goodbye to the Americans. They released me.'[26]

THE ASSAULT ON AACHEN

By 15 September the Allied forces that had invaded southern France came under the direct control of Eisenhower as Supreme Commander of the Allied Expeditionary Force. This added the Sixth Army Group to the forces opposing the enemy along the German frontier, making a total of 48 Allied divisions in the European Theatre of Operations poised to move into Germany.

According to General Collins, the prone left flank of his VII Corps might be better served by seizing high ground overlooking Aachen rather than by occupying the actual city. Collins instructed the 1st Infantry Division to take the high ground to the east of the city and avoid becoming embroiled in urban warfare. The 1st Division's 16th Regiment had already made incursions into the scant line of pillboxes to the south of Aachen. This was one of the two bands of the Siegfried Line that coursed both in front of and behind Aachen. Then there was the Siegfried Line itself to negotiate and the ancient city of Aachen.

At the time Collins was planning his attack, his opposite number commanding German forces in the Aachen sector was General Erich Brandenberger. On 31 August he had been given command of the Seventh Army in the west. General Gerhard Graf von Schwerin was in command of Aachen itself. His meagre force was composed of the remnants of the 116th Panzer Division, three Luftwaffe fortress battalions and a few other miscellaneous units. It transpired that Schwerin had other ambitions that were going to directly oppose the specific orders of his Führer. This German general had fought through Normandy with his division, but by the time it was in proximity to Aachen, the once formidable 116th had been reduced to 600 men, 12 tanks and no artillery pieces. It desperately needed to be removed to the rear for refitting and rearming.

An authorized press release from SHAEF on 11 September 1944 remained triumphalist and stated that while the British Second Army was smashing through hastily organized German forces north of the Albert Canal and was moving steadily toward the northern end of the line, the American First and Third Armies were hammering the Germans back into the Siegfried Line. It went on to say that American 155 mm guns were pouring shells into Germany from positions less than 18 km (11 miles) from the German border. According to reports from the front, American patrols were probing the German defences in front of their vaunted Siegfried Line. Thousands of Allied warplanes, heavy, medium and light bombers and fighter bombers, were also hammering the Germans, by hitting railroad centres on which the enemy depended for the movement of his reserves and front-line targets. The Allies had secured objectives and progressed along a line that pre-D-Day planners hadn't anticipated reaching before May 1945 or thereabouts. They were way ahead of schedule, but that caused more problems than it solved at the time.

SHAEF now acknowledged that the fighting was reaching a new hiatus on three army fronts and that the Germans were committing an increasing number of troops to the combat areas. Field Marshal Gen. Walter Model's efforts to stiffen German resistance on the front before the US First Army didn't prevent Lt. Gen. Courtney H. Hodges' units from reaching Luxembourg. Northeast of Liege, Belgium, they reached a point 13 km (8 miles) from Aachen that came within range of heavy artillery. The first American shells to burst in Germany were fired into Bildchen by First Army artillery.

Paris radio reported that American troops had taken the city of Luxembourg, capital of the Duchy, and the Associated Press released

*Graf von Schwerin's severely depleted 116th Division was tasked with
defending the city. On 14 September 1944 Schwerin was relieved of his
command because he had allegedly hampered the evacuation of the
population and defied Hitler.*

information that the German forces were unable to prevent the cities of Verviers, Hasselt, Limburg and Neufchateau in eastern Belgium falling to the First Army.

The September rains persisted, and when the sun infrequently managed to break on the horizon it cast long, ominous shadows. At the time the Allies were poised to cross into Germany and there was still hope that Operation Market Garden might succeed. Either way it was going to be a hard fight. It was generally accepted that Nazi forces would fight the hardest on their own turf. The overriding questions were, how well provisioned were the enemy and could they still field a fighting force? The other pervading question concerned supplies for the Allied armies. The harbour at Antwerp was still inaccessible for Allied shipping and forward divisions were beginning to feel the pinch.

US forces had already begun to encroach across the German border and the roads that led into the German heartland appeared to be an enticing prospect. As soon as SHAEF Commander General Eisenhower realized this, he wasted no time in relaying orders that the conquest of the Ruhr, Germany's industrial region, be given top priority among the current phase of operations. The Ruhr Valley was the pumping heart of Germany's industrial might; moreover, the Allies wanted an economic objective that, if achieved, would substantially hinder Germany's means of continuing the war. If they could capture the Ruhr industrial area this would effectively deprive Germany of 65 per cent of its production of crude steel and 56 per cent of its coal.

Sergeant Harley Reynolds of Company B, 16th Regiment, 1st Infantry Division, 'Big Red One', said: 'I can remember the talk and comments about the city of Aachen, that no way would the Germans give up this city without a fight to the last German standing. It was very unnerving and mystifying that they let us get as close to the city as we did. We were aware of the importance of this ancient city to the Germans and would have given good odds that they would never give it up. We talked about this among the ranks. I felt that there was a good chance that they would possibly drive us back with a big counterattack. We were a finger sticking out in front of the U.S. line, a very dangerous position.'[27]

Physically taking the city of Aachen was going to be problematic. Armies on the offensive rarely enjoy becoming embroiled in house-to-

American soldiers at the Battle of Aachen.

house urban warfare because it provides multiple advantages to the defenders, and almost none for the attacking force. The Germans had discovered the real horrors of urban warfare at Stalingrad and it had cost them dearly. Was Aachen going to be the Allied Stalingrad?

Urban warfare means that previously innocuous streets can become natural funnels and channels that skilful defenders can easily transform into killing zones. Armoured support could be compromised because artillery and vehicles would be vulnerable to close-quarter attacks. Fields of fire are restricted, as is the ability to manoeuvre, and the team on offence is usually reduced to attacking with small, decentralized units.

Then there's the inevitable collateral damage when civilians are caught in the crossfire, not to mention the structural damage to ancient and antiquated buildings that are often reduced to rubble.

Preparing to undertake this task was General Omar Bradley's Twelfth Army Group, the largest concentration of American troops ever to serve under the auspices of one field commander. It consisted of four field armies, around 40 infantry and airborne divisions, and 15 armoured divisions. General Charles Harrison Corlett, nicknamed 'Cowboy Pete', informed SHAEF that he planned to hit the Siegfried Line close to Aachen on 20 September, before the Germans had time to reinforce their positions.

Harold Williams of 105th Engineer Combat Battalion remembered: 'We spent days preparing for the attack on the Siegfried Line. We had to rig pole charges using sticks of TNT. We didn't use dynamite, everything was TNT. Pole charges were 3–5 feet long. We would put 4–5 sticks of TNT with a detonator. The poor fellas who carried these charges at the Siegfried Line placed them in the openings of bunkers to take care of the gun emplacements. Some of them succeeded but some of them did not. A lot of them were used. The Siegfried Line had dragon's teeth, which were big cement formations in the ground. It had pillboxes and big cement bunkers with machine guns and big guns. Some of the engineers were involved in the actual attacks. I knew one of the engineers personally who was killed there at the head of an attack with one of those pole charges, but I was not involved in that. The engineers and infantry worked hand in hand.'[28]

It transpired later that the Allies actually held the Siegfried Line in higher esteem than did the Germans, who by 1944 had allowed it to fall into quite serious disrepair. After the resounding military achievements of the Nazi war machine in the west in 1940, it was regarded as superfluous and unnecessary. That was until the Allies raced across Europe to the German frontier. At that juncture there was a desperate hunt to find the keys to the many locked bunker defences, which were subsequently re-opened and re-equipped. Soldiers were sent to man them in preparation for the Allied advance.

The 1st Infantry Division was the first in almost everything. After Normandy it drove across France. On 7 September it turned east from

Mons and by September 12 had reached the Siegfried Line southwest of Aachen. Company C, 16th Infantry Regiment, crossed the last frontier on 12 September at 3.15 pm, whereupon it began attacking the Siegfried Line. Deployment of division forces on this day had a truly international feel about it. There was a battalion in Germany, an outpost in Holland, the main body of the division in Belgium, and a rear echelon in France. A reinforced battalion continued the drive forward, and the same day pierced the first belt of defences a few miles west of Aachen.

Rather than directly attacking Aachen in mid-September, the 1st Division circumnavigated it, moving the bulk of its forces to the east, to complete the penetration of the Siegfried Line eastward of the city and isolate Aachen in anticipation of a direct attack. It was around this time that supplies, particularly gasoline, had become very scarce, directly affecting operations of the First and Third US Armies. Opening the harbour at Antwerp to shorten the supply lines now became an imperative, but although some progress had been made at the Scheldt estuary there was still a hard fight ahead.

Meanwhile, in Aachen General Graf von Schwerin, commander of the 116th Panzer Division *Windhund* (Greyhound), was fully aware of the build-up of Allied forces along the German border and knew that their intended attack on Aachen could have only one possible outcome: the total annihilation of a beautiful city. When he arrived in the city Schwerin attempted to restore order and gave instructions to his men to shoot looters on sight. He was completely unaware that, at the same time, General Collins had decided to bypass the city entirely. His VII Corps had penetrated the first band of the West Wall along a 19 km (12 mile) front, and the second band had already suffered an 8 km (5 mile) breach. By 16 September, every single unit of VII Corps had been committed to the front that spanned 48 km (30 miles) from Aachen to Schevenhutte, culminating at the Hoefen-Alzen ridge. For all the advances it had achieved, VII Corps was in a delicate situation. Both of its flanks were exposed, rendering it vulnerable to a potential counterattack.

While the Allied ground forces hammered away relentlessly and struggled to establish their presence, the air forces maintained the pressure. But they were incurring casualties above and below.

As September progressed and the Allied threat in the Aachen sector increased, the situation regarding German forces deteriorated. Field Marshal von Rundstedt was dispatching daily reminders from his headquarters at Koblenz to the effect that Hitler's planned offensive had to occur irrespective of all potential difficulties. Rundstedt seriously considered his options. He had already pleaded with Hitler to rush new divisions to the Aachen area to little avail. The other option was to buy time by seizing the initiative on another part of the front. Hitler had already decided to ignore Rundstedt's request completely and assemble all available armour on the Cologne plain. Hitler remained intransigent as always and simply reiterated that the line from the Scheldt estuary along the face of the West Wall to the western borders of the Alsace should be held under any circumstance.

He had little regard for the difficulties facing his armies in the west, and didn't propose any solutions on how his forces were to maintain their positions. This prompted Rundstedt to send a further memo to Field Marshal Jodl on 7 September, requesting that OKW support the Fifth Panzer Army with the necessary materiel, fuel and planes to orchestrate a successful counterattack. Field Marshal Model, who had preceded Rundstedt as Commander in Chief West, had done his utmost to relay information on what he regarded as an impending crisis.

As the days passed Rundstedt's consternation increased. He dispatched an urgent memo to Berlin requesting at least five infantry divisions, along with tanks and tank destroyers to counter the imminent threat to Aachen. Unfortunately, at that time the only available reserves were a significantly depleted 9th Panzer Division, an understrength *Sturmpanzer* battalion and two assault gun brigades that were already making their way to Aachen. The German situation was rapidly worsening.

THE NAZIS SURRENDER?

The war wasn't going as well as expected on the Eastern Front and the Allied vice on the Third Reich was tightening. On 4 September Hitler reluctantly gave priority on all new artillery and assault guns to be dispatched to the western theatre. On 11 September the swiftly approaching American forces triggered panic among the civilians in Aachen. Most Nazi Party officials, Luftwaffe flak detachments, local civil servants and functionaries, the police and troops promptly abandoned the city and headed east towards Cologne.

The chief of staff of the German Seventh Army reported that the tableau of retreating Luftwaffe and SS troops he had witnessed, with the commanders leading the retreat, was very bad for morale. It even prompted a riot in Aachen, but before the situation descended into total anarchy Hitler ordered that the civilian population should be evacuated, forcibly if necessary. He suspected that they might have preferred American occupation, which would among other things have effectively ended the bombing. Hitler, as expected, threatened terrible retribution against all those who didn't leave as ordered, stating that they would be considered traitors to the Reich. He was at best volatile, at worst completely murderous. His faith in his generals had been greatly tested after the attempted assassination against him on 20 July that year. Hitler had exacted a terrible retribution on both the conspirators and innocents alike, and it is estimated that over 7,000 Germans were killed or sent to concentration camps as he took revenge on what he deemed were enemies of the Third Reich.

General Graf von Schwerin must have been aware of the possible consequences of his actions, but nevertheless he wasted no time in countermanding the implicit evacuation order. He decided that Aachen was indefensible. In a letter to the commander of the US forces he wrote: 'I stopped the absurd evacuation of this town; therefore, I am responsible for the fate of its inhabitants and I ask you, in the case of an occupation by your troops, to take care of the unfortunate population in a humane way. I am the last German commanding officer in the sector of Aachen.' Schwerin entrusted the missive to a telephone service manager, the only official he could locate who was still at his post, who it transpired was a dedicated Nazi.

At the very moment the Wehrmacht general chose to offer surrender, the US forces temporarily deflected their attention away from Aachen. When Schwerin discovered that an attack wasn't imminent he attempted to retrieve his message, but that boat had sailed. His message had already fallen into the hands of Nazi party functionaries, who relayed its contents to Hitler. Apoplectic with rage, the Führer immediately ordered Schwerin's arrest and trial for treason. It was only the timely intervention of Field

German prisoners march through the ruined streets of Aachen shortly after its fall.

Marshal Gerd von Rundstedt and Field Marshal Walter Model that saved Schwerin from execution, and he was incredibly fortunate to receive only a severe reprimand. Nevertheless, his military career was more or less over. He had failed in the eyes of the Führer and had to be replaced. The man who took over from Schwerin was Colonel Gerhard Wilck, commander of 246th *Volksgrenadier* Infantry Division, which assumed responsibility for this sector from the 116th Panzer Division in late September 1944.

By 15 September the 1st Infantry Division had occupied the high ground on three sides around Aachen. The US First Army then planned a pincer attack. The northern part of the pincer was the 30th Infantry Division, with the southern part allocated to the 1st Infantry Division, which was also tasked with clearing the city. As the autumn weather deteriorated and temperatures dropped, the 30th Division went in on 1 October, followed by the 1st Division one week later. The 1st Division had three main objectives: holding its current ground southeast of Aachen and facing Germany to ward off any German counterattack; attacking north to reach the 30th Division and seal off the city; and actually entering and clearing the city. These tasks were assigned to the 1st Division's 16th, 18th and 26th Infantry Regiments.

'Day by day we were making small gains in the endeavour to complete the encirclement on the eastern side of Aachen. At times the fighting was severe. The Germans had been given an "eyes of Germany are upon you" order by Hitler himself, and told to defend their sacred Fatherland to the last man,' said Colonel Stanhope Mason, Chief of Staff of the 1st US Infantry Division. 'Each day also saw a lessening of the previous German army disorganization. Artillery and troops were being moved into the Aachen area and on an occasional clear day they would send over fighter bombers to bomb and strafe us. On several occasions I had a chance to see some dramatic dog fights high up over the area when our own fighters, who had complete supremacy of the air, would take on these German planes. By then we had learned that German Gen. von Schwerin who commanded the 116th Panzer Division (Wehrmacht) was in command on the German side.

'We had encountered him briefly back in France when on Mortain position. There Hitler had put Schwerin in a coiled position with orders to attack the American forces and make a break through to Avranches. If accomplished, this not only would have been a miracle of German capability, but also would have been a bad blow to the American advance then moving rapidly from the beachhead area against disrupted opposition. Our Division Artillery discovered this concentrated Panzer division and when they got through pounding it, aided by called-in fighter-bombers, the 116th Panzer Division wasn't capable of making any attack at all. Prisoners we had taken from the 116th seemed to be highly respectful of General von Schwerin and considered him a good soldier with lots of common sense. In this case, he must have known that his orders to slice through at Avranches was another of Hitler's pipe dreams, but he had no choice. So finding him in Aachen, we knew we had a good soldier as an opponent, but one who might see the futility of fighting to the last man, the last round of ammunition, the last building in the city. Leaflets were air dropped into the city demanding surrender with threats of dire consequences if refused. Within twenty-four hours our observation posts reported countless windows displaying white sheets, but no move was made to "parley". The next day the sheets were no longer in evidence. We later learned that misfortune again attended General von Schwerin's reasonableness. He recommended to his higher headquarters that the city be surrendered, thus saving what was left of it and its civilian population. His recommendation had been turned down by the German High Command and Schwerin was summarily relieved of his Aachen duties and sent to some out of the way place in the Balkans. He survived the war but I was never able to meet him, though I think I would have liked him, professionally and as an individual.'[29]

General Huebner, commander of the 1st Division, paced the earthen floor of his HQ in contemplation. He was deeply reluctant to commit his men to a house-to-house battle among the bomb-ravaged buildings of Aachen. He knew what that would entail and the potential consequences. He continued establishing a 13 km (8 mile) wall of infantry defences that almost circumnavigated the city perimeter. He just had to hold on a little while longer until elements of the 30th Division could assist in completing its encirclement. Despite the fact that no actual link-up had been achieved, on 10 October Huebner ordered the delivery of an ultimatum to the commander of the German garrison in Aachen. The ultimatum stated in no uncertain terms that, if the commander failed to capitulate unconditionally within 24 hours, US forces would in effect reduce the city to rubble with artillery and bombs, and then take what remained by ground assault. A few days earlier a number of RAF bombing raids had inflicted serious damage on the city, a taste of what was to come perhaps.

The actual wording of the ultimatum ran: 'The city of Aachen is now completely surrounded by American forces who are sufficiently equipped with both air power and artillery to destroy the city, if necessary. We shall take the city either by receiving its immediate ultimate surrender or by attacking and destroying it. While unconditional surrender will require the surrender of all armed bodies, the cessation of all hostile acts of every character, the removal of mines and prepared demolitions, it is not intended to molest the civil population or needlessly sacrifice human lives. But if the city is not promptly and completely surrendered unconditionally, the American Army Ground and Air Forces will proceed ruthlessly with an air and artillery bombardment to reduce it to submission. In other words, there is no middle course. You will either unconditionally surrender the city with everything now in it, thus avoiding needless loss of German blood and property, or you may refuse and await its complete destruction. The choice and responsibility are yours. Your answer must be delivered within 24 hours at the location specified by the bearer of this paper.'

The American soldiers, 1st Lt. Cedric A. Lafley, 1st Lt. William Boehme, and Pfc. Ken Kading delivered the ultimatum. They were blindfolded by German troops and then received by a Lieutenant Keller, who read the ultimatum but displayed no outward expression of consternation. Keller relayed the document to the garrison officer *Oberstleutnant* Leyherr, one of 246th Division's regimental commanders. At that time the number of German troops defending Aachen and its surrounding area was estimated to be around 12,000, including the reduced 246th *Volksgrenadier* Division, a battalion of Luftwaffe ground troops, a machine-gun fortress battalion, and a *Landesschutzen* battalion, all under the direct command of Lieutenant Colonel Maximilian Leyherr, who felt dutifully compelled to refuse the ultimatum, which in essence sealed the fate of Aachen.

Throughout the ensuing 12 days, a bitter fight to decide the fate of this ancient city raged on from door to door and street to street. According to the Allies, taking the city would provide relatively easy access to the road network heading east and facilitate a direct advance to the Ruhr industrial complex before moving on to Berlin.

On the other hand, Hitler believed that the West Wall was impenetrable. He considered holding the city would provide the valuable time he needed to organize a counterattack and sever Allied spearheads, which would establish a stable front line whereupon Allied forces would inevitably be contained for the foreseeable future. Ironically, although by rejecting the Americans' ultimatum Colonel Leyherr was faithfully carrying out Hitler's 'last stand' order, this was not enough to prevent him becoming yet another victim of his leader's volatile nature. Just two days after defying the Allies Leyherr was replaced as commander by Colonel Gerhard Wilck.

Wilck was at the time of taking command unaware that man for man his garrison was numerically superior to those troops at General Huebner's disposal. The US forces did, however, possess more artillery pieces and they could rely on concerted Allied air support. This became apparent on 11 October, when around 300 P-38s and P-47s of IX Tactical Air Command opened the assault by releasing 62 tons of bombs on targets selected by the infantry and indicated with red smoke primarily on the perimeter of the city. A deafening barrage delivered by 12 battalions of VII Corps artillery followed the air attack that sent in a further 169 tons of bombs. Over the next two days more air raids were conducted, and further artillery shells rained down on the city. Then, the 3rd Battalion, 26th Infantry of the 1st Division, launched its main assault along a more than mile-long front heading towards the centre of Aachen.

Within days the besieged citizens of Aachen had almost reached their nadir. Life in the city had long since lost any semblance of normality, but the situation was now at its absolute worst. The absence of running water and electricity, compounded by ceaseless bombing, pushed everyone to the limits of their endurance. Life had devolved to a semi-subterranean existence as the city's inhabitants flinched and shuddered inside their cellars with each brain-numbing impact.

Mrs Kunigunde Holtz was living with her family in Aachen in 1944. She remembered that 'My husband was drafted, but not yet as a soldier. He was probably too weak and had to stay in a recovery camp, and I was on my own with everything. The child was born in December 1944 and by this time, when we waited for the Americans, I had to leave the apartment and look for a new home several times. Since here in Aachen-Steinebrück, we were in the front line of fire, in a no-man's-land so to speak: the Germans on one side, the Americans on the other and the bombs from above for weeks and months. Horrible!

'And then, sometime in September, the evacuation of the city was ordered. But as the leading engineer in a strategic business, my father had always said, "No, when the time comes, we will stay here." He was against the "Brown Shirts" and probably he was on their "black list", because he was often careless with critical statements or political jokes.

'So, we were sitting in the bunker when it was said: "Everybody out!" The SA was standing in front of the bunker, everybody had to leave the city! When I saw that, I said to myself, "No, you won't let your evacuation to somewhere happen!" So, in the middle of this confusion I somehow went away. I was terrified. And I heard them: "Halt or I'll shoot!" – But nothing. It was all in my head and in a panic I had thought up an excuse to be on the safe side. But nothing ... ! I just went on. This was the toughest decision for me and my child, but it was the right one.

'Where to go? As a precaution I had rented an apartment near the border in the Eynatten [in Belgium]. I went there. Defenceless and completely alone I first crossed the German and then the American lines! And then I saw the first dead German soldier lying in the street at the Jahnplatz. A terrifying scene. He must have been there for days. As I said: no-man's-land!

'But then I was fortunate again: an American jeep stopped, I was controlled, interrogated and then they took me to Eynatten – safely. I stayed there as long as possible. The owner of a house in the neighbourhood – a real guardian angel – gave me a stroller with children's clothing. You never knew what was to happen and where you would be then. Some days later, my family followed. My parents and my sister in law – they have been liberated by the Americans and temporarily evacuated to an old Belgian barrack in Hombourg.

'As Aachen was liberated I could go back to the hospital at Lütticher Straße, "Sanatorium" as it was called at that time. And after that things finally got better. But later we had to change our residence several times with the small child that got seriously ill because of the general shortages – but that's another story.'[30]

Combat on the streets of Aachen quickly started to follow a pattern reflecting the urban nature of the battlefield. This is precisely what Huebner had feared, but under the circumstances it was inevitable. The attacking forces divided into compact assault teams; each platoon accompanied by a tank or tank destroyer. The purpose of these was to maintain continuous fire on each designated target until the riflemen moved in to make the assault. Then the armour would point its turret at the next building and, supported by heavy machine guns, the process would be repeated. If the defenders proved too difficult to dislodge the riflemen could call on demolition teams and flamethrowers. It was a laborious, terrifying and extremely dangerous way to fight a battle, as light artillery and mortar fire swept forward one block at a time ahead of the attacking infantry supported by heavier artillery that hammered German communications deeper in the city.

In his headquarters at the resplendent Palast-Hotel Quellenhof, in Farwick Park in the northern section of the city, General Wilck urgently requested reinforcements. By the evening he had received the last available 159 men from his own 404th Regiment. An SS battalion that had once been part of the 1st SS Panzer Division *Leibstandarte Adolf Hitler* also attempted to reach him but they were diverted by an attack launched their old adversaries the 30th Division near Wurselen. The following day, to Wilck's relief, eight assault guns managed to reach him but this was considerably less than he was expecting. During the afternoon of 19 October Wilck issued an order of the day: 'The defenders of Aachen will prepare for their last battle. Constricted to the smallest possible space, we shall fight to the last man, the last shell, the last bullet, in accordance with the Führer's orders. In the face of the contemptible, despicable treason committed by certain individuals, I expect each and every defender of the venerable Imperial City of Aachen to do his duty to the end, in fulfilment of our Oath to the Flag. I expect courage and determination to hold out. Long live the Führer and our beloved Fatherland!'

Clarence Huebner at the Siegfried Line during the Battle of Aachen in October 1944.

This communiqué made a veiled reference to General von Schwerin, undoubtedly one of the 'certain individuals' Wilck referred to. Despite Wilck's encouragement, the Nazis did not quite fight to the last man, and on 21 October, at 12.05 pm, Brigadier General George A. Taylor accepted the German surrender at Colonel Corley's headquarters. The bloody battle for the first major German city was over. But it was a victory that came at some cost, with 85 per cent of this once-proud city now lying in ruins.

First Division G2 Lt. Robert Botsford had been a reporter with *The New York Times* before the war and was asked to provide a report of his observations. He wrote: 'The customary terms in figuring damage to a building, monetary value or a detailed inventory of the wreckage, cannot be applied even in extension to the city of Aachen as it now stands after twelve days of assault by bombing and artillery. The city is as dead as a Roman ruin, but unlike a ruin it has none of the grace of gradual decay. The end of Aachen came so suddenly and so completely that it is now of no historic interest except as an object lesson in the power and application of modern warfare. The products of more recent civilization have only increased the disaster. Burst sewers, broken gas mains and dead animals have raised an almost overpowering smell in many parts of the city. The streets are paved with shattered glass; telephone, electric light and trolley cables are dangling and netted together everywhere, and in many places wrecked cars, trucks, armored vehicles and guns litter the streets. Most of the streets of Aachen are impassable, except on foot; many of the narrower alleys are impassable by any means at all. A few of the main thoroughfares are still open to vehicular traffic, chiefly because they are wide enough to permit passage around buildings, which have sprawled into the street. Although it is true that some sections of the city have suffered less than others, comparison can only be set in terms of damaged or destroyed. In a tour through four-fifths of the city, not one building was observed which had been untouched by blast at least, and many sections, of course, had been piled into shapeless rubble by saturation bombing.'[31]

Lt. General Clarence R. Huebner was born and raised in a small town in central Kansas. A career soldier, he enlisted in the army as a private in 1910 and served in World War I. Huebner wrote: 'We reached the

German border on September 12th, saw Aachen from the surrounding hills and realized we had a "hard nut to crack". We didn't know it would be the 21st of October before the last German surrendered and the Imperial City of Charlemagne would be ours. The Siegfried Line defences around Aachen were a spur of the main defences which were to the rear of the city, but they were the same type; dragon's teeth to hamper tank action, pillboxes and casements from which were sited the automatic weapons, and mines and wire entanglements.

'Rather than attack directly into Aachen, the Division plan of action called for an easterly encirclement of the defences. A slow, grinding advance by the 16th Infantry against frequent counterattacks captured Munsterbusch and menaced Stolberg.'[32]

A COSTLY VICTORY

Aachen was a hard-won victory. What remained after the fighting had dissipated was a smouldering spectre of this former seat of emperors. Miraculously, as with the city of Cologne, the cathedral of Aachen was scarred but intact. Among the ruins and dispersed masonry decomposing bodies and limbs of civilians and soldiers alike festered in the autumn rains. The rubble was interspersed with blue flames from ruptured gas mains that added to the rancid, sulphuric stench of decay and death. It would take decades to rebuild the first city to fall to the Allies. Although Allied bombing had devastated many German cities, US ground forces had proved that German cities were not invincible and the Third Reich was beginning to fracture both externally and internally.

While General Courtney Hodges was focusing on his push to the east, he neglected to study regional maps of what appeared to be a densely forested area between the German cities of Aachen, Düren and Monschau. The US 9th Infantry Division had ventured into the forest in September 1944 and discovered that it was a challenging environment. Mighty Douglas firs and other tree varieties allowed little sunlight to infiltrate the ethereal, dank depths, which were pockmarked with muddy puddles that never evaporated due to the September rains. Approaching the Hürtgen Forest, a forward US reconnaissance team saw a vast, undulating sea of green that stretched as far as the eye could see. One of them was heard to say, 'We're going to send our boys to fight in that?'

CHAPTER NINE

MEANWHILE AT FORTRESS METZ

ONE OF THE STRONGEST POINTS on the famous French Maginot Line was located between the hills of the Ardennes and the Vosges in France. Metz had been a fortified city since ancient times, heavily rebuilt by France in the post-Napoleonic period, modernized by Germany in 1870–1914, and modernized again by France during the Maginot effort in 1935–40. Metz was inarguably the most heavily fortified portion of the Maginot Line, yet these defences had still been expertly circumnavigated by the Germans in 1940.

But in 1944 the situation was entirely different, with General George S. Patton and his Third Army planning an all-out frontal attack. He would use every means at his disposal to compromise the Maginot Line's fortifications and push forward into Germany. The boisterous general had energetically coursed 650 km (400 miles) across central France to the Lorraine region in a single month. As early as 8 September, the American 5th Infantry Division had established a bridgehead on the east bank of the Moselle to the south of Metz and hopes were high.

The Germans were to all intents and purposes retreating in disarray, and no one expected them to make a concerted effort to defend the

Moselle Line. But under the command of *Panzertruppen* general Otto Knobelsdorff and his First Army they would make a determined stand.

Even with the 'Red Ball Express' (the system of convoy trucks established in autumn 1944 to supply the Allied armies) running full out, Patton complained incessantly about the lack of adequate supplies he demanded in order to sustain the momentum, which by 23 September had ground to a stuttering halt. This was in part due to the tenacious German defence, but also due to the Allied shift in priority of focusing on moving north toward Belgium and Holland. Patton was allowed to conduct limited attacks, but remained under strict orders from SHAEF not to make any moves to surround and besiege Metz.

From September onwards, Patton's Third Army had been hammering at Metz but soon realized that taking the fortress system there was going to be considerably more difficult than Old Blood and Guts had initially assumed. Considered to be the most heavily fortified city in Europe at the time, it comprised 43 forts arrayed in an inner and outer belt that extended 10 km (6 miles) west of the Moselle and reached back another 6 km (4 miles) to the east of the city.

The most imposing forts in the complex were Driant and Jeanne d'Arc. Both were gargantuan constructions of steel and reinforced concrete, complete with guns housed in revolving steel turrets and the garrison protected in subterranean quarters surrounded by dry moats and multiple rows of barbed wire. Back in September, acting on the basis of erroneous intelligence reports that stated that Fort Driant was thinly held, Colonel Charles Yuill, commanding the 5th Division's 11th Infantry Regiment, drafted a plan of attack that was personally approved by Patton.

Although sporadic fighting continued throughout October it came to be regarded as a kind of hiatus, a time to prepare for the next moves. Troops were treated to movies and Bing Crosby. S/Sgt. Ed Stone, a correspondent for the US military newspaper *Stars and Stripes*, wrote in his 25 September 1944 column: 'Singing in mess halls, fields, from the backs of trucks in the squares of captured towns, Bing Crosby, together with his USO Campshow troupe, has traveled more than 1,500 miles and put on as many as five shows a day for American soldiers since his arrival in France Sept.

'Dressed in OD's and a fatigue hat, with his inevitable pipe in his mouth, Crosby has sung his way across France, putting on shows for troops spread from the beach heads to the front lines. On several occasions, the group has appeared within gunshot range of German positions. While in the Valognes area, Crosby joined forces with Fred Astaire, the star of another USO group, and during his visit to the troops of the 3rd Army, he sang with Dinah Shore and her entertainment unit. Crosby usually closes his programs by singing "White Christmas" and expressing the hope that Christmas, 1944, will find them home.'

On 3 November 1944 orders were issued for the attack and a reduction of the forts around Metz. Once this was achieved the Third Army could resume its offensive operations and push on to the Rhine. The plan would entail an encirclement of Metz, followed up with reconnaissance to the River Saar, the securing of a bridgehead in the vicinity of Saarburg and, in compliance with further orders, the continuation of the attack to the northeast. Regarding Metz, the order stated in no uncertain terms that the intention was to destroy or capture the Metz German garrison without having to lay siege to the forts, which in itself would be nigh on impossible.

What would ensue demanded a meticulous and perfectly orchestrated pincer movement. The 90th Infantry Division was allocated to implement the plan for the primary envelopment of the city from the north while the 5th Infantry Division was to hit Metz from the south. Once the concentric pincer had been closed, the 95th Infantry Division would be tasked with containing the salient west of the Moselle and securing the city. The 10th Armored 'Tiger' Division was earmarked to follow the 90th Division. At that time, the 10th Armored Division was commanded by Major General W. H. H. Morris, a West Point graduate and World War I veteran. He had led an infantry battalion in the famous St Mihiel and Meuse–Argonne operations, and had received the DSC for gallantry in action.

Of all the forts to be attacked, Driant was one of the strongest and most modern. Located in the outer belt surrounding Metz, 8 km (5 miles) southwest of the city on the west bank of the Moselle, it sat at the top of a 356 m (1,200 ft) hill, surrounded by rows of barbed wire on the outer perimeter and within by a dry moat that measured 18 x 6 m (60

A tank from the 10th Armored 'Tiger' Division on the move after the Battle of Metz. They would be the first American unit to reach Bastogne a few weeks later after the 'Battle of the Bulge' erupted.

x 20 ft), originally designed to slow down infantry and tracked vehicles. Its 100 mm and 150 mm guns were mounted in turrets visible above ground; the bunkers and the central fort were underground, linked by a complex network of tunnels, all protected by a roof of reinforced concrete 4.5 m (15 ft) thick.

Efforts to take Driant quickly assumed the characteristics of famous counter-mining battles such as the one fought at Messines in World War I. Attempts to eject the German defenders by aerial bombardment and shellfire met with little success due to the density of the fort's reinforced concrete.

Around 30,000 German troops defended the city of Metz. To the north, the 416th Infantry Division, with a strength estimated at 8,300 men, held the sector that extended from Koenigsmacker to the northern boundary of XX Corps. The 19th Infantry Division, which exceeded 5,000 troops, held the Moselle from Koenigsmacker south, 8 km (5 miles) shy of the city. South of Metz was the 17th SS Panzer Grenadier Division, numbering approximately 6,000 men. Other General Headquarters units, such as flak and artillery battalions, totalling 2,000 men, were liberally distributed throughout the area.

General Lieutenant Kittel, an expert in fortress defence, was transferred from the Eastern Front to take command of the 462nd *Volksgrenadier* Division. However, he didn't arrive in Metz until the operation had begun, and could only then position his units to meet the attack and issue orders to defend at all costs, echoing Hitler's standard 'last man, last cartridge' instructions.

THE TROUBLE WITH TANKS

October had been a leisurely month for most of Patton's Third Army. As torrential November rains pelted down a further attempt was made to cross the Moselle. Corporal Louis Gruntz was with the 712th Tank Battalion, 90th Division. In his recollection: 'As we attempted to cross the Moselle River, German artillery was finding the bridge sites with deadly and punishing accuracy. The rain had caused the Moselle River to burst its banks and at some places it was over 800 yards wide. This didn't stop those American engineers from struggling on.

'Every so often word would be received to "prepare to cross". When this came though, the tanks, sporting their newly attached floaters, which had been put on in record time, would crawl down the murky, muddy roads in the black of night, only to be informed that the river's strong currents had smashed the bridge, or mines had blown it, or direct shell hits had ruined it. A new bridge site would be chosen and the tanks would wade through the mud to get in proximity, only to find that the previous one had been re-designated for the job. The tankers spent wakeful nights in haylofts in the vicinity and listened to the nearby Long Toms sending barrages against the Germans.'

On 7 November, the 90th Division began to assemble its troops on the west bank of the Moselle across from the town of Koenigsmacker, from where it intended to make its river crossing. Meanwhile, the 5th Division had returned to its old positions in the bridgehead south of Metz. The XX Corps plan of attack entailed the 5th Division making its main effort in the south, commencing on 9 November. On 4 November General Walker decided that the 5th Division would not attack simultaneously with the XII Corps.

During the first week of November the 10th Armored Division was initially assigned to work with the 90th Division to affect the wide envelopment north of Metz, and had been given a narrow front west of Metz. The 10th Armored Division wouldn't be relieved until 8 November, by which time it had exceeded expectations and was already charging north.

The situation on the far bank finally reached such a critical stage that supporting armour became essential if it was to be retained and exploited. On 13 November, at 2 pm, B Company platoon from the 712th Tank Battalion pulled down to the river bank and, under an elaborate smoke screen, cautiously ferried across on rafts as German shells impacted the waters around them. The firepower of these five Shermans was far outweighed by the morale boost they gave to the exhausted GIs on the far bank who had been taking a hammering from the German artillery. It was an emotive moment as both B platoon and the C Company tanks that followed on shortly afterwards made it to the other side, where they were greeted with cheers and tears.

In no time at all armour disseminated to provide support for forward troops and the atmosphere changed from an overall feeling of last-ditch retention to aggressive offence. Meanwhile, work on the bridge continued, despite continued German attacks, and success came at last to the dogged engineers. By the evening of 14 November the entire battalion was across the pontoon bridge, along with great quantities of supplies. Louis Gruntz was in one of the first five tanks to cross on the rafts. General Patton immodestly said: 'The crossing of the Moselle by the 90th Division was one that will ever rank as one of the epic river crossings of history.'

As soon as they arrived on the far bank Louis was faced with another problem. During the afternoon of 13 November, just before dusk, one platoon of three tanks made an advance with infantry into an area called Reitholtz Woods. Louis described what happened next: 'We were advancing and we entered a mine field. My tank struck a mine and blew off one of the tracks. The infantry was walking along beside us. One of the infantry stepped on a mine and had his leg blown off. I could not get out to help him because we were under orders not to get out of the tank because it was too dangerous; if we tried to get out and help him we would probably step on a mine also. It was night and I could hear him crying. I yelled at him to put a tourniquet on his leg. We were ordered to stay put until the engineers could clear the minefield at daylight. I listened to the infantryman most of the night and yelled words of encouragement to him telling him everything would be alright. When daylight came I no longer heard the infantryman. His tank was pulled out of the minefield but I never discovered whether the infantryman was rescued or whether he died in that field.'[33]

By the end of November, and after a protracted and bitter struggle, only four forts, the ones that Kittel had chosen to fortify when he assumed command, were still occupied by German forces. On 8 December, the garrisons at St Quentin, Plappeville and Driant had all surrendered, and on 13 December the last stronghold of Fort Jeanne d'Arc finally capitulated. The fight was far from over and there was still work ahead for the Third Army but other matters would soon take precedence.

CHAPTER TEN

IF YOU GO DOWN TO THE WOODS

THE BATTLE OF THE HÜRTGEN Forest began in September 1944 and would endure until mid-February 1945. It was the longest and most protracted engagement the Americans ever fought in the history of the United States military. The US army would incur over 34,000 casualties in what became one of the bloodiest and most disastrous campaigns of World War II. It's still a contentious subject and historians continue to argue today whether or not it was necessary to enter those woods and fight the Germans on their own turf. The name Hürtgen doesn't appear on many memorials, and while some other battles in the autumn of 1944 were more dramatically decisive none was tougher or bloodier than this one.

Tightly ranked towering firs made the Hürtgen Forest a foreboding, sinister world where, once the rain clouds cleared, moonlight was muted to an eerie twilight that filtered through an almost impenetrable canopy on to tall pine trees surrounded by sodden pine needles and rotting forest debris. Every so often man-made ditches dissected the undergrowth, which had been dug as fire breaks. Occasionally, a woodsman's cottage could be spotted hidden among trees in a scene straight out of a Germanic fairy tale. The *Hürtgenwald*, to give it its German name, is sombre enough in peacetime, but in 1944–5 it was a grisly death trap complete with concealed enemies, whizzing bullets and thunderous bursting shells that reduced trees to matchwood and punctured the ground with shell craters, decomposing corpses and broken men.

By 12 September the 1st Infantry Division and 3rd Armored Division had reached the western border of Germany at the small town of Roetgen, south of Aachen. The 3rd Armored Combat Command B Task Force Lovelady, under the command of Lt. Col. William B. Lovelady, was the first Allied force to enter the area. Inclement weather, an unreliable supply system and a very organized enemy soon began to hamper its progress. This region would ultimately become synonymous with unprecedented tragedy and terrible suffering for all who fought there. The decision to go in would deprive the American soldiers who fought through this green hell of all previous tactical advantages.

The 60th Infantry, 9th Division, had already experienced an ominous taste of what lay in store. It was commanded by Major General Louis A. Craig, who had led his men through some tough times, from the deserts of North Africa and across France. By the time it reached Hürtgen the division's 60th Infantry Regiment was operating at less than 40 per cent strength. The 9th's other two regiments, the 39th and 47th, were also understrength. Throughout most of September they had operated on an extended front that stretched from Schevenhuette, near Stolberg, south through the Hürtgen Forest and the Monschau Corridor and to the Hoefen-Alzen ridge, southeast of Monschau, a distance of more than 30 km (20 miles). They had entered the forest and been badly mauled by small but tenacious German units. Bloodied and stunned, they soon recoiled in disorder. They had discovered to their chagrin that inside the triangle was a densely forested region of deep gorges, high ridges and narrow trails. This terrain was ideally suited for a defensive position and would prove a tremendous impediment to the First Army's drive to the River Roer.

Within the boundaries of the forest are numerous ridges and hills with vertiginous gradients and hardly any navigable roads. It is home to some of the most rugged terrain in Europe. Nestled at the base of the two main ridges that divide the forest is the River Kall, a waterway that isn't actually much more than a stream depending on the time of year. To add insult to injury, two bands of the Siegfried Line also ran right through the middle of the forest. In its densest corners, visibility in the forest extended to just 15 m (50 ft).

The Allies had been getting used to warm welcomes and exuberant receptions, but that only applied when they arrived anywhere as an army of liberation. Once they entered the German-speaking area of Belgium and physically crossed the border, there were no shouts of '*Vive les allies*'. Now they were an invading army, an army of occupation, and the indigenous populations weren't so happy to see them. There were portentous precursors of the shape of things to come, and this was something Allied soldiers felt as they approached the perimeter of the Hürtgen Forest region at the small town of Roetgen. One GI was heard cynically singing, 'If you go down to the woods today, you're sure of a big surprise.' Most soldiers were superstitious by nature and the omens were most definitely not favourable.

Alfred F. Knaack of 9th Infantry Division, 60th Regiment, experienced the Hürtgen Forest in September and October 1944. 'We were firing support for another company that was trying to advance,' he later recalled. 'No.2 gun was doing the firing, I was in the bunker at my gun, No.3, with the telephone relaying fire orders to No.2. Suddenly the guys on No.2 said they were out of action and I was ordered to put my gun in play. I had just fired five rounds and the order was for 5 more same place. So I got 5 more ready and had dropped two and had the next two in my hands ready to drop when it happened.

'Next thing I remember, I was flat on my back looking up, except I couldn't see. My hands were numb but everything else seemed to work. Without thinking about falling shells I got up and walked back to my bunker. So this is what it's like to be a casualty. In a way it was a relief, nearly everyone who is under fire gets it sooner or later.'[34]

Knaack could not bring himself to talk about his experiences until almost 70 years later. In March 2003 he went to Europe to visit his old battleground. Thanks to the assistance of his son, John, his nephew Jim Mitchell and former Hürtgenwald Museum proprietor Manfred Klinkenberg, they were able to find the exact spot where Alfred was wounded. The Hürtgen remains a pristine, almost untouched battlefield and together they managed to discover Alfred's actual foxhole, along with the foxholes of No.2 and No.1 guns. They also saw two obvious square depressions where the CPs had been located.

THE CALM BEFORE THE STORM

As American troops entered the forest they trod cautiously, watching every tentative step forward and knowing that their opponents were laying in wait on familiar ground. The Germans had managed to transform the forest into an impenetrable labyrinth of well-camouflaged pillboxes complete with interlocking fields of fire, reams of barbed wire and minefields. The few roads and trails that did run through the forest had been zeroed by enemy artillery. Months earlier, the German Todt Organization had established a checkerboard complex of pillboxes constructed from both reinforced concrete and wooden logs.

Chester H. Jordan was a first lieutenant in Company K, 47th Infantry Battalion. According to him: 'For two days we saw nothing but trees. We saw no Germans, no buildings. Nothing. On the second day, we were so close to Zweifall that their air raid sirens sounded as though they were in the next row of trees. Our radios picked up their air raid warning: "*Achtung! Achtung!*"' By the third day, Jordan and his companions were attacking northeast, and were perched on a hillside trail. Below them, in plain sight, people in the hamlet of Schevenhütte pursued their business seemingly without regard for the war. The astonished lieutenant then saw a German officer strolling along near his position studying a map. Jordan recalled that 'None of us had ever heard of a Kraut officer going anywhere alone, so we expected the shit to fly at any minute. We grabbed guns and ran or fell down the steep slope. It was a German colonel, who was not only surprised but pissed off something terrible. We de-souvenired him and sent him back.' The platoon continued over a road and climbed another ridge. 'Sergeant Myers was the last to cross the road, and as he did, he heard a motorcycle coming from the east. Myers knelt next to a tree and fired. He blew the rider into the ditch. I called a halt and radioed for instructions. They said, "Take the village." We did a left face and raced down the hill to the village. Our speed was the product of the steep hill rather than combat zeal.

'As we ran through the backyards, I looked for the handiest back door. The one I opened led into a small commercial kitchen and then directly into the taproom of a small hotel. The only inhabitant was a dignified old man with a large moustache who was wearing a frock-tailed coat and a shirt with a winged collar. I motioned him behind the bar and had him draw beer for the three of us in the room. I was getting ready for a second round when I heard rifle fire outside. As I emerged from the bar I could see the [American] machine gun section standing by the church on the Gressenich road [another town within the forest]. The section had been going down the road to set up the MG when a Volkswagen jeep with four Kraut soldiers came barrelling by. The Germans waved, and our men reciprocated and both realized at the same time that they were fraternizing with the enemy. They had managed a few rifle shots, but by that time the car had turned left at the church and headed for Düren. The foe vanished, abandoning the vehicle by a creek whose bridge had been blown.'[35]

Throughout the ensuing three days Wehrmacht soldiers, not realizing the Americans were in control, wandered into Schevenhütte. The GIs utilized a massive communications bunker in the village for their headquarters. Jordan's battalion commander sent a German-speaking sergeant up to intercept messages detailing assembly points. He promptly relayed the data to the artillery. Isolated from the remainder of the company, Jordan and his small band endured several days of sparse rations and the unsettling noise of vigorous activity by enemy troops nearby. Eventually, the platoon pulled back to the ridge above Schevenhütte, while others from the 47th took up positions in the area.

Elsewhere, other 9th Infantry Division soldiers entered a far more deadly environment. The 39th Regiment pressed an attack at Lammersdorf on the edge of the forest about 13 km (8 miles) south of Schevenhütte. From a hill overlooking that village, the Germans hammered the Americans with everything from small arms to heavy artillery. 'The enemy attacked five or six times,' a German officer reported. 'The regularity was amazing, the more so since each attack was repulsed mostly with great losses. For the latter reason, the enemy requested a short, one-day armistice to recover wounded and bury dead. That was granted. Nevertheless, the attack was repeated the following day at the usual time.' It took two weeks for the 39th to dislodge the defenders.

The advance of the 60th Regiment toward the Höfen-Alzen ridge south of Simmerath proved equally frustrating. Command and control broke down as tree bursts showered deadly shrapnel upon prone soldiers and those crouched in foxholes. Enemy fire drenched open areas, and the available maps provided little information on the few trails that could be found. Radios functioned poorly in the thick woods and mines lurked just beneath the surface. The steel-reinforced concrete bunkers, often protected by layers of earth, were impervious to satchel charges. It often required as many as a dozen hits from 155 mm artillery shells to force the inhabitants to surrender. The pillboxes defied even Allied fighter-bombers. Buttressed by their massive defensive positions, the Germans counterattacked, hitting the 39th and 60th regiments hard. Nevertheless, aided by tanks from the 3rd Armored Division, the Americans slowly forged ahead.

The Germans rushed in reinforcements to confront the deepest penetration by the GIs, at the town of Germeter, 5 km (3 miles) from the strategic hub of Schmidt. Between 6–16 October the 9th Division gained about 3 km (2 miles) at a cost of 4,500 men killed, wounded or missing. Having battled its way only a short distance into the forest, the 9th Division was depleted and exhausted. Heavy rains also took a heavy toll on personnel and equipment, the ground becoming a virtual quagmire. Even when the weather improved slightly, it never lasted long enough for the saturated ground to dry out properly. Soldiers in the Hürtgen often found themselves wallowing in a sea of mud reminiscent of World War I.

Lieutenant General Courtney H. Hodges as commander of the First Army would oversee the eventual incursion into the forest. Ensconced in the beautiful Belgian Ardennes town of Spa, he took comfortable quarters in Hindenburg's old suite at the Britannique Hotel from where he settled in to consider his options for the late autumn campaign. Hodges was in command of three corps that belonged to the First Army totalling more than 256,000 men. They were deployed on a line that ran from north to south. Major General Charles H. Corlett's XIX Corps was on the northern section of the German–Belgian border, while Major

General J. Lawton Collins' VII Corps held the centre and Major General Leonard Gerow's V Corps were arrayed to the south. As early as 6 September 1944 Hodges had somewhat audaciously told his staff that, with ten more days of good weather, the war would be over.

Unlike most of his contemporaries, Hodges had failed at West Point Military Academy. He'd had to start from scratch, rising through the ranks after enlisting as a private in 1905. He was the son of a newspaper publisher from southern Georgia. Physically he was of average height with a deportment that made him appear taller. His long face was crowned with a capacious domed forehead and prominent ears. Hodges was generally regarded as a stoic, inarticulate and unimpressive figure. He seldom visited his corps and division commanders in the field, preferring to have them visit his headquarters and brief him there. He had earned a reputation of being extremely intolerant of any mistake and he was always quick to relieve subordinate commanders when he suspected that they were lacking drive and initiative. It was said that he delegated much of the command and control of the First Army to his chief of staff, Major General William B. Kean. Eisenhower once said of Hodges, 'God gave him a face that always looked pessimistic.'

At the southern edge of the forest is one of the largest Roer barricades, the imposing Schwammenauel Dam. It provided vital hydroelectric power for Germany's industrial heartland, but surprisingly didn't even feature in the planning for the offensive in the Hürtgen Forest. Young Ludwig Fischer was only seven years old in late 1944 and lived in the village of Schmidt on the western edge of the forest. He had seen US army vehicles and knew that the war was getting closer. It would soon get too close for comfort. 'We were evacuated shortly before the fighting started but I returned to live in Schmidt after the war. There was almost nothing left of my once beautiful little town.'

By the end of September it was acknowledged at SHAEF that Monty's foray into the Netherlands had been an abject failure. Moreover, the Allied armies in general had only achieved limited territorial gains that month. This was blamed on factors such as bad weather and German resistance, but the real problem facing all the armies in the field was the lack of supplies due to a crippled logistical structure. And things only got worse as September turned into October.

THE BATTLE OF HÜRTGEN FOREST

The German army situation after the fall of Aachen was difficult to ascertain. OKW (*Oberkommando der Wehrmacht*, or the German armed forces' High Command) was fully aware of the inevitability of a fresh Allied offensive. Whether it would be ready to meet it was another matter entirely. A concerted counterattack by the Germans at that moment in time was out of the question, but they would doubtless give everything they had to defend the *heimat* (homeland) and were in better condition to implement a resolute defence than they had been in September.

Generalfeldmarschall Walter Model was in full control of the situation and, moreover, he was one of the few commanders in the field who dared to contradict Hitler. Also, despite the almost continuous bombing orchestrated by the Allies, he was still able to draw from a considerable pool of manpower. Patton instinctively suspected that the German army was far from being a spent force, as it would inevitably prove later.

In October 1944 radical changes were occurring in the German armed forces. That month saw the introduction of the *Volksgrenadier* and *Volksturm* units. Anything in German with the prefix *volks* implied that it was 'of the people' or 'the folk'. The *Volksgrenadier* units were in fact the remnants of the *Heer* (regular army) units that had been given a new name to emphasize that they were now fighting for their people and performing a patriotic duty. *Volksturm* were quite different. These ad hoc units had been largely assembled from those who were previously considered outside the normal parameters for conscription, such as teenage boys and pensioners.

The problem from Model's perspective was slightly more disconcerting. He was strictly against removing units from the Eastern Front and deploying them in the west. This was due to the massive build-up of Red Army forces that were currently bearing down on German positions in the autumn of 1944. He saw it as essentially robbing Peter to pay Paul and that in the long run it would cost the German army dearly (only one in nine German soldiers died fighting in the western theatre). Yet even though the Eastern Front accounted for a much heavier German death toll, after the war the German general Rudolf Christoph Freiherr von Gersdorff still maintained that, 'I have engaged in the long campaigns

GIs of Co. E, 110th Regiment, 28th US Infantry Division in the Hürtgen Forest near the Raffelsbrand road junction.

in Russia as well as other fronts and I believe the fighting in the Hürtgen was the heaviest I have ever witnessed.'

The Battle of Hürtgen Forest did not officially end until February 1945, with the major fighting taking place during the three wet, cold, miserable months of mid-September through to mid-December 1944. The battle claimed 24,000 Americans, killed, missing, captured and wounded, plus another 9,000 who succumbed to trench foot, respiratory diseases and combat fatigue.

In this same period, 120,000 American soldiers advanced upon the Germans through the forest and took 70 square km (27 sq miles) of real estate that had questionable tactical value for future operations. On the other hand, they had destroyed enemy troops and reserves that the Germans could ill afford to lose. The Germans, for their part and with only meagre resources, delayed a major Allied advance for three arduous months. By the end of November, the area's dams along the River Roer were still in German hands. Their importance would not be realized until late in the fighting, and between 4–11 December the RAF dropped approximately 2,000 tons of bombs on these dams – ineffectively, as it turned out. In fact, calling for air support in the Hürtgen was often superfluous and counterproductive because of the dense canopy, so it was usually left to the infantry to do the hard work on the ground.

If Hodges and his First Army had gone for the River Roer dams early in the fighting, entering the Hürtgen Forest would have been surplus to requirements. An attack directly from the south to capture the dams would have reduced the number of Allied casualties and been tactically more effective. It has long been agreed among historians that those who fought in the Hürtgen Forest engaged in a misconceived and basically fruitless battle that could, and should, have been avoided.

Hodges, arguably the least talented of all US generals in the ETO, remained inflexible; he had every intention of sticking to his agenda. He decided that before he could push on to his objective it was imperative to clear and secure the area from Monschau to Schmidt, and that entailed clearing the Hürtgen Forest. His intelligence officers errantly assured him that this goal could be achieved in a matter of weeks. General 'Lightning Joe' Collins later defended the incursion into the forest when he said, 'Somebody had to cover the Hürtgen Forest. I happened to be the unlucky one this time. But not all of it, because later on, the area was turned over to a different corps, and it did the real fighting in the forest. We fought on the fringe of the forest, most of it. We did finally clear the top end of it but it was tough going. Anybody who had to fight there would have had the same problem. Nobody was enthusiastic about fighting there, but what was the alternative? The Germans didn't counterattack against my flank, because we had some troops there that would have prevented them from doing so, but if we would have turned loose of the Hürtgen and let the Germans roam there, they could have hit my flank. It's easy to go back to second-guess and say, "Well, you shouldn't have done that." Then what would you have done? Who would have cleared it? How much time would it have taken? Nobody was enthusiastic about it, least of all the 704th, but we had to do it. That was part of our job, but we didn't fight it all. The V Corps later took over. The forest covered a series of dams that our intelligence people had alerted us about.'[36]

Collins, who often lectured that the three most important initial aspects of any campaign were 'terrain, terrain, terrain', apparently had not absorbed his own lesson when he decided to move his corps through the Hürtgen. Moreover, it was one American soldier who had lived in the area as a boy that alerted the US forces to the presence of the dam. No one at SHAEF had any idea that it was in such close proximity to the attacking forces.

The German defenders found it quite inexplicable that the Americans would launch an offensive in this inhospitable and almost impenetrable forest terrain. German strategists believed no sensible adversary would seek to infiltrate the place they had honeycombed with thickly shielded emplacements capable of providing murderous crossfire.

After VII Corps had tried unsuccessfully to pave a way through the forest, Hodges allocated the task of capturing Schmidt to Major General Leonard T. Gerow's V Corps. Gerow, in turn, was perfectly happy to pass on the mission to General Norman 'Dutch' Cota's 28th Infantry Division. Cota had been the hero of D-Day, the oldest and possibly most senior officer to lead the assault on Omaha Beach at the head of his so-called 'Bastard Brigade'. Defying his 51 years, Cota repeatedly crossed the beach under fire, leading, directing and encouraging hundreds of American soldiers, many of whom were sheltering behind beach obstacles, disabled Sherman tanks and the shingle wall below the German pillboxes. Revered by his men and fellow officers, Cota and his 28th Division were seen as the ideal replacements to take over attacks into the Hürtgen Forest.

'THE WORST CONDITIONS I EVER HAD TO FIGHT UNDER'

At the time of the first infiltrations into the Hürtgen region, Field Marshal Walter Model's Army Group B and General Erich Brandenberger's Seventh Army occupied positions there. Brandenberger could only field two understrength corps to hold both Hürtgen and Aachen. His left flank was held by the 353rd, with five battalions of *Landsschutzen* (security troops) and several second-line Luftwaffe fortress battalions. In August, a new unit called the *Panzer Jager* 519 was formed with a company of 14 Panthers, two companies armed with 14 Stug assault guns and three *Jagdpanthers*. The new unit was first given to the 1st SS *Panzer Korps* but was later reallocated to the 116th Panzer Division in the Hürtgen Forest.

Now it was the turn of the 28th Division to go on the offensive in that foreboding forest. Schmidt was regarded as an important objective because of its geographic location on high ground in proximity to the Schwammenauel Dam. The first problem the 28th encountered was the maps. The topographic maps they used were primarily the standard 1:25,000 versions and were considered to be accurate. The problem was that they indicated roads running between the two villages of Vossenack and Schmidt that were in fact just narrow paths. The maps didn't provide the correct elevation of the two ridges in the vicinity either. Between those steep ridges there is a precipitous gorge and, at the base, the River Kall, which was usually a quiet, picturesque, babbling stream but a few weeks of torrential rain had transformed it into a fast-flowing river.

The general purpose of the second attack on Schmidt was expected to provide additional supply routes for the planned VII Corps attack to the north, while covering its right flank from counterattack. This would all culminate in a massive offensive against the Roer dams. It was also hoped that an attack on Schmidt would cause the German army to syphon off reserves that could be deployed against the First Army's main drive east. It looked good on paper, but the 9th Division had already tried and failed to take Schmidt in October. Despite this, military planners indicated that it remained a thorn in the side of VII Corps' offensive plans. It was generally acknowledged at First Army HQ that in providing a force to take Schmidt they would be compelled to tap strength from the main effort. Hodges amended the situation by redrawing the corps boundaries so that V Corps would assume responsibility for taking Schmidt from VII Corps.

Corporal Bob Bradicich of 110th Infantry Regiment, 28th Division, later wrote: 'The weather was miserable, very cold, muddy roads, and snow managed to seep through the heavy trees of the forest. The thick covering of pine needles managed to keep the mud underneath from

US tanks make their way along a narrow road in the Hürtgen Forest, 18 November 1944.

freezing. Walking through the forest your feet got wet and, with the freezing temperature, it went right through to your bones. Just walking to the front, I was ready to leave. If this was not enough, we had to contend with Germans and the 88s which always exploded high in the trees. These were called "tree burst". The tops of the trees were broken off and came falling down, you hoped not on you. Along with the branches and the tops of the trees, the exploding shells rained shrapnel down on top of you. To sum it up, I was fighting the cold, the wet under foot, the snow, the tops of the trees, the 88s, the shrapnel and let us not forget the Germans. These were the worst conditions I ever had to fight under. We didn't have any artillery support because they couldn't hit the bunkers, and the shells would explode in the trees, which was where we were. Something to do with the angle the shell comes in at, and you can't fire mortars in a forest. This was the hellhole of all hellholes. I don't think hell could be this bad.'[37]

The 28th US Infantry Division was given the order to take the area of Vossenack, Schmidt and Lammersdorf with the objective of circumnavigating the Germans that were in the Monschau corridor. Zero hour was 2 November at 9 am. The date was poignant for the Germans because it is All Souls' Day.

The densely wooded ridges of Vossenack, Brandenberg, Hürtgen, Kommerscheidt and Schmidt were a daunting prospect for any army on the offensive owing to the steepness of their inclines, with 1-in-2 and 1-in-3 gradients not unusual. The forest canopy had prevented any air reconnaissance and potential air support, so it was going to be left to artillery units in Roetgen to soften up the targets, if they could zero them. The German defenders were fully prepared and had anticipated another assault on Schmidt, they just didn't know precisely when it would occur. General Cota later admitted to having 'grave misgivings' regarding the operation, but at the time he reluctantly sanctioned the attack.

Neither Cota nor his staff had ordered sufficient reconnaissance of the target area. Consequently, they had little idea of the enemy's dispositions and strengths or the locations of obstacles and reinforced pillboxes. Corps intelligence had identified the 275th and 89th German divisions defending east of Schmidt. What they didn't know was that the 272nd *Volksgrenadier* Division, along with the 1023rd Reserve Grenadier Regiment, the 189th Fusilier Battalion and the 1403rd *Festung* (Fortress) Infantry Battalion were preparing to relieve the 89th when Cota's 28th Division attacked. The 28th would in effect be outnumbered four to one. To the south of the 28th Infantry's position was Hill 400 that was occupied by a German artillery unit. It was on the highest elevation in the forest and had a perfect panoramic view of the whole area. At the top of the Kall trail there's an open plateau that effectively rendered all Sherman tanks vulnerable as soon as they emerged. It was a perfect killing zone for the Germans.

Hans Herbst of 116th German Panzer Division, LXXIV Corps, 5th Panzer Army, Army Group B, said that 'Model had ordered us to move into the sector in early November. We knew exactly where the Americans were. I didn't understand why they wanted to fight there, it was not a good place for them. Even our armour had trouble moving through those

General Norman 'Dutch' Cota, 28th Infantry Division at his headquarters in Rott, near Hürtgen, Germany, 8 November 1944, shortly after the attack on Schmidt.

woods, but we soon got to know our way around. That was thanks to some of our men who were from the region and knew it very well. In open ground the Americans had the advantage like they had in Normandy but not in the Hürtgen, no, no, we had them there. This was the first part of the Battle of the Bulge for us and we gave them a very hard time. I had a *panzerfaust* antitank weapon and thanks to the good cover in the Hürtgen it was possible to get right up close to the American vehicles, and fire almost point blank. The weather was a serious problem though. I never got completely dry the whole time that I was in there. I was always damp and cold down to my underwear the whole time.'[38]

Sixty minutes before zero hour a deafening but largely ineffective US artillery barrage opened the proceedings. The first attack was ordered to begin at 9 am on 2 November with the 109th Infantry supported by the 2nd Battalion of the 112th leading the way in a northerly direction toward Hürtgen. They ran into trouble almost immediately when they stumbled across a densely packed minefield. 110th Infantry supported by two battalions of the 112th were timed to join in at midday. As the GIs from the 109th clambered out of their foxholes, the 112th Regiment moved forward over a thin smattering of snow and it soon became glaringly apparent that three factors were going to impede the progress of this battle: terrain, weather and the enemy. The 112th fared slightly better. Its 2nd Battalion captured Vossenack and began digging in, unaware that Germans on a nearby ridge were watching their every move. Further south, the 110th Regiment's attack on Simonskall prevaricated after it received heavy enfilading fire emanating from a network of minefields, concertina wire and pillboxes near Raffelsbrand. In the resulting confusion, soldiers became separated from their units and general chaos ensued.

Cota was hoping that the cart track across the Kall gorge, the main supply route, would be navigable. As things transpired, getting tanks across the Kall gorge from Vossenack to Schmidt proved nigh on impossible. On the day, the early morning light snowfall had turned to a saturating drizzle that drenched the GIs to the skin and caused US vehicles to slip and slide in all directions. General Cota made no bones about the fact that he thoroughly disliked the original battle plan that called for dividing his division and sending it on three divergent missions. Yet back at V Corps HQ General Gerow remained intransigent, a factor that determined the eventual outcome of the engagement.

Pushing on, the 28th Division entered a disfigured forest area that was littered with debris from the battered 9th Division and the German defenders. Torrential autumn rains pelted the troops. According to the initial plans, the attack was supposed to have air support, but bad weather kept the aeroplanes grounded when the first attacks went in. It would take until noon to get them in the air, and even then their effect would be limited. These planes inflicted collateral damage by accidentally bombing an American artillery position, killing seven and wounding 17 GIs.

Back in September, the 893rd Tank Destroyer Battalion had been heavily engaged with the enemy along the Siegfried Line and had played a major role in the battle at Aachen. On 4 November, in support of the 28th Infantry Division, it was dispatched to capture the village of Schmidt under the leadership of Lieutenant Turney W. Leonard. It was also charged with protecting the Schwammenauel Dam from being sabotaged by the Germans. Leonard was wounded but did not require evacuation. His tank unit helped turn back the German attack and captured the village of Vossenack in the process.

As the bitter cold and rain poured down, German Panzers counterattacked on 4 November, pushing the American units back to Kommerscheidt Hill. Security along the icy Vossenack–Kommerscheidt road became a tremendous problem as US tanks slid into ditches and were delayed by land mines. On 5 November, Company C, commanded by Captain Pugh and Lieutenant Leonard, again engaged the enemy. Casualties were high and ammunition was low as the American forces were ordered to hold their position and push forward. On the morning of 6 November intense fire continued on both sides, again resulting in the loss of men and tanks in Charlie Company. Leonard was wounded again, yet stayed with his men. To assist Leonard's unit, Captain Pugh called in supporting or covering artillery. To prevent being overrun, Leonard took charge and reorganized the leaderless and confused infantrymen, led them to cover, consolidated their ammunition and set up a line of resistance before getting wounded a third time.

Sergeant John R. Vitchock, of Republic, Pennsylvania, recalled: 'When we entered the fighting at Kommerscheidt, Lt. Leonard advanced alone under heavy enemy fire to scout German tank platoons. Moving out and returning to direct our fire, he went up and down a wide hill in concentrated fire of enemy tanks and mortars. He found enemy tanks in a haystack that was boarded at the bottom, and our Destroyers knocked them out. When the leaders of several Infantry units were killed, he took over these groups and reorganized them to keep them in the fight.'[39]

The resulting attack by German Mark VI Tiger tanks was directly over Leonard's position. In the fight he was credited with taking out six enemy tanks before being disabled. An exploding shell shattered his left arm just below the shoulder but, somehow, he managed to apply a tourniquet with his belt before heading for the field aid station. He was critically wounded and too ill to be carried on a litter so army medics covered him with foliage to conceal his position. He was later declared MIA and his body not recovered until after the war. He was 23 years old at the time of his death.

In the after action report, Captain Pugh reported that all the platoon leaders in Charlie Company had been killed. US units in Kommerscheidt were ordered to withdraw on 9 November and infiltrate through enemy lines to return to American-held positions. Company C destroyed 17 enemy tanks, lost 11 of its own tanks and sustained massive casualties, with only one officer and 27 men able to pull back, many on stretchers.

Lt. Turney W. Leonard's Medal of Honor citation reads: 'He displayed extraordinary heroism while commanding a platoon of mobile weapons at Kommerscheidt, Germany, on 4, 5, and 6 November 1944. During the fierce 3-day engagement, he repeatedly braved overwhelming enemy fire in advance of his platoon to direct the fire of his tank destroyer from exposed, dismounted positions. He went on lone reconnaissance missions to discover what opposition his men faced, and on 1 occasion, when fired upon by a hostile machinegun, advanced alone and eliminated the enemy emplacement with a hand grenade. When a strong German attack threatened to overrun friendly positions, he moved through withering artillery, mortar, and small arms fire, reorganized confused infantry units whose leaders had become casualties, and exhorted them to hold firm. Although wounded early in battle, he continued to direct fire from his advanced position until he was disabled by a high-explosive shell, which shattered his arm, forcing him to withdraw. He was last seen at a medical aid station, which was subsequently captured by the enemy. By his superb courage, inspiring leadership, and indomitable fighting spirit, 1st Lt. Leonard enabled our forces to hold off the enemy attack and was personally responsible for the direction of fire which destroyed 6 German tanks.'[40]

THE GERMAN COUNTERATTACK

Ironically, the name of the original German commander that had opposed the earlier attack on Schmidt was General Schmidt of the 275th Division. He still held the front in early November. The 275th was part of General Straube's LXXIV Corps that operated under the indolent auspices of General Brandenberger's Seventh Army. German defenders in the

Hürtgen were at that time a peculiar collection, comprised in some cases of remnants requisitioned from other German units for the duration.

Hubert Gees of the 275th Infantry Division wrote: 'On the morning of November 2nd (All Souls' Day), a massive barrage erupted on our positions. The 109th US Regiment struck north. All our telephone and radio connections failed us so our forward observers and myself were ordered to report to the battalion as soon as possible on the situation.

'We hurried along and saw the shattered telephone cable about 500 yards from our position. Suddenly barely 20 paces in front of us a group of Americans appeared with rifles ready to fire. We were shocked, but even before the GIs had time to fire we disappeared back into the forest. We ran for our lives. One of our officers screamed and began staggering. A bullet had hit him. As soon as we got back to our positions, we took a closer look at his wound. He had been shot through the elbow. He had a "blighty wound" that would get him sent home, I envied him at that moment.

'On the afternoon of Nov. 2 we immediately deployed to the "Wild Boar" minefield, which had already been laid on the western side of the road behind us. We held this position until the 20th of November.

'On Nov. 3, our leaders threw the 116th Panzer Division into the fray between Schmidt and Hürtgen. On Nov. 4, determined counterattacks began. In the area of Vossenack and Schmidt fierce fighting raged, accompanied by heavy artillery fire and tank fire. The US Air Force constantly intervened in the ground battles. Thankfully, on some days the bad weather (fog) hindered them.'[41]

At 9 am, the 112th Infantry, led the 28th's main effort and began its attack to assault Schmidt. But as soon as the lead companies had jumped off and crossed the line of departure, they began taking casualties from German artillery fire. The Germans had evolved a method of firing at the treetops to cause what the GIs referred to as 'tree burst'. This method combined deadly wood splinters with the fragments of their artillery shells that rained down on the heads of GIs in proximity and caused horrific injuries and death. Apparently, the best way to deal with this situation was to hug a tree. The splinters would rain down umbrella style to the ground so the closer one could get to the tree trunk when the shells impacted above the safer one was.

Captain (*Hauptmann*) Erwin Kressman, Heavy Tank Destroyer Unit 519 (*Jägerabteilung*) earned a Knight's Cross in the Hürtgen. He recalled: 'I was a captain of my unit, 519. In October 1944, we became attached to the 116th Panzer Division and transferred to the Western Front. At that time my company had 14 *Jagdpanthers*. We moved to Nideggen not far from Schmidt on November 3. On that day the Americans had taken it. Our whole division was cleverly concealed in the small town, and our vehicles, which had considerable size, were camouflaged in-between the houses. I immediately began exploring the possibilities to launch a counterattack.

'Until then, we had seen combat at Wurselen in the Aachen area and in Stolberg. On the morning of November 4 we advanced towards Harscheidt, where we contacted the German 1055th Infantry Regiment of the 89th Infantry Division. It was feared that the Americans would continue their attacks so General Bruns, Commander of 89th Infantry Division, gave the order to begin an assault against American positions. Our attack began at 08:00 from the left of Schmidt. We attacked a location held by enemy infantry. We didn't know if the Americans had upper tanks. So I wanted to infiltrate the enemy infantry and draw them out because while we were static our heavy panthers were very vulnerable to them. One of the big advantages we had over the Americans was the high range of our 88 mm guns, and we wanted to take full advantage of them. Of course, we also shot at individual foxholes when we recognized American soldiers in them. Around 11 o'clock, our forces managed to take Schmidt.

'One of my commanders was a corporal who wore a gold Knight's Cross, but I don't remember his name. He was the most composed person under fire that I had ever seen. Even in battle he was calm, his crew liked and trusted him implicitly. When we reached the north exit of Schmidt at midday, things changed. About an hour later we were ordered to continue the attack. I could not believe my ears, attack in broad daylight with strong enemy artillery superiority and good visibility, which could make the use of enemy fighter-bombers possible at any time. We managed to hold our positions and inflict a lot of damage. When it was over we cheered for our commander.'[42]

On 3 November, assisted by a combat command of the 5th Armored Division, the 112th Regiment captured Schmidt. As reinforcing armour hit the Kall trail it became obvious that the road was far too narrow and unstable to support vehicles. Engineers were immediately dispatched to widen the trail, but as the first tank moved down the trail it rolled over a mine and lost a track. Consequently, only three tanks were able to reinforce the battalion in maintaining a tenuous grasp on Schmidt. The following morning the Germans counterattacked with tanks of the 116th Panzer Division, supported by infantry. Cota had already committed his reserves to assist the 4th Infantry Division who were in Monschau, so no help could be expected for the American battalion in Schmidt.

The German defenders were quick to seize the opportunity to counterattack and overran Schmidt in a matter of hours. As the reports reached Cota, sensing impending doom he gave orders to reorganize the remainders of the shattered 3rd Battalion, 112th Infantry, and 3rd Battalion, 110th Infantry, and provided them with seven tanks. Then, in

A US infantryman helps his buddy up a slope in the Hürtgen Forest, 18 November 1944.

an uncharacteristic error of judgement, ordered them to recapture Schmidt. As American infantry and tanks moved up the Kall trail they began receiving accurate enemy small arms and artillery fire. The ensuing fight was a vicious and costly encounter as both sides attempted to gain the advantage. By nightfall the situation had reached stalemate. Exhausted American survivors began a costly withdrawal down the trail that signalled the end of the second attack on Schmidt. The 28th Infantry Division incurred 6,184 casualties, with the 112th Infantry alone losing 2,093, including 544 that succumbed to frostbite and trench foot due to the terrible weather conditions.

The division was relieved on 13 November by the 8th Infantry Division and dispatched to the seemingly innocuous Ardennes sector to rest and refit. During their time in the Hürtgen the Germans ignominiously referred to the 28th Division's keystone emblem as the 'Bloody bucket'. American sacrifices that occurred there during this battle of attrition would be largely overshadowed by the ensuing Battle of the Bulge, but German veterans would frequently refer to the fighting in the Hürtgen as the 'Battle of the Bulge, part one', and subsequently claim it was their victory.

'It seemed so strange to see a wire strung between two trees with turkeys strung on them for Thanksgiving as I was riding in the back of a truck with other replacements in the Hürtgen Forest. The next thing I saw was a dead German soldier laying close to the mud road and I thought he should be moved to avoid being run over,' said Sergeant Robert Westerman when he spent his first and last Thanksgiving in the Hürtgen Forest and experienced some of the worst fighting during those final weeks of November 1944. 'I went on and joined my platoon. I will always remember days later it appeared we had come to the end of the forest, but no one said so.

'One night Nicolas Antounex and I were told to take a Jeep to the battalion commander. Nick drove and on the way we got stuck in the mud all the way up to the bottom of the Jeep. He raced the motor so hard the Germans apparently heard us. They shot 88s at us, and as they came pouring in we laid in a ditch beside the Jeep. Nicky, a Catholic, prayed so loud, almost screaming, and I felt included. As a Protestant I didn't understand all of those beads, but I did the cross and it was a comfort. Later Nicky gave me a rosary.

'We finally got the Jeep out of the mud and took it to the battalion commander. He was at the front giving instructions to his battalion. There we were in the woods alongside a wide-open field about the size of a football field. The Germans were across that no man's land in the woods. We were told that a 105 antitank gun on wheels needed to be moved to a place in the woods where our antitank platoon was waiting, but could not be moved through the trees where we were. It was hooked to the Jeep and Nicky and I were told to tow it another way through the woods and get it to where the antitank platoon was waiting. We did, and was told later that it helped. We were both given Bronze Stars.

'In the Hürtgen the Germans built some good foxholes, and at times we would take them over. In the forest we picked up one of our dead from one of those German foxholes. I always wondered if he had been hit and crawled in there and died, but the answer is unknown. ... In the Hürtgen, walking in the woods close to a muddy road, [I] heard and felt a loud explosion. One of the jeeps had hit a road mine. I walked over and saw that the right front of the jeep was heavily damaged. The GI in the right front was unconscious, and the driver was talking out of his head. Company commander, Capt Mullins, walked up, told him I was okay. The jeep driver then made a comment that didn't made sense: "Captain, sorry I messed up the jeep."

'In the Hürtgen I only saw one of our tanks and it had no one in it, but it had been left in an awkward position. The front end of it was stuck about 6 feet up a big tree. I did get under the rear of it for protection because the German Messerschmitts were skimming along the treetops strafing us. That was a most helpless feeling. We could tell the difference between our planes and the German planes.

'I remember the massive number of our bombers flying over and I was concerned when I saw the black flak from the German guns exploding in the air around them. Another thing I just remembered, on a clear day it appeared to be snowing, but instead our planes were throwing out little shreds of tin foil to mess up the German radar.

'It was the most wonderful feeling when the American troops came in to replace us. From the Hürtgen we moved south. My platoon was in the town of Echternach in the Grand Duchy of Luxembourg.'[43]

'WE CAN'T GO ON LIKE THIS'

A day after their arrival, the 4th Division troops began an attack designed to eliminate a salient that extended into the Weisser Wehe Valley. Marcus Dillard of 12th Infantry Company M was 18 years old, and he later remembered that, 'As we started through a fire break, there was a minefield and barbed wire. The company commander stepped on a mine. Then the Germans started shelling us. They must have had an observer in the woods. Almost all supplies had to be hand carried over trails and paths barely wide enough to walk [on]. We had never encountered terrain like this. When the regiment renewed its drive on November 9, Companies I and K were designated as the main assault units, but a 500-yard-wide minefield separated them. Company I had to withdraw from its frontline position, and a support platoon from Company L replaced it. Company K moved rapidly until it reached booby-trapped concertina wire covered by machine gun fire. All this time we in Company M were laying down a mortar barrage in front of K. Company I, which circled around the minefield, came up in the rear of K, then swung to the left. They too caught intense small-arms fire. Both of our infantry companies were calling for our 81 mm mortars, but the Germans were well dug in. [Companies] K and I had to dig in for the night, all the time under intense artillery and mortar fire.'[44]

On 28 November, Major Goforth led his 1st Battalion, 22nd Infantry, 4th Infantry Division, in the attack on Grosshau and Gey at the eastern perimeter of the Hürtgen. Pushing over a series of wooded hills along the forest rim in his gloomy CP, a lantern-lit dugout, Major Goforth discussed the situation with his executive officer, Swede Henley. A new company commander arrived and said, 'We're hunting for officers, G Company's got only two left. Lost three this afternoon. We can't go on like this, Major.' Goforth shook his head. 'I know, boy, but where am I going to get them? Division says we can commission any good man right here in the field. But who?' He scanned the arc of dirty, unshaven faces watching through the meagre light. 'There's McDermott,' said Swede. 'Can't spare him,' retorted Goforth indignantly, 'Practically runs G-1. He's the last available sergeant. We've already commissioned six.' 'Guess we'll have to depend on replacements,' Swede replied. Then the company commander interjected: 'The trouble with replacements is that they don't last long enough. Trucks brought up 30 for me this morning; 18 were hit even before they could get into the line.' As he spoke, the blanket covering the dugout doorway was pushed aside and three young lieutenants entered, saluted and said they were reporting for duty. 'There you are, Jack,' said Goforth. 'Replacements for you. Take 'em with you when you go back.'

Goforth's battalion managed to navigate those precipitous wooded hills, edging closer to the road connecting Grosshau with Gey. Meanwhile, another battalion struggled to hold on to their positions a little way outside the forest facing Grosshau, while taking losses from artillery. During the night an order came down from headquarters that Grosshau had to be taken by 29 November. This would lead the troops into open country but would also entail a murderous frontal assault.

The following day, at 9 am and under an overcast sky, the first infantrymen emerged from their foxholes, shell holes and dugouts into a veritable torrent of enemy machine-gun fire from the ruined village. The GIs were supported by two M10 tank destroyers that moved in front of the attacking infantry and they proceeded to the outskirts of the village, close enough to the German positions to silence their guns. Then American riflemen advanced to within 150 m (500 ft) behind the M10s toward the village. As they approached, 50 haggard-looking Germans scrambled from their hideouts and cellars with their hands above their heads shouting 'Kamerad'. From the turret of his M10 a sergeant gestured to them to move out of the way and surrender to the attacking infantry. A punishing house-to-house fight ensued.

It took three hours to take the village, but the Americans finally managed to reach open country beyond its perimeter. Major Goforth's battalion struggled to fend off violent counterattacks. He used every man at his disposal, a collection of cooks, guards and even a group of engineers from Colonel 'Buck' Lanham's headquarters and he eventually succeeded in repelling the Germans.

Lanham's friend Ernest Hemingway would memorably describe the Hürtgen Forest as the equivalent of the Great War's bloody battle of Passchendaele, except 'with tree bursts'. One night, during an all too brief hiatus, two notable American writers met up. Hemingway was briefly stationed just a mile from J. D. Salinger's encampment. Salinger was still with the 12th Infantry and a few months earlier the two had met during the liberation of Paris. While fighting in the Hürtgen, Salinger turned to a fellow soldier and suggested making a visit to see Hemingway. The two men made their way through the dense forest to Hemingway's quarters, a comfortable small cabin lit by its own generator. For two or three hours they yarned together and drank champagne from canteen cups. Neither Hemingway nor Salinger would ever forget their experiences in the unforgiving Hürtgen.

THE HELL OF HÜRTGEN

Matthias Hutmacher of *Sturmgeschutzbrigade* 116th Panzer *Windhund* (Greyhound) Division, was only 17 when he joined the German army.

Ernest Hemingway with his friend Colonel Charles T. (Buck) Lanham of the 4th Infantry Division, 18 September 1944. Hemingway said the Hürtgen forest was like Passchendaele with tree bursts.

He wrote: 'I was born in Schmidt. The Battle of Hürtgen was the most terrible slaughter that I ever witnessed. There were dead bodies from both sides lying everywhere. Our officers told us that the Americans were going to be easy but this was not the case because they fought valiantly. Early in November my unit drove to Kreuzau, and from there to Brandenberg. We had been told that we should attack Vossenack. I remember the Americans firing at us with bazookas and causing serious damage. We didn't have enough good infantry to fight back with but we caused many American casualties. There were many futile attacks in that forest, but eventually the Americans were too strong for us. The weather was bad that November. Rain and snow most of the time, but we had been on the Russian front and so this wasn't so bad for us. The Americans fought very well and they kept their positions despite everything we threw at them. It was a terrible battle and I will never forget it.'[45]

Many US Divisions would be poured into what became known as the 'Meat Grinder' before final victory was achieved. The final attack by American forces into the Hürtgen would occur the following year, on 5 February 1945. A few weeks later the First Army would finally bring to an end its protracted and costly incursion into the region before pushing on to Cologne and the Roer.

The emotional and physical toll on the soldiers was exceedingly high. A staggering casualty rate of more than 25 per cent implies that more than 24,000 American soldiers were battle casualties, with an additional 9,000 succumbing to disease or combat fatigue. Over 120,000 American troops fought and suffered in the Hürtgen Forest, in the most deplorable conditions imaginable.

The US forces faced resistance from around 80,000 German adversaries, six full divisions, along with auxiliary units from other divisions. In addition to the protection they got from the dense forest, these troops also had reinforced concrete pillboxes and dug-in positions to cover them from US enfilades. Enemy soldiers were often barricaded inside buildings and used small towns for protection. The cover and concealment used by the Germans drastically limited the effectiveness of US indirect fire, as well as aerial bombardment when it was available. The dense undergrowth and capacious pines rendered the movement of armour almost impossible, except along well-established roads, and there were not many of those. The marshy ground also hindered any mechanized cross-country movement. The Germans had multiplied the effectiveness of the natural obstacles many times over through the effective use of wire, booby traps and minefields. The wire was well protected by small arms and machine-gun fire, making it difficult for advancing troops to progress more than a few feet or yards at a time.

One of the main problems encountered by US forces was due to a major underestimation of the Germans' capacity to defend this area, and an overestimation of the US army's capacity to maintain the momentum and advantage that had sustained it since the successes of the Normandy campaign. Moreover, the offensive action that was undertaken covered a front that was far too wide to successfully navigate. This resulted in having to reduce and funnel the area of attack and frequently bypass objectives, which on occasion led to the attacking troops becoming completely surrounded.

German forces may have been severely depleted in Normandy but they still had reserves and ammunition at their disposal, and contrary to popular belief at ETO, they were not on the verge of total collapse. The divisions sent into the Hürtgen Forest discovered that the fighting there had no precedent or comparison in their previous battles. In the Hürtgen Forest the Germans had the advantage of being able to contain most assaults from their well-defended and entrenched positions, meaning that hundreds of needless US casualties were sustained because of excessive exposure to front-line conditions that resulted in battle fatigue and debilitating weather-related ailments such as trench foot and hypothermia. Replacements were often inexperienced and unprepared for the horrors that confronted them in the Hürtgen. This often resulted in a terrible waste of much needed men and equipment.

In time the hell of the Hürtgen would be overshadowed by the ensuing Battle of the Bulge, but it would never be forgotten by those who had survived it.

CHAPTER ELEVEN

A PATH TO THE SEA

WHEN, DURING THE AFTERNOON OF 4 September 1944, the British 11th Armoured Division reached Antwerp, it meant that one of the greatest ports in northwest Europe was now in Allied hands. Monty was relatively unmoved by this vital achievement, being at the time preoccupied with his plans to get to Berlin, and later admitted that one of the greatest mistakes of his career was underestimating the importance of the port of Antwerp. The Germans may have lost Antwerp, but the Allies had not gained the use of its harbour. The city lies about 80 km (50 miles) inland from the North Sea, and in September 1944 both banks of the estuary of the Scheldt that runs through the city were controlled by the Germans.

Adolf Hitler may have been physically and mentally deficient at this time, but he understood completely the importance of denying this harbour and its facilities to the Allies. Nothing if not consistent, he resolved in time-honoured fashion to hold the area to the last man and issued the following directive: 'Because of the breakthrough of enemy tank forces toward Antwerp, it has become very important for the further progress of the war to hold the fortresses of Boulogne and Dunkirk, the

Calais defence area, Walcheren Island with Flushing harbour, the bridgehead at Antwerp, and the Albert Canal position as far as Maastricht. For this purpose the Fifteenth Army is to bring the garrisons of Boulogne and Dunkirk and the Calais defence area up to strength by means of full units. The defensive strength of the fortresses is to be increased by means of additional ammunition supplies from the supplies of the Fifteenth Army, especially antitank ammunition, by bringing up provisions of all kinds from the country, and by evacuating the entire population. The commanders of the Calais defence area and of Walcheren Island receive the same authority as a fortress commander.'[46]

On 15 September the Canadian general Henry Duncan Graham 'Harry' Crerar sent a directive to his corps commanders outlining what would be required to make the port of Antwerp operational. The task had been entrusted to the Canadian First Army. The title 'Canadian First Army' was actually a bit of a misnomer, because although it was designated as such, it contained a significant amount of British and Polish troops, including the entire British I Corps. Crerar's contemporaries regarded him as a politically astute man, but not a particularly gifted strategist, and there had been rumours circulating that he wasn't in the best of health.

By 27 September, a few days after the abject failure of Market Garden, Monty relented over the opening of Antwerp's port when he said it was now 'absolutely essential before we can advance deep into Germany'. The timely capture of Antwerp had to a large extent seriously compromised the three corps (67th, 86th and 89th) of the German Fifteenth Army, which was ensconced in a potential cul-de-sac west of the city and south of the Scheldt. On the day Antwerp fell the German Commander in Chief West's headquarters diary noted that the British advance on Antwerp had in effect encircled Zangen's Fifteenth Army. An opportunity was squandered here because an Allied push north a few miles to the Dutch town of Breda would have severed the Fifteenth Army's escape route across the Scheldt by way of Walcheren and South Beveland. Unfortunately, military inertia on the Allied side allowed the Fifteenth Army to flee unimpeded.

Canadian units already in the city may have lacked some provisions but they were quite content to entertain the locals. Regiments such as the Essex Scottish benefitted greatly from this temporary hiatus and allowed significant numbers of men to take their leave in Antwerp, which in effect turned the place into a profligate Canadian fun town, where the troops did a lot of alcohol-fuelled liberating and feasted on previously unavailable foods. They had endured a hard fight getting out of France and charging up the west coast of Belgium, so it was understandable that they wanted to let off a bit of steam. The problem was the timing.

On 14 September Eisenhower wrote to his boss, General George C. Marshall, the US Army Chief of Staff. He informed Marshall that the unexpectedly rapid advances in northern France had caused him to opt for one all-out advance to the German border and possibly the Rhine before pausing to regroup. In this letter he emphasized that a 'rush right on to Berlin' was impossible and was 'wishful thinking'. He then related the details of his strategic vision as he had done earlier to the Combined Chiefs of Staff, Montgomery and Bradley. Among other previously mentioned objectives he tasked Montgomery with clearing the approaches to Antwerp, thereby opening that vital port for Allied use. The Combined Chiefs of Staff approved Eisenhower's plan. They also mentioned the absolute necessity of opening Antwerp before the onset of inclement weather.

It was becoming apparent that the Allies had made far too many assumptions regarding the strength and morale of the German forces. This had been clearly demonstrated during Operation Market Garden, when two SS divisions, supposedly understrength and in need of refitting, had successfully checked the Allied advance to the Rhine.

Eisenhower wasted no time in ordering Monty to make the capture of Antwerp his first priority. It's entirely possible that Eisenhower was motivated by the recent capture of France's second largest port at Brest, which had been used by the Germans as a vital submarine base.

Monty had realized the gravity of his mistake in not making more of the capture of Antwerp, but it would be years before he publicly admitted this. He did, however, reciprocate Eisenhower's concerns and promptly dispatched all the available offensive power of the British Second Army to assist the Canadians in the opening of the port. It wouldn't be an easy task though, due to the terrain on all sides of the estuary. This is canal country, and much of the land is below sea level. The Dutch, through necessity, had become masters in the skill of land reclamation, but this would ultimately be to the detriment of the Allies. In 1914, at the start of World War I, the diminutive Belgian army had effectively demonstrated that water could be used as a weapon when it halted German army progress dead in its tracks by opening the sluice gates and flooding sizeable areas of West Flanders. Hitler had been serving in the region and now he wasted no time in ordering the German forces to flood the Walcheren peninsula in the hope of augmenting defences there.

There was no ambiguity on either side regarding the importance of capturing the Channel ports. The Germans had clearly demonstrated that they intended to fight for them tooth and nail. Air reconnaissance had erroneously reported the Boulogne, Calais and Dunkirk areas as deserted, but this was far from the truth. Dunkirk wouldn't surrender until May 1945. Adolf Hitler had designated the Channel ports as fortresses (*Festungen*) and they proved to be hard targets for the Allies. Le Havre fell on 12 September, but the other ports fielded a stronger defence and Monty became a little exasperated with the situation. He told Crerar in no uncertain terms to redirect his efforts to Antwerp and leave Boulogne and the other Channel ports alone for the time being at least.

OPERATION WELLHIT

The British staff officers' philosophy throughout the European theatre differed greatly from the American perspective. British staff officers developed a habit of audaciously referring to military operations as a 'show'. Well, no show is complete without an audience, and in the case of one particular planned military engagement officially called Operation Wellhit, specific instructions were issued which set out the arrangements for visiting spectators. The purpose of the plan was to attack Boulogne. One military memo referring to the forthcoming 'show' wrote: 'It is becoming apparent that a large number of spectators are planning to attend Operation "WELLHIT"; these include naval, military and air force personnel as well as correspondents. It is imperative that such spectators do not position themselves at an operational headquarters where the staff is engaged in fighting the battle. Accordingly it was provided that all such spectators will be sent to the spectator's stand, which has been suitably marked.'[47]

Monty finally redirected his attention to Antwerp. It was imperative to clear the Germans out of South Beveland and the Walcheren peninsular just over the border in the Netherlands. The operation to achieve this would demand the combined deployment of amphibious forces, along with joint naval, air and ground forces. Concerted planning was immediately undertaken during the latter part of September and early October at the Headquarters of the Canadian First Army.

THE BATTLE OF THE SCHELDT

There was work to be done. So far, the Twenty-First Army Group had managed to take French ports such as Boulogne, which was captured after Operation Wellhit on 22 September, but which didn't open for business until 14 October. Calais fell on 30 September, but it wouldn't be operational until 30 November. The last port taken by the Canadians on the Belgian coast was Ostend, which surrendered on 9 September and was receiving Allied shipping by 28 September.

Allan Notman of the 17th Duke of York's Royal Canadian Hussars (7th RECCE Regiment) said: 'The liberation of Holland was probably the most memorable experience of my whole service in Europe. It was called the Battle of the Scheldt. The main battle was in the Scheldt Estuary, which was situated just above Antwerp in Belgium. This was an area that the Germans wanted to hold at any cost because it was a direct supply route from the port of Antwerp through Holland for the Allied armies in northwestern Europe. The Germans in the Scheldt Estuary controlled all of the shipping into that port with their heavy guns; and the Allies had to take the area away from them at any cost.

'We worked closely with the Dutch Resistance and the White [Resistance] Brigade forces from Belgium. We were almost always in water up to our knees for hours at a time due to German snipers. We liberated many villages during the month, some of the names were Waterland, Uitdam, Watervliet, Sint-Margriete, Maldegem. As a matter of fact, in Maldegem, our colonel, Colonel Lewis, was killed; and he is buried in the cemetery in Maldegem in Row D, Grave 23. Other places in proximity were the Dutch towns of Sluis, Oostburg and Aardenburg.

'Aardenburg has a particularly sentimental memory for me because my section of nine men were the first troops to enter that town. We stormed the house there and the Germans rushed out the back door. The coffee that they were drinking was still warm when we entered the house. The headquarters for the enemy was in the house cellar. The mayor gave us a great welcome when all the Germans were cleared out the next day.

'On one particular dangerous mission, our officer, Lieutenant Banks called out, "Notman, you lead". So McKewan, the driver, Bill Thompson, the gunner and I moved to the front of the section and the column. And the other armoured cars and carriers followed it along this narrow road, somewhere in the Scheldt.

'We passed Dutch people pushing their belongings on pushcarts, wheelbarrows, bicycles and anything they could find, trying to get out of the area that we were going into because we were heading into a stronghold of the Germans. It was a terrible sight to see the mothers carrying babies and old people with the look of sheer horror on their faces, trying to get away from their town, which was just a few miles away. We finally reached the town. We had hardly a chance to bathe or change clothes. If you got soaked, no matter what time of the day it was, you just had to wear your uniform and let it dry on your body.

'After the Germans were cleared out of the islands, we moved to Nijmegen, where our regiment was responsible for the security of the large bridge that was there. We were stationed under the bridge on the city side and went on duty, fired machine guns at any moving object floating down the Rhine River. This was done to prevent frogmen from bringing explosives to attach to the bridge and blow it up.'[48]

Once the Allies had agreed a practicable strategy for liberating the Scheldt, the Canadian First Army began making preparations to execute the plan. General Crerar had returned to England due to a bout of dysentery and the First Canadian was placed under the command of Lieutenant-General Guy Simonds. Monty was pleased with this change of command because he didn't trust Crerar and had already cast certain aspersions regarding the man's tactical ability. What Monty couldn't detract from was the fact that Crerar was a highly decorated World War I veteran, an excellent staff officer and, after Market Garden,

Monty should have reserved his opinions. Those who live in glass houses...

Bill Davis of the Black Watch, Royal Highland Regiment (Canada), recalled: 'After we fought our way out of Antwerp, we were given the job of sealing off the bottom of this peninsula and by taking a town called Woensdrecht, which sat at the very neck of the peninsula. That was one of the occasions when the order came down from up above, that this was how we do it and no ifs, ands or buts, just do it.

'And we moved in, we left our reserve position about 2:30 in the morning [of 13 October 1944] and marched to where our take off spot was and about 6:00 or 6:30, we made the attack and we didn't make it 50 feet and we were cut down by heavy machine gun fire and I don't know, everything you could catch.

'So we went back to our starting point, which was a ditch going down a road and then again, about noon hour I believe it was, they ordered

Bill Davis of the Black Watch, Royal Highland Regiment. They fought against tough opposition in terrible conditions through the inundated Walcheren peninsula.

in a second attack. We were going across a thousand yards of so-called polder land, where the Dutch had built dikes all around and then drained the water out and they used those for vegetable farms.

'We went across there, a thousand yards, with no cover, no nothing. The only thing that was there was beets. How the hell we ever got across, I don't know, because the Germans were dug into a big dike at the other side, which contained the railway and a roadway, the only way to get to Walcheren [Island]. We stayed there until, I don't know, 2:00 or 3:00 in the morning and the word finally come to pull out and all that was left of my company were 19 of us, 18 of us walking.

'Our company commander, Popham, had been shot earlier in the day in the head. I was the senior one left, so I went to take his map case and any papers he might have and he scared the hell out of me, he was alive. So I put a dressing on his head and we walked out back to the clearing area where they had ambulance Jeeps to take people back to the hospital and they loaded us in trucks and took us back where we'd started from the day before. That guy was shot right through the head and he lived and practiced law in Montreal for many years afterwards. He was a tough beggar.

'You may find this hard to believe but it wasn't the fighting that bothered you. You would give your right arm to have a decent night's sleep in a nice warm, dry place. That became the objective. The Germans were in the way of keeping you from having that. It wasn't the fighting really that bothered most people. It was the conditions. It was a terrible, terrible autumn and winter in Holland, the worst they'd had in 50 years.

'We were moving up to a little town called Goes on the Beveland Peninsula. And everybody took to the ditch all of a sudden and I jumped in and then went back to see what was going on. One of my guys had fallen on the road and the boys all thought it was a sniper had hit him. He just fell asleep walking and fell down. It was raining and snowing and everything. But that's how beat up the guys were.

'So when we got out of there and they took us to Cuijk, it was like being on a holiday for us, you know. Four or five days in the line and out for maybe three days or even a week, and just doing, cleaning weapons and doing a little fieldwork. To us, it was just like having a holiday.

'War is a terrible thing. And people survive the war by having a little humour. Oh, they used to do all kinds of silly things when we'd be out of the line. I had a fellow with me that, today they call it post-stress disorder or something. In those days, we called it bomb-wacky. Guys would just go kind of nuts and run around and do different things but this fellow had already been back to what they'd call the sleep camp.

'If you went bomb-whacky, they'd send you back to this place, give you a needle and put you to sleep for 48 hours. They're supposed to keep you there for a few days until you settle down and send you back up. The second time, they were supposed to put you in a labour battalion, so you didn't go back and do any fighting. But we were so short of guys that they'd give you the 48-hour sleep, hand you a rifle and send you back.

'Now, this fellow had been back twice and the other platoons didn't want him because he'd get up in the middle, as soon as any shells or mortar shells landed, he'd start running around and hollering. But he was a good soldier otherwise. I said I would take him. When he'd get up, I kept him with me, if he tried to get up and run around, I'd just bat him one and knock him out and we became very good friends. And on more than one occasion, he saved my skin.

'We used to call him the Duke, because when we were up in Groesbeek, where they'd drop the paratroops and the gliders, there was thousands and thousands of parachutes hanging in the trees and on the ground. We were collecting them up. I sent a bunch of the silk home to my family. There was the best of silk in those days, in parachutes. He made himself like a cravat and wore around it his neck. He always looked like a dandy.

'And everybody used to have some kind of German weapons, Luger pistols or what have you, and the order come from up on high, "All German weapons were to be surrendered". So we were in this little town of Cuijk, and there was a pub next door that sold beer that was about as strong as water but better than nothing. We were standing there, about 20 of us, when the MPs rolled up in two or three Jeeps. Everybody had a German pistol or something. The sergeant of the MPs said, "You have to surrender those or I'll put you under charge."

'And the Duke pulled off a John Wayne. He was wearing two pistols. "If you want these, you've got to come and get 'em." Of course, the MPs are looking. Here's 20 guys armed to the teeth. They just got back in their Jeeps and drove off. Those kind of things became rather legend in the army and gave everybody a good belly laugh.'[49]

The challenge presented to the Canadian First Army was particularly daunting owing to the unique geography of the targeted area. To the north of the Scheldt estuary was the Dutch province of South Beveland, low-lying country that gave those holding defensive positions a marked advantage. Beyond South Beveland lay the island of Walcheren, which had been reinforced and transformed into a powerful German stronghold. The Allied plan to open the estuary entailed implementing four key operations. The first objective was to clear the area north of Antwerp and secure access to South Beveland. Secondly, it was absolutely necessary to attack the town of Breskens and clear what became known as the Breskens pocket behind the wide Leopold Canal. The third phase would require the taking of South Beveland and finally the capture of Walcheren Island. The Breskens pocket was a place of fortified German resistance against the Canadian First Army. It was mostly situated on the southern shore of the Scheldt estuary in the southern Netherlands, in proximity to the Belgian border.

OPERATION SWITCHBACK

The German Fifteenth Army had escaped back east but General von Zangen was a cautious man. As a precautionary measure he left two garrisons to hold the north and south of the Scheldt. The 64th Infantry Division was told to defend to the last man in the Breskens area, while the 70th Infantry Division held Walcheren Island. In Zangen's opinion the purpose of these fortress troops was bilateral. First, to deny the port facilities to the Allies and, second, to pin down as many Allied troops as possible. He later claimed that he had no definitive idea as to how long Walcheren would hold, but he expected that it would take at least three to four weeks for the Allies to secure the areas. The Germans still had a lot of fight left in them and they were going to demonstrate this.

The Canadians had already had a taste of what it was going to be like fighting through lowland positions when they had attacked the Ghent Canal. This is the winding waterway that linked the historic towns of Ghent and Bruges. The Germans made full use of the blown bridges to slow up the advance to the Scheldt. As dusk fell on 8 September the Argyll and Sutherland Highlanders of Canada attacked in force across the canal near Moerbrugge, 5 km (3 miles) south of Bruges. It was thought the crossing would be relatively simple and unhindered. As the Argylls launched two punts German artillery hit them with a withering barrage of mortar and 88 mm ordnance that inflicted terrible damage and forced the Argylls to take cover. It took until midnight to effect the crossing.

On 6 October, the Canadians launched Operation Switchback, whereby the 2nd Canadian Infantry Division began its advance north of Antwerp, while the 3rd Canadian Infantry Division, supported by the 4th Canadian Armoured Division, began the assault over the Leopold Canal.

Private Les Garnham of the Algonquin Regiment 10th Infantry Brigade, 4th Canadian Armoured Division, said: 'The Leopold Canal, that was another scary place. They sent out a detail by boat; and before I went in there, I used to be a guide that paddled canoes. Anyway, they put me on a boat crew. They took 18 men across in the boat, across the Leopold Canal, and there was about four of them. I knew it was a suicide outfit. God, I thought, what the heck are they trying to do, kill us all off? But they were good Germans. We pulled in with the boat and I had 18 men in my boat; and as soon as I got the oars of the boat in, there was a machine gunner about four feet out from my boat with a Schmeisser [submachine gun]. And, I guess, there was only a couple of Germans.

'So all the guys that was in my boat, they give themselves up. Of course, I was trained for D-Day and you don't stop for not, you go through the end. I bailed out of the back of the boat and run. And I guess them two Germans were searching them 18 men, they didn't see me go. So I laid down beside a river cart there. And when I was laying down there, it was dark alright. I could see they took about 75 of our guys prisoners. Dear God, I didn't know what to do. I'll sneak over to the barn there. I sneaked over there; and I thought, God, I could hear some Canadians talking over by the house. So I sneaked over to the house. There was a little lean-to on that house and around the corner, a little apple tree there. So I hid in there; and God, I didn't know what the hell to do. I was all by myself and I was scared skinny; and I didn't know what to do. All the rest of the guys were taken prisoner.

'After a while, I'm going to sneak back the way I come. I'll sneak back there; and I'll swim that damn canal. Come out around the corner of this and God damned, there's four Germans coming from where I'd come from. They had their rifles slung over their shoulder; and they were laughing and talking. I leaned my rifle against a wall and I was going to give myself up and I thought, oh, no, God, they took them 75 prisoners of ours 15 minutes ago, they don't want to take me, they'll shoot me likely. They wouldn't bother with one man. I thought, God, I grabbed my rifle again and I said, hands up! *Nicht bewegen!* [Don't move!] Their rifles fell off their shoulders. I got them up against a wall, four of them, I thought, oh God, now what I am going to do? My rifle was shaking there and I thought, oh, what the heck? Now I was thinking fast there. God, I don't want to shoot the poor guys. I thought, well, I didn't know what to do.

'I was a great believer in carrying hand grenades on both sides of my web belt. And I had the rifle on them and I pulled one hand grenade off my web belt and I pulled the pin. When you squeeze the lever down, the pin will pretty near fall out. I pulled it out with my teeth; and I showed it to them. And I had them up against the wall and their rifles were, God, 15 feet away from them. I just showed it to them and I just, what the heck? So I threw it in amongst their feet. They had to get the hell away from that hand grenade before it went off, by that time, I'd run like hell. My hand grenade didn't go off until I was hitting the canal. I dropped my rifle in and I swam it, son of a gun. I still got on the other side, all I had then was one hand grenade left on my web belt. And then I thought, oh God, I took my socks off and wrung them out, put my boots back on.

'My uniform, my tunic, was getting tighter and tighter; and I thought, what the hell's going on? It's wool and seemed to have shrunk up. And I had to undo it. Well, I had enough nerve to sneak up over the dike. God, there was an old vacant house there. And there was a pair of Dutch wooden cloppers there. So I took my boots off again and I put them damn wooden cloppers on; and I walked with them. And tied my boots together. So I had to get back to the Algonquins before they left. And I thought, God, now I don't know the password for the next day, so anyway I went back and before they stopped me, I said, I'm an Algonquin; I

Pvt. Les Garnham. Algonquin Regiment, 10th Infantry Brigade, 4th Canadian Armoured Division experienced the bitter fighting that occurred at the Leopold Canal in Belgium in 1944.

don't know the password. They stopped me, you know. Said, halt, who goes there?

'But, anyway, corporal come and said, colonel wants to see you. I said, what the hell for? I don't know. So I went; and he said, What happened? I said, well, I took my 18 men in my boat. I said, they were all taken prisoner. And I said, I run, I was trained for D-Day and I run. I said, I met these four guys and I told them what I'd done; and I said, and I swam that canal. And well, he said, you're the twenty-eighth one that came back out of the whole works of us. I don't know why [they] sent us over there, it was suicide actually. They should have known better, we couldn't handle that many, you know. Anyway, that was one scary outfit'.[50]

The Leopold Canal was a formidable obstacle and extensive flooding to the north of the canal left only a narrow strip of land where the Canadians could establish a bridgehead. Both divisions faced tough opposition and the fighting was fierce in both areas. The well-entrenched German forces made it difficult for the Allied forces to advance. The first challenge for the 3rd Canadian Division was to traverse the Leopold Canal spanning about 18 m (60 ft) with steep banks. With the support of Wasp flamethrower carriers, two bridgeheads were achieved on the opposite bank of the canal, but the Canadians met with stiff resistance and progress was laborious.

SECURING THE LAND

At midnight on 9 October, after a few false starts and a 24-hour delay, an amphibious assault force embarked at Ghent in Terrapin and Buffalo tracked landing vehicles and sailed down the canal leading to the Dutch town of Terneuzen. The objective was to hit the rear of the Breskens pocket and make landfall east of the village of Hoofdplaat. Both attacking Canadian battalions managed to get ashore near Biervliet against negligible opposition. By 9 am a bridgehead had been established and soon the reserve battalion was landed, advancing to Hoofdplaat. The defending Germans withdrew into concrete bunkers along the coast and more fighting followed. By 3 November the south shore of the Scheldt had been secured.

The 2nd Canadian Infantry Division, advancing north to close the eastern end of South Beveland, made good progress against General

Kurt Chill's paratroopers who were attempting to bar the way. Casualties were heavy as Canadian troops attacked over open, inundated terrain, but by 16 October they had seized the town of Woensdrecht at the entrance to South Beveland. Walcheren Island was attacked simultaneously from three directions: across the causeway from the east, across the Scheldt from the south and from the west by sea. To hamper German defences, the island's dykes were breached by heavy Royal Air Force bombing, which flooded the central area and allowed the use of amphibious vehicles.

Things didn't go exactly according to plan for the British 248th Armoured Assault Squadron of the Royal Engineers, who took up position in a field near the village of Ijzendijke. No. 3 troop was assigned the task of operating a mine-clearing device known as a Condor, which consisted of a 90 m (300 ft) length of canvas hose launched empty across a mined area and then pumped full of liquid nitroglycerin which was then detonated, clearing a wide path through the minefield. While unloading the nitroglycerin from three Canadian lorries, a tremendous explosion rocked the area, sending shock waves that flattened everything in its path. Trees, farm buildings and military vehicles were set on fire or completely wrecked by the blast. The three lorries carrying the nitroglycerin simply evaporated, leaving three large craters on the site. This accidental explosion, presumably one of the largest during Operation Switchback, took the lives of 26 British and 15 Canadian soldiers and wounded 43 others.

Lieutenant General Simonds concentrated on the area north of South Beveland. The 4th Canadian Armoured Division, which had been engaged at the Leopold Canal, moved north of the Scheldt and drove hard for the Dutch town of Bergen-op-Zoom. By 24 October, the entrance to South Beveland had been breached and secured, allowing the 2nd Canadian Division, assisted by an amphibious landing by the 52nd British Division, to move on South Beveland. By 31 October the Allies had secured the area.

Between 31 October and 7 November, Allied troops executed Operation Infatuate. This involved two British amphibious assaults on the heavily defended island fortress of Walcheren, located at the northwestern corner of the estuary. Simultaneously, 52nd Division attacked Walcheren's eastern coast. On 6 November, the Walcheren Island capital Middelburg was secured, and by 8 November all enemy opposition in the area had been eradicated.

Finally, between 3–25 November, Royal Navy minesweepers undertook Operation Calendar to clear the Scheldt of mines. As early as 1 November an attempt had been made to pass minesweepers up to Breskens, but they were driven back by German batteries near the Belgian port of Zeebrugge. It was only after the 3rd Canadian Division occupied Zeebrugge on 3 November, having endured tenacious German opposition, that the threat of shore-based attacks was removed and the minesweepers were able to clear the channel, at last enabling merchant ships to make a safe passage up the estuary to Antwerp.

By 26 November Operation Calendar had been successfully completed, with a total of 267 mines removed from the estuary. On that same day the first three Allied ships reached Antwerp. On 28 November the first convoy, led by the Canadian-built freighter *Fort Cataraqui,* entered the harbour and Antwerp was once again open for business. More importantly, this crucial supply line could now provide vital fuel and provisions for the Allied advance to liberate Europe. But there was still work to be done. It wasn't over yet.

In those autumn months of September, October and November, it has been estimated that the Allies suffered over 56,000 battle casualties. As daunting as that number is, it pales by comparison with Russian casualties. During the opening months of the Soviet army's Operation Bagration, while making their 650 km (400 mile) drive from Vitebsk to Warsaw's outskirts, the Soviets incurred 178,000 killed or missing and 590,848 wounded. One of the reasons why the Soviet army sustained so many casualties was due to its often deplorable tactics. When its front-line soldiers needed artillery support they were in trouble because most units didn't have radios and they were never allowed to request any kind of support.

The strategy and tactics employed by east and west differed substantially. Anglo-American generals used tactics that were aimed at encircling and capturing their adversaries. In the east the Red Army wasn't weighed down by any tactical considerations. It frequently employed almost suicidal frontal attacks hammered home with brute force that didn't stop short of annihilation. The disparity in numbers reflects the difference. In the course of World War II, Allied forces in the western theatre numbering over three million claimed the lives of 834,314 German soldiers. In the east, where neither side had a strategic bombing force, less than six million Germans killed 11 million Soviet soldiers and at least seven million civilians. General Eisenhower wrote in his memoir: 'When we flew into Russia, in 1945, I did not see a house standing between the western borders of the country and the area around Moscow. Through this overrun region, Marshal Zhukov told me, so many numbers of women, children and old men had been killed that the Russian Government would never be able to estimate the total.' Most historians concur that the level of mass barbarity inflicted by both sides on the Eastern Front was almost indescribable.

In the west, innumerable villages, towns and cities were liberated in the autumn of 1944. Some permanently, some temporarily. Whatever the result, while the civilians and soldiers who participated during those turbulent months would never forget, many preferred not to remember. Many Allied soldiers were deeply traumatized by their experiences during World War II, both by actual combat and by the subsequent interaction with local civilians. One such soldier was Albert Salomon Charest who served as a private in Canada's *Le Royal 22e Régiment*. He said: 'If ever you go to Holland, you'll feel more than at home. This is true – it's nearly impossible to imagine how welcomed we were in that country. For them, French Canadians are gods, it's us who saved their lives. I remember in Amsterdam, the Germans were really terrible, real pigs. They had crucified nine people at the bottom of a huge monument – if you're in Amsterdam, it's the big monument that they have all their large ceremonies in front of, there's a huge monument – they crucified them, killed them in front of thousands of people. The Germans were rotten scum.

'I saw even worse things. In Italy, I saw a mother with her three little children. They had a hay stack for their mules, their goats; that was all they had for winter. [The Germans] took the woman, tied her near to it, along with her three little children, and they lit her on fire and stole the animals. That's the Germans for you! It's true what I am saying to you, I am not making up a word of it.

'I saw some poor women. They would come by in the morning when we were eating breakfast. We weren't allowed to give them our leftovers, our toast. We had to take them and throw them in the garbage, rather than give them to the women. The women had two little infants with them, about two or three years old. Poor things, they were clothed shabbily but they were wearing all they had. They came to see us with these little pots to gather something to eat for their children. I wasn't put out; sometimes I would go without my toast and drop it in their pot. A couple of times, I got caught, but I said, "Look here. These are human beings just like any other. We're going to throw this all out, when we could be giving it to them to help them eat and survive. If you're going to punish me, I'm ready, it won't be as bad as doing nothing."

'They saw what war is on the television, but on TV war is only a thing. It's a game, a game that they're playing. It's a comedy.'

CHAPTER TWELVE

FIGHTING FOR YOUR COUNTRY

THE ALLIED ARMIES THAT RACED across Europe in the autumn of 1944 were a mixed bag. American, British and Canadian accounts have a tendency to overlook a fine army that contributed to the Allied advance and proved indomitable in battle. The Polish 1st Armoured Division had helped to inflict a crushing defeat on the Germans at Falaise, and after Normandy the division doggedly fought its way across Belgium and the Netherlands, liberating Ypres, Ghent and Passchendaele. They proved beyond any doubt that they were tenacious and dedicated fighters. A brilliant flanking manoeuvre by General Stanisław Maczek, a talented Polish tank commander, forced the Germans out of Breda in the Netherlands, allowing the Poles to take the city without even firing a shot. Shame that it didn't occur before the German Fifteenth Army escaped!

The 1st Polish Independent Parachute Brigade, commanded by General Stanisław Franciszek Sosabowski, had participated in Operation Market Garden. Part of the brigade was lost during the heavily contested landings. However, the brigade's 2nd Battalion and elements of the 3rd were dropped at Driel, directly opposite Arnhem on the south bank of the Lower Rhine on 23 September, which caused a radical dislocation of the

German siege around the isolated 1st British Airborne Division in Oosterbeek, and ensured its further survival by a few more days. It was a vain and brave attempt that was ultimately doomed. One British commander even had the audacity to suggest that the Polish Brigade was responsible for the failure at Arnhem, when this was very far from the truth (see chapter six).

Slawomir Kwiatkowski was a lance corporal with the 3rd Battalion, 1st Polish Independent Parachute Brigade Group. He said: 'I was with a group of Poles who took over from British the defence of 5 houses in Eastern perimeter of Oosterbeek ... We stayed there till night from 25th to 26th. At night British Airborne Division began to withdraw for evacuation upon the riverbank. There was a distinct shortage of motorboats available and the evacuation proceeded at a very slow pace. It occurred on "no man land" area called after "the killing ground" because it was all covered by German fire. The Poles were the far rear-guard and our group arrived to the riverbank almost at the break of the day. We saw the row of soldiers waiting and eventually no more boats to cross. Then a white flag came out and with the rest of waiting men I became a prisoner.'[51]

Polish soldiers were among the best, ostensibly fighting for freedom and daring to hope that their sacrifices would be suitably rewarded when it was all over. But they were suspicious of the Allies, too. In 1939 the Molotov–Ribbentrop Pact had sealed the fate of Poland and left the country devastated and divided between Stalin and Hitler. The Allies had promised to send help, but in truth the British and French had been quite content to do absolutely nothing.

In 1944 the war was going relatively well for the Allies in the west, and on the Eastern Front the Germans had suffered a series of devastating defeats and appeared to be withdrawing to the west. Soviet tanks had reached the eastern suburbs of Warsaw and broadcasts from Moscow called on the Polish people to rise up against the Germans. This was something the Poles were more than ready to do. On 14 February 1942, the Polish Supreme Commander General Sikorski, in exile in London, established the Home Army (*Armia Krajowa*) to operate in Poland, commanded by General Rowecki. Using the unqualified support of the civilian population, the clandestine Home Army established secret meetings in small groups in accordance with the plans for a future uprising. Secret schools trained officer cadets and non-coms, while underground factories produced weapons and ammunition. Radio methods provided for daily communications between the Home Army Commander and the Chief Delegate and their counterparts in England. The Supreme Commander was able to arrange for air supply drops of weapons and trained specialists.

All of this was targeted to one goal: an uprising against the brutal Nazi regime in Poland. This duly began in Warsaw on the afternoon of 1 August 1944. It was expected to last about a week, but, following the Germans' decision to dig in and make a stand to defend 'Fortress Warsaw', the uprising lasted nine weeks. It became the longest and bloodiest urban insurgency of World War II.

Despite the Home Army's initial success in liberating most of the city from the Germans, the tide soon turned. Although the Home Army was numerically stronger, with around 40,000 fighters at its peak, including 4,000 women, only around 10 per cent of its troops were armed, and only then with light weapons. The Germans, on the other hand, were well equipped, with guns, tanks, artillery and fighter planes. As the tide turned in the Germans' favour the civilian population bore the brunt of their retribution. Between 5–6 August more than 40,000 inhabitants of Warsaw's Wola district were slaughtered. This mass killing of men, women and children was the work of the SS, police, penal battalions and units of the Russian People's Liberation Army, made up mostly of Russian collaborators.

Polish losses ultimately totalled 150,000 civilian dead and about 20,000 Home Army casualties. German forces lost about 10,000. The fighting finally petered out on 2 October, with the formal capitulation of the Home Army forces. The remaining 700,000 civilians in Warsaw were deported. When the dust finally settled, just 1,000 people remained in what had been a city of 900,000 souls. Those few survivors were then sent to concentration camps or into forced labour in the Reich. To add insult to injury, over the next three months the Germans proceeded to systematically eradicate what was left of the city, building by building.

Young Andrei Borowiec was frequently mired in the thick of the action, fighting in the rubble of the capital, crawling through sewers and over the dismembered limbs of his comrades, all the while waiting for Stalin's Red Army, currently sojourning on the far bank of the River Vistula, to come to the city's aid. When the situation had reached its nadir Andrei recalled seeing another young man close by firing a machine gun at the Germans until his ammunition was expended. He waved at him and got a friendly wave back. As the fighting intensified more and more Polish resistance fighters began to run out of ammunition, leaving them unable to fight back as bullets and shrapnel flew in all directions around them. Every few moments Andrei looked over to see if the young man was still there until, suddenly, a German tank shell impacted the wall directly behind him. The percussion wave knocked Andrei off his feet. When he finally got up again, covered in dust and blood, the young man with the machine gun was gone. Those who did survive the onslaught attempted to crawl through the wreckage and make it to the river.

Andrei later described his part in the uprising: 'I was a very young man, just fifteen years old. The whole thing was met with enthusiasm at the start by everyone in Poland. But then everyone realized that the Germans would not be so easily defeated without outside help. So people just hoped for the best. I was not accustomed to the idea of killing someone. But when the time came to pull the trigger it was a strong feeling and you just hoped that you got the enemy.'[52]

Like Andrei Borowiec, Ted Stopczynski was a mere teenager when he fought in the uprising. In 2017 both men unexpectedly found themselves reunited when they discovered they were living in adjacent bungalows in a Devon care home. Andrei, 87, and Ted, 89, were not even aware of each other's existence until a Polish care worker who was looking after Andrei realized the war connection between them. The men were eventually introduced, and Andrei was astonished to realize that Ted was the young man with the machine gun that had waved to him and then disappeared all those years ago. 'Someone had to tell me who he was,' he admitted. 'But once I realized who he was, I remembered him. It's an enormous coincidence.'[53]

It's generally agreed that the Warsaw Uprising failed for a number of reasons. The relationship between the western Allies and the Soviets was tenuous at best. British and American diplomats were unwilling to vociferously demand that Stalin extend assistance to their Polish allies. The root of this problem originated in the spring of 1943, when Stalin had severed diplomatic relations with the Polish government in exile after it sought to establish who was responsible for the deaths of thousands of Polish officers at Katyn. This was a forested area close to what is today Smolensk, in Russia, where 21,000 Polish officers had been captured and later murdered by the Soviets in early 1940, following the Red Army's 1939 invasion of Poland (by the terms of the Molotov–Ribbentrop Pact, once Germany declared war on Poland in September 1939 it was agreed that Hitler's regime would occupy the west of the country while the Russians would take over the eastern half). The Polish government in exile demanded an International Red Cross investigation into the mass execution once the bodies were discovered in 1943, but Stalin prevaricated and attempted to lay the blame at the door of the Germans. The truth of the Soviets' responsibility for this atrocity would remain uncovered for another 50 years.

The simple fact of the matter was that the Soviets had no interest whatsoever in assisting the Home Army in the liberation of Warsaw. Just like in 1939, it was Stalin's intention to annex eastern Poland and keep it in the Soviet sphere of influence once the war ended. Moreover, the western Allies had secretly agreed to this annexation at the conference in Teheran in December 1943. The Poles, oblivious to these terrible political machinations, remained confident that they could rely on the British and Americans to keep Soviet ambitions in check. They were all allies, after all. Although the RAF and the US Air Force made a few weapons drops over Warsaw toward the end of the uprising it was too little too late. These air drops were further compromised by the Soviets refusing permission for Allied planes to land or refuel on airfields under their control. The Red Army may have been fighting the same adversary but they were never true allies.

The Polish had taken a calculated gamble and they had fought with passion, tenacity and incredible courage. But their trust and their faith had not been rewarded and never would be. They relied on those whom they thought were allies to help them and they had lost. The ultimate blame lay squarely at the feet of the Red Army, which had incited the

Polish Boy Scouts fighting in the brutal Warsaw Uprising.

uprising, was in close proximity and had the power to affect the outcome. The bitterness that the uprising spawned would fester along with the feelings of having been utterly betrayed by the Allies. The Red Army had watched from across the river as Hitler's forces exacted their terrible revenge, destroying and depopulating a magnificent city. What happened to Warsaw far exceeded the damage incurred by the Russians at Stalingrad and Leningrad.

THE 'OLD HICKORY' MEN

Meanwhile, Frank Towers and his unit were taking some well-earned R&R after a punishing few months of almost continuous combat. They had no idea that they would take the field again against their old adversaries the 1st Division SS (*Leibstandarte SS Adolf Hitler*) in the biggest confrontation since the Battle of Mortain. Those 'Old Hickory' men, the name given to the 30th Infantry Division in honour of Andrew Jackson, had seen the worst and been pitched against the best the Nazis had to offer. Frank Towers served in M Company of the 120th Infantry and as the regimental liaison officer between the 120th and 30th Division headquarters. His duty position during the war allowed him to witness the making of 30th Infantry Division history like few others. After the war he became a very active member of this association, holding numerous offices from president to executive secretary and treasurer from the 1960s well into the 2000s. They had recently incurred 160 men killed and 1,058 wounded. General Simpson, commanding Ninth Army, was so impressed by this achievement of combined armour and infantry tactics used by the 30th Division that he actually persuaded them to re-stage them for the benefit of newly arrived commanders. Frank wasn't out to impress anybody. A hot shower and a hot meal was his only consideration, and it was a pressing one.

The 28th Infantry division had been decimated. Eighty per cent of its number had been casualties in the Hürtgen. It needed time to re-equip and replace those men. To accomplish this, it was sent to a quiet sector known as the Ardennes. Nothing was happening down there but back at Bletchley Park in late November they were intercepting some rather ominous messages regarding the movement of

German troops from east to west. They would be dispatched to the 'quiet sector' of the front line along the German/Luxembourg border to await their next commission. Like the 30th Division, they wouldn't have to wait long.

CHAPTER THIRTEEN

ACCORDING TO MY INFORMATION

IN THE AUTUMN OF 1944, Allied intelligence services came under increasing pressure as they entered Germany. Apart from suffering almost insurmountable logistical problems, the commanders in the field were complaining about the lack of reliable intelligence. Some commanders were claiming that Operation Market Garden had failed as a result of the intelligence community not providing adequate information. The real problem was that adequate information was available but that it was largely dismissed due to the euphoria brought on by recent successes.

On 10 September 1944, for example, a Twenty-First Army Group intelligence summary stated unequivocally that elements of the Second SS Panzer Corps, the 9th (*Hohenstaufen*) and 10th (*Frundsberg*) SS Panzer Divisions, were refitting in the Arnhem area, information that was confirmed by Dutch resistance forces. But Monty and his planners only had one week to put together a complex and risky operation, and were dealing with multiple other sources of information, too, some of it contradictory. In short, there simply wasn't enough time to collect and process all the data needed to ensure Market Garden was as perfectly planned as it could be.

Added to this was the problem that the Dutch resistance was known to have been infiltrated by the *Abwehr*, the German army intelligence service. Could the information the resistance provided always be trusted?

ULTRA

While the Allies were breezing across France and Belgium, facing largely ineffectual opposition, they had created a false sense of security. This was rapidly dispelled once they began to encroach the borders of the Third Reich. Now, more than ever, they needed to know the strength of the opposition. Where were these units of old German men and pubescent youths they'd been told about, for example? When the first American patrols surveyed and crossed the frontier, Allied intelligence on the Siegfried Line was at best vague, at worst almost non-existent. Most intelligence dated back to 1940, and in the intervening four long years many of the Siegfried Line's bunkers and pillboxes had become inconveniently overgrown with camouflaging foliage. The aerial recon that had worked so well in Normandy was less effective when dealing with the forests and woodlands that now lay before the Allied advance.

In September 1944, a member of Eisenhower's intelligence staff had optimistically predicted that victory in Europe was 'within sight, almost within reach'. The First Army chief of intelligence went one step further, declaring that it was unlikely that organized German resistance would continue beyond 1 December 1944. It all sounded too good to be true, and it was.

From October 1944 the Allies began encountering disconcerting levels of German resistance as they advanced to the Rhine. On 25 September, ULTRA had intercepted and decoded a message sent between German commanders. The message had been sent a week earlier and stated emphatically that all SS units on the Western Front were being withdrawn and assigned to a new Sixth Panzer Army.

Germany was losing the war, but on some days it was difficult to tell if the Allies were winning. Everything now hinged on accurate intelligence. From 1944 onwards three American detachments were assigned by SHAEF to work with the British intelligence-gathering services at Bletchley Park. This marked the beginning of the sharing of high-level decrypted German communications traffic between Britain and the US.

The information SHAEF G-2 issued in its weekly intelligence reviews generally reflected reports received from the Intelligence Divisions at both Army and Army Group levels. G-2 was a section of the military intelligence staff of a unit in the United States Army. These summaries incorporated additional information obtained from the British Red Cross and other sources. There were restrictions because not all intelligence could be conveyed for fear of endangering or revealing their sources. Specific and frequently highly reliable information provided by ULTRA would rarely, if ever, be included in SHAEF weekly summaries.

In early November, acting on intelligence reports Major General Sir Kenneth William Dobson Strong, SHAEF's chief of intelligence, mentioned the existence of the new German Sixth Panzer Army and that the Fifth Panzer Army had somehow evaporated from the line in the Alsace where Patton's Third Army was fighting. There were also reports of heavy rail movements in the Eifel region below Aachen. Strong knew the Germans well. He had served as assistant military attaché in Berlin shortly before the outbreak of war in 1939. In February 1943 he was appointed G-2 of Allied Force Headquarters in the Mediterranean and had assisted in armistice negotiations with the Italians. In the spring of 1944 he was appointed G-2 of SHAEF.

Allied intelligence was frequently maligned during the autumn of 1944, but no one could detract from the wonderful deception that had occurred prior to D-Day. Operation Fortitude had been specifically designed to support the invasion of Normandy. Using double agents, ersatz coms and the Ghost Army, the operation successfully helped to convince Hitler and his staff that the primary invasion site in France would be Pas de Calais, while giving the impression that other potential invasion sites, such as Normandy, were merely diversionary tactics to detract from the real Allied landing beaches.

On 23 November 1944 ULTRA intercepts indicated that German air forces were being moved west and had been ordered to protect large troop movements into the Eifel region. Montgomery's Twenty-First Army Group G-2, Brigadier Williams, stated emphatically that 'there was no need for worry about any possible German initiative, because Hitler's forces were in an advanced state of erosion'. In effect, 'Keep calm and carry on', as long as one has good intelligence.

SHAEF's failure to act on reliable intelligence was highlighted as early as 4 September 1944, when ULTRA intercepted a message reporting Hitler's briefing to a senior Japanese official that he was 'forming a force of a million men, augmented by units pulled back from other fronts, and a replenished air force that would strike a large-scale offensive in the west, probably in November'. This was dismissed as being wishful thinking on the part of Hitler, who was known to be not in the most stable frame of mind at that juncture of the war.

Suspicions weren't even aroused when on 25 September a further message decoded and intercepted by ULTRA stated that 'All SS units on the Western Front must be withdrawn and assigned to a new Sixth Panzer Army.' In early November, the Bletchley Park team decrypted the codes used by the German rail network. The information gleaned reported that more than 400 trains were transporting men and materiel toward the Eifel area that bordered Belgium and Luxembourg.

Strong, who Monty had once described as 'that chinless horror', had mentioned the existence of the new Sixth Panzer Army, adding that the Fifth Panzer Army had somehow disappeared from the line in the Alsace–Lorraine region where Patton was based with his Third Army. Patton had also remarked to his G-2, Colonel Koch, that the Germans had failed to follow their own doctrine and standard practice of counterattacking against Third Army operations in the Saar region, despite the fact that German forces were reportedly available there. What on earth was going on? Despite indications to the contrary, Allied intelligence still predicated all its estimates on the expected early collapse of the German war effort, even though it was becoming increasingly apparent that the Germans were on the move.

It is estimated that between October 1943 and January 1944, over 11,000 German messages were intercepted; this meant between 40 and 50 ULTRA intercepts every day. It should be noted here that ULTRA was not an acronym. The name simply referred to an innovative British invention that was used to crack the famed Enigma Code. This was achieved mainly thanks to the work of the much-maligned genius Alan Turing and many others (mostly women) who worked at Bletchley Park. Even today Turing's pioneering work in the 1940s continues to have an impact on computer science and technology.

There were still around 100,000 operative Enigma machines being used by the Third Reich in late 1944, and, although some of the communications were little more than insignificant conversions of German abbreviations, the staff at Bletchley Park forwarded each decoded message by secure radio and teleprinter network to the relevant military headquarters. Inter-Allied committees dealt with most of this work, to add to their remit that included censorship, intelligence, psychological warfare, displaced persons and counterintelligence, as well as forestry and timber supply along with communications, prisoners of war and radio broadcasts.

For armies in the field there were numerous other ways of gathering intelligence, such as patrol reports, radio intercepts, signals traffic analysis, prisoners of war, civilian and refugee interrogations, assessments of captured letters and documents, interpretation of aerial graphs and artillery sound-ranging. In military CPs G-2 personnel, polyglots and prisoner interrogation teams assessed and disseminated most of the information. Another prime source of information on enemy activity was gleaned by aerial photography, but this was severely hampered during the winter months when mist and low cloud covered most of Europe, rendering this method temporarily obsolete.

Outside the ULTRA network, gathering reliable intelligence was a spurious and perilous game. A former British secret service agent who worked during the war said, 'Intelligence work necessarily involves such cheating, lying, and betraying that it has a deleterious effect on the character. I never met anyone professionally engaged in it whom I should care to trust in any capacity.' But by 1944 ULTRA was making a difference – at a certain point it became afflicted with a complacency that caused one of the great intelligence fiascos of the whole war: the failure to identify the true purpose of the significant build-up of German forces in North Rhine-Westphalia.

Omar Bradley noted in his autobiography that, 'One major fault on our side was that our intelligence community had come to rely far too heavily on ULTRA to the exclusion of other intelligence sources.' By December 1944 Bradley's Twelfth Army Group was one of the largest US ground combat forces ever created. Inside Bradley's HQ, the Appreciation Group operated an 'ULTRA room' which received and assembled Bletchley material with other sources to provide estimates of German army numbers and dispositions. The Twelfth Army Group held two daily ULTRA briefings, both of which would have been attended by Bradley. The intelligence that ULTRA provided was considered so sensitive that the data provided by Bletchley was forbidden from inclusion in Allied written intelligence reports or summaries.

Another problem was that the Germans were so convinced of the infallibility of their codes that they had no concept that they could have been breached, but there were dissenters. When German U-boats were tracked down in obscure locations the head of the country's navy, Admiral Doenitz, suspected that messages were being intercepted but didn't take any action to either confirm or deny this.

As 1944 came to an end, the men in the field doing the fighting had little knowledge of what lay ahead. They had endured terrible weather and supply problems in the post-D-Day push to liberate Europe, and now hot food, warm clothing and a bed for the night were their immediate priorities. With no access to the reports provided by their armies' intelligence-gathering service they had little or no idea of the bigger picture that was being formed by the top brass, although some had noticed increased activity from the enemy and guessed that something was about to happen.

In the meantime, with Christmas coming, SHAEF ensured that all festive deliveries to combat outfits were given priority. By the end of November 1944 no fewer than six million packages had arrived on the Continent and were being manually transported to the front and base sections. This was a mere 20 per cent of the estimated total the postal services were preparing to process that winter. One particular transatlantic ship was loaded with a record-breaking 130,000 sacks of packages and 2,593 pouches of letters. It unloaded in Boulogne along with other similar vessels scheduled to carry the bulk of the 30 million packages expected. The War Department announced that 50 million packages were mailed to all theatres between 15 September and 15 October 1944. It was regarded as the greatest mass movement of packages from the US in history.

A FALSE SENSE OF SECURITY

By August 1944 the Allies were in control of nearly all of France, Belgium and Luxembourg and were within 80 km (50 miles) of the Ruhr, the industrial base of the Third Reich. The Allied strategic bombing campaign was severely hampering German petroleum production and it was obvious that the once mighty German war machine was getting hammered on both the Eastern and Western Fronts. Allied commanders and intelligence officers still believed that the Germans were so beaten that they could not mount an effective counterattack. Now it was just a question of digging in and holding on until the weather improved, with new offensives planned for February. Many SHAEF commanders believed that any build-up of German defences was simply because they were expecting an Allied attack. The idea of any sort of counteroffensive was dismissed out of hand. There was far too much of this dismissive hypothesizing among the higher echelons.

Meanwhile, bad weather and the recent offensives had severely afflicted the numbers of Allied infantrymen available for duty. The only untapped and readily available resource of new manpower was African American service units. Lieutenant General John C. H. Lee, General Eisenhower's deputy commander, proposed using African American servicemen as volunteer infantry replacements. Since African American soldiers were already in situ, and seemingly under-utilized, Lee correctly hypothesized that these men could provide a potential solution to the army manpower predicament. There was still racial segregation in the US army and the issue of integrating African American and white units remained contentious. Some senior officers who remained obdurate on the matter maintained that the military needed to remain segregated, come what may. As diplomatic as ever, General Eisenhower attempted to assuage the problem by insisting that Lee requested volunteers of both races to fight together. The emphasis would be on offering the opportunity to fight rather than the promise of racial integration. Lee insisted publicly that if the number of suitable African American volunteers exceeded the replacement needs of African American combat units, these men would be suitably incorporated in other organizations.

At the same time, the Allies had made a serious miscalculation regarding the state of Germany's infrastructure in the autumn of 1944. Despite the loss of resources and production centres, the implementation of strict central management structures orchestrated by Germany's

Minister for Armaments and War Production Albert Speer, the Nazi economy was actually peaking towards the end of the year. The country was still capable of manufacturing a record 1.25 million tons of ammunition, 750,000 rifles, 100,000 machine guns and 9,000 artillery pieces. The only serious deficit was Germany's capacity to produce tanks, but even this was compensated by the increased production of self-propelled assault guns such as the *Stug III*, *Jagdtiger* and *Jagdpanzer* models. Any country capable of maintaining production levels such as these, especially while under sustained attack, was still a dangerous adversary. Precisely how dangerous would soon be revealed.

CHAPTER FOURTEEN

WHAT MAY COME

IT HAD TAKEN WEEKS OF fierce combat to open the Scheldt estuary, but by the end of November the port of Antwerp was open and receiving Allied shipping. Optimism was the order of the day. The opening of the harbour went some way to alleviating the mounting supply problems, but suspicions were beginning to be aroused by the apparent inertia of enemy forces. It was reminiscent of the old cowboy movie adage: 'I don't like it, it's too quiet.' There was a reason for this consternation.

The torrential rain that had beset the Allied armies in the western theatre was turning to sleet and snow, causing temperatures to dip below freezing along the whole Allied line. The fighting in the Hürtgen had petered out and no one questioned why. ULTRA had inadvertently been rendered ineffectual by a perplexing German radio silence and the consensus of opinion among the ranks was that something was about to happen but nobody knew precisely what.

The Third Reich could still call on close to 10 million men in uniform, including 7.5 million already serving in its army. On the strength of this Hitler believed heart and soul that if Germany could hold on to the Ruhr he still had the capacity to force a stalemate and bring the Allies to the negotiating table. He wrote: 'In the whole of world history there has never been a coalition which consisted of such heterogeneous elements with such diametrically opposed objectives. Ultra-capitalist states on the one hand, ultra-Marxist states on the other. On the one side a dying empire, that of Great Britain, and on the other a "colony", the United States, anxious to take over the inheritance. The Soviet Union is anxious to lay hands on the Balkans, the Dardanelles, Persia and the Persian Gulf. Britain is anxious to keep her ill-gotten gains and to make herself strong in the Mediterranean. These states are already at loggerheads, and their antagonisms are growing visibly from hour to hour. If Germany can deal out a few heavy blows, this artificially united front will collapse.'[54]

In late autumn 1944 Hitler was suffering from some serious health problems, exacerbated by the assassination attempt against him at the Wolf's Lair in July of that year. His doctor, the half-Jewish Theodor Morell, kept a medical diary of the drugs, tonics, vitamins and other substances he administered to Hitler, usually by injection (up to 20 times per day) or in pill form. Hitler had a weak stomach, so he preferred injections to pills that he often had trouble digesting. The problem was that Morell's experiments sometimes contained toxic and addictive compounds such as heroin. It has even been suggested in some quarters that Morell's drug combinations were instrumental in accelerating Hitler's already deteriorating health. In November 1944 some of those close to Hitler became so concerned that they even attempted to remove Morell, whom the Führer trusted so implicitly.

There's every indication that Hitler was addicted to an opiate drug known as Eukodal that was frequently administered by Morell. Witnesses said that the effect of the drugs on the Führer was nothing short of miraculous. One minute Hitler was so frail he could barely stand, the next he would fly into an apoplectic rage and rant at whoever was unfortunate enough to be in close proximity. This erratic and unpredictable behaviour is highly characteristic of addicts and Hitler was no exception.

Health issues apart, Hitler had been ruminating for some time on the prospect of mounting a major offensive in the west. He thought that it was time for the German army to seize the initiative and take the fight to the Allies. He'd been pondering various scenarios while he was recu-

Dr Theodor Morell, Hitler's personal physician, administered all sorts of treatments, from nerve tonics to Pervitin, a type of amphetamine common in Germany at the time. Morell's personal journals list no less than 74 medications that he gave to the Führer.

perating from an assassination attempt, which the OKW narrowed down for him to two basic concepts. Field Marshal Walter Model, commanding Army Group *Heeresgruppe 'B'*, suggested a classic pincer offensive codenamed *Herbstnebel* (Autumn mist), designed to ensnare and destroy Patton's Third Army and Lieutenant General William H. Simpson's Ninth Army between Luxembourg and eastern central France in the region to the north of Colmar.

The other plan, designed by Rundstedt's staff, was simply called 'Martin' and was based on the tried and tested Nazi *Blitzkrieg* formula by driving through the thinly defended Ardennes, dividing the Allied armies in two and leading to the recapture of Antwerp. The only problem with the plan was Germany's glaring lack of available aircraft after the Allies had largely decimated the Luftwaffe.

Hitler preferred Rundstedt's plan and decided to adapt it to his own designs. Operation Martin became *Wacht am Rhein* (Rhine Guard). By the middle of September Hitler had imposed the plan on the German High Command, committing everyone involved to the strictest secrecy. Only the actual planning staff would be informed of developments, and even though it was overtly apparent that hundreds of officers would have to be involved in the actual handling of troops and supplies during the concentration period, the number of those in the know would be drastically limited. This entailed a major reshuffle of headquarters staff that began around 10 November 1944.

While most of France, Luxembourg and Belgium were returning to some semblance of normality, this wasn't the case in the Netherlands. In the autumn of 1944, the southern part of the Netherlands had been liberated, as far as the Rhine, but the northern and eastern part of the country remained strictly under German control. After the failure of Market Garden the Germans implemented a range of punitive measures on the Dutch. Arnhem was destroyed beyond all recognition and its people were evacuated. All food transports were restricted for six weeks and the movement of coal from the liberated south also ceased. Gas and electricity supplies were disconnected. People chopped down trees and dismantled empty houses to get fuel. The amount of food available on ration began to steadily decrease. Soon, the effects began to result in terrible suffering and resulted in what the Dutch still call the 'Hunger

Winter' of 1944–5. Roughly 20,000 Dutch men and women perished as a result of this cruel, man-made famine. One survivor recalled: 'Yes, we ate tulip bulbs when we could get them. We lived in The Hague where there was little agricultural area around. I remember the soup kitchens very well. If you were lucky you got red cabbage stew that was lukewarm and watery. My mother went on a foraging trip with the pram to the Westland. There was no fish either because the whole coast was a restricted area.'[55]

The black market thrived during the Hunger Winter, with illegally obtained food sold at extortionate prices beyond the means of regular working men or women. Soup kitchens were set up. People began foraging for food in the wild. Nobody was immune from the shortages, and the elderly, the young, men, women and children sold everything they owned, from their most precious belongings to everyday household utensils, in order to buy food. Malnutrition and vitamin deficiency were rife. Some even perished from hypothermia because they didn't have sufficient clothing to protect themselves from the biting cold. To make a bad situation worse, thousands of men between the ages of 16 and 45 were rounded up during raids and forced to join the German army or work in German factories, as was the case in all Nazi-occupied territories.

THE WEAPONS OF WAR

By now months of continuous Allied carpet-bombing of Germany's industrial heartland was beginning to have some effect. But it still didn't deter the German war effort from coming up with new, innovative ways to repel the Allies.

The 2nd Armored Division reported that it was highly impressed with Germany's new Royal or Tiger II tank, which boasted a devastating high velocity 88 mm cannon on its turret that could easily penetrate 12 cm (5 in) of armour at a range of up to 2 km (1.2 miles). Moreover, the shells used smokeless powder that made them hard to detect. By comparison the Allied Shermans had just 5 cm (2 in) of frontal armour, which made its five-man crew vulnerable to various German projectiles. Despite its shortcomings, Allied troops still praised the reliable Shermans, but admitted that their American tanks were outgunned, outclassed and outpaced by the King Tiger II, which, on top of everything else, had a road speed of 40 k/ph (25 mph).

The King Tiger II weighed in at a massive 68.5 tons and featured sloping armour 15 cm (6 in) thick on the front hull, which at ordinary distances could easily deflect American 75 and 76 mm shells. It featured an automated turret, which could turn a full 360 degrees in 19 seconds, which was impressive, but which also theoretically allowed a fast-moving Sherman or M10 Tank Destroyer to outmanoeuvre it. And while the Tiger II was capable of surprisingly excellent tactical mobility in open ground, with its wide, 90 cm (35 in) treads it was less effective on narrow cobbled streets in towns and villages. German troops on the move discovered that it was best to dig in and camouflage the tank around built-up areas, whereupon they would wait until the advancing Allies were within range before opening up. The results were often devastating.

German technical innovation extended to aviation too, but as impressive as their new jet fighters were, it was all going to be too little too late. As early as July 1944 Allied pilots had reported seeing German jets in the skies above Normandy. With the Me 262 the German aviation industry had created an aircraft which could in theory have restored command of the skies over Germany to the Luftwaffe. Compared with Allied fighters of the day it was faster and packed a much heavier punch. Despite the obvious potential of these jets, for years its development was beset by lack of official interest, and by the personal insistence of Hitler that the world-beating jet should be used solely as a bomber! In the autumn of 1938 Messerschmitt was asked to study the design of a jet fighter, and the resulting Me 262 yielded remarkably positive results during test flights. Despite numerous snags, production aircraft were being delivered by mid-1944.

It was a clear day over Munich on 26 July 1944 as a lone RAF Mosquito reconnaissance aircraft flew 8,500 m (28,000 ft) above the city. Its pilot, Flight Lieutenant A.E. Wall of 544 Squadron, kept the aircraft steady. Its navigator, Pilot Officer A.S. Lobban, operated the camera that captured black and white images of the city's key targets.

At that height they felt relatively safe from anti-aircraft fire and were confident they could outrun any of the Luftwaffe's Bf-109s and Fw-190s. Nevertheless, their aircraft was unarmed and constructed almost entirely of wood, making it defenceless and vulnerable. Its crew had been on high alert ever since taking off from their base at RAF Benson, Oxfordshire, early that morning.

After a few minutes circling over the city, Wall and Lobban got the shots they needed. Lobban resumed his seat and they began to head for home when suddenly he called out, 'Hey, what's this? Bandit at 6 o'clock! And closing fast!' Wall was taken by surprise. How could an enemy fighter have reached their altitude so quickly, without being spotted? There was no time to ponder the problem, the pilot had to pull away from the attacker in a hurry. He shoved the throttles forward, and reset the fuel mixture to full rich. The Mosquito's powerful engines immediately responded, and they sprinted ahead.

The Mosquito's official maximum speed was 675 k/ph (420 mph), but Wall knew that it could exceed that when pushed. All he had to do was keep the throttles full open and fly straight, and the enemy would be left far behind. He underestimated his attacker. Wall was incredulous that even though he was reaching maximum speed their pursuer was rapidly closing down the distance between them. To help accelerate, Wall put the aircraft into a shallow dive. The airspeed indicator peaked at 760 k/ph (470 mph), causing incredible vibrations that left the Mosquito in danger of falling apart. Wall drew the stick back and brought the Mosquito level. Not only had the enemy aircraft stayed with them, it was closing in. Then it began firing its cannons, sending tracers streaking past the Mosquito, inches above the cockpit canopy.

Wall responded by backing off the throttles, and swinging left. The attacker zipped by, and as it did they got their first good look at it. They noticed that the bandit had no propellers. It was a low-winged monoplane with two large engine pods, and a configuration unlike any they had seen before.

The strange aircraft was now turning towards them but it didn't seem to be all that manoeuvrable, probably due to the incredible speed it was travelling. It appeared to require a great amount of space to turn about. Wall realized that if he could turn more tightly than the other aircraft he might be able to keep it from getting a clean shot him. He added power and reversed course, heading directly towards it. Like an aerial game of chicken, the two aircraft began closing on each other again at a combined speed of nearly 1,600 k/ph (1,000 mph). The enemy aircraft fired again, but was not lined up well enough to hit. At the very last possible moment, Wall flicked the ailerons and sent the Mosquito past the attacker. Then with G-forces pushing him deeper into his seat he continued to turn hard. Once more it took longer for the enemy aircraft to swing around. The same thing happened again. On the next pass the opponent made a smart move and began his turn only a fraction of a second after Wall began his. Then he dived, and climbed toward the British aircraft from underneath, firing his cannons as he came.

A resonant bang rocked the Mosquito, causing it to tilt and shudder. Wall struggled to maintain control, but the aircraft was still flying. The only response he could think of was to try another dive. He pushed the stick forward, and as he did caught sight of cloud cover below. He raced downward, and an instant later was inside the cloud's solid white sanctuary. When he eventually emerged the enemy aircraft had gone. It was a lucky escape and one that both crewmen would never forget. They had encountered a Messerschmitt Me 262 and lived to tell the tale. The Me pilot, Luftwaffe ace Lieutenant Alfred Schreiber, would later claim that encounter with the Mosquito was the first aerial victory by a jet fighter in aviation history.

On 28 August, the first Me 262 was destroyed by Allied pilots when Major Joseph Myers and Second Lieutenant Manford Croy of the 78th Fighter Group shot one down while flying P-47 Thunderbolts. The new German jets were impressive but not indestructible. When the Allied pilots became aware that a jet was tailing, like the Mosquito, they would turn as hard as they could just before the jet came into range. The Me 262 could not turn as fast or as tight, so the German pilot would have to go in a big circle and get behind the Allied plane again, whereupon the Allied fighter would repeat the manoeuvre.

German technological innovation was unprecedented and caused some terrible headaches at SHAEF. The Nazis had both the methods and the technical acumen, but owing to a lack of basic resources they no longer had the means of mass production by that stage of the war. German research into the development of nuclear weapons was competitive with American research. German physicists may have made important ground-breaking discoveries in nuclear reactor construction, isotope separation and heavy water production, but their exclusionist, racist policies and twisted ideologies proved ultimately detrimental to advancement. There were a variety of factors that prevented Nazi Germany from achieving the breakthroughs they required to actually construct a nuclear bomb, including governmental interference, and the expulsion, imprisonment and even murder of gifted Jewish physicists and other scientists that could have helped their cause.

In World War II both the Axis and Allies were developing helicopter technology, but Germany was first past the post in terms of actual production. In 1941 it produced a prototype called the Flettner FL 282, which became the world's first mass-produced helicopter, and a full order for 1,000 machines was placed in 1944. Only 24 had come off the production line before Allied bombing completely levelled the Flettner factory, but the machines that were made were used for artillery spotting and reconnaissance until the final days of World War II. Three actually survived the war.

The best history provokes cognitive dissonance and it is easy to marvel at and even admire German innovation, but what remains is the indisputable fact that under the Nazis there was but one goal: the destruction of fellow humans. They didn't need to invent WMDs (weapons of mass destruction), they had them already, as they efficiently demonstrated with the death camps and their inane capacity to destroy families, whole communities, and exterminate millions of innocent, promising lives.

The Nazis first introduced poison gas as a means for mass murder in December 1939, when an SS *Sonderkommando* (special unit) used carbon monoxide to asphyxiate and murder Polish mental patients. One month later, Philipp Bouhler, the head of the Nazis' Euthanasia Programme (the term 'euthanasia' literally means 'good death') employed carbon monoxide to kill those who the Nazis regarded as useless to society such as the handicapped, chronically ill, the aged and others who had been placed at his mercy. By August 1941 the lives of approximately 70,000 Germans had been extinguished in the country's five euthanasia centres, which were equipped either with stationary gas chambers or with mobile gas vans.

On 18 August 1939, the Reich Ministry of the Interior circulated a decree requiring all physicians, nurses and midwives to report newborn infants and children below the age of three who showed signs of severe mental or physical disability. Beginning in October 1939, public health authorities began to encourage parents of children with disabilities to admit their young children to one of a number of specially designated paediatric clinics throughout Germany and Austria. This was a deadly feint because, in reality, the clinics were places of infanticide.

The first mass killing centre was located in the Warthegau area of Poland annexed to Germany in December 1941. Those murdered were mostly Jews, but Roma (Gypsies) were also exterminated using mobile gas vans. In 1942, as a component of *Aktion Reinhard* (the programme to exterminate Jews), the Nazis commissioned and constructed three fully operational death camps equipped with hermetically sealed stationary gas chambers at Belzec, Sobibor, and Treblinka. At first, the chosen means of elimination was suffocation by diesel engine exhaust fumes. But this was soon deemed to be an inefficient practice and the search began to find a new method.

After some experimentation on Soviet prisoners of war, the Nazis discovered that a commercial insecticide called Zyklon B produced an appropriate gas for their needs. A form of hydrogen cyanide, Zyklon B was immediately put to use at the mass extermination centre at Auschwitz–Birkenau. Zyklon B gas chambers were also constructed at the Mauthausen, Neuengamme, Sachsenhausen, Stutthof and Ravensbruck concentration camps, although none of these were used for routine mass killing as at Auschwitz. By spring 1943 Auschwitz had four operational gas chambers. At the height of the deportations, up to 6,000 Jews were murdered every day at Auschwitz–Birkenau. By November 1944 over a million Jews and tens of thousands of Roma, Poles and Soviet prisoners of war had died there.

In autumn 1944 the SS began attempting to cover its tracks at Auschwitz–Birkenau, ordering the killing of some of the Jewish prisoners assigned to the *Sonderkommando* that operated the crematoria and gas chambers. This resulted in a small mutiny that erupted on 7 October and left 450 dead and one of the crematoria demolished. On the orders of *Reichsführer* SS Heinrich Himmler preparations were made in November and December of that year to destroy the three remaining crematoria at Auschwitz–Birkenau. Most of the technical installations in the gas chambers and furnace halls of Crematoria II and III were dismantled. Crematorium V and its adjacent gas chambers remained fully operational until the second half of January 1945. In Himmler's delusional mind, destroying two of the three remaining crematoria was a way of putting himself in a more favourable light with the Allies as it became clear that Germany was going to lose the war. The man who had sanctioned and orchestrated the greatest crime against humanity was attempting to cover his own back and the Führer be damned.

THE RULES OF MILITARY GOVERNMENT

It's been noted that there was the occasional lack of cohesion among the Allied staff at SHAEF, and this was on occasion problematic. But this was minor compared with the malicious collusions of Hitler's closest aides and deputies. This sycophantic group of misanthropes was constantly jostling for position and favour. As the irreversible tide of war began to turn in favour of the Allies, the power struggles in Germany intensified and gathered momentum. Meanwhile, Hitler was preparing one last vain attempt to damage the western alliance and bring them to the negotiating table.

When the first Allied soldiers encroached the Reich in September 1944 they were issued with strict instructions to prohibit fraternization with the German population. As Allied armies moved in even further female auxiliary members of the United States and British forces were moved into the rear areas for safety reasons. SHAEF insisted that Allied soldiers should present a morally impeccable image to the civilians. To assist this SHAEF organized a 14-day series of five-a-day proclamations to the German people on 'how to act under the Allied occupation authorities'. The broadcast emphasized the following stipulations:

1. The Military Government in occupied Germany will act with severity and determination but with justice. Its aim will be the destruction of the Nazi system and the extermination of German militarism imbued with aggression.
2. The Military Government will govern on the basis of written laws. The Allied Military Government will protect the German population against corruption, greed, obscure machinations and all acts of the terror of the present National Socialist leaders.

3. The laws of the Military Government will be drawn up and published. Everyone should be acquainted with the contents of these laws. The present laws remain in force provided they are not in contravention to the laws published by the Military Government. The Military Government will see to it that its laws are strictly enforced. The meaning of these laws will be clear and unequivocal. Everyone must abide by them at once.

4. The procedure of the courts instituted by the Military Government will be just and swift. All violations of the law will be punished in regular legal procedure and without delay.

The rules and regulations stipulated by the military authorities looked good on paper, but in reality fraternization between the Allies and German civilians was ubiquitous. Coffee, nylon stockings and food in general could buy a lot of temporary friendships and sex could be procured for a cigarette. Many German women were shot and killed by their husbands for consenting to sexual relations with Allied soldiers. Fraternization made them prone to retribution from returning German soldiers who castigated them as 'Allied whores'. Some woman 'adopted' Allied soldiers who supplied them with food and other basic necessities as well as luxury items in return for sex. This kind of procurement for sexual favours was particularly popular among the German bourgeoisie and the middle classes.

In the liberated countries of France, Luxembourg, Holland and Belgium some friendships became more permanent as GIs and Tommies made romantic connections with the locals. The language of love was rarely lost in translation and usually rendered all linguistic barriers superfluous.

APPROACHING THE RIVER SAAR

Not known for keeping his opinions to himself, General Patton was uneasy about the large gap that existed between the First and Third Armies in a place called the Ardennes. He had remarked that, 'The First Army is making a terrible mistake in leaving VIII Corps static, as it is highly probable that the Germans are building up to the east of them.' Patton was sure that the Germans were still capable of mounting a major counterattack and wrongly assumed that it would occur in the Twelfth

Army Group's southern sector. Metz had proved to be a particularly difficult objective and fighting there had continued almost unabated since 8 November. Patton's attempts to take Metz and plough on through the rest of Lorraine in France had been impeded by bucketing rain almost throughout the whole campaign. When he wrote to his wife he whined incessantly about how the weather was preventing his army from killing more Germans. In a letter to the Secretary of War, Henry L. Stimson, Patton light-heartedly requested that 'in the final settlement of the war, you insist that the Germans retain Lorraine, because I can imagine no greater burden than to be the owner of this nasty country where it rains every day.' In his memoirs Patton semi-seriously revealed how, 'The weather was so bad that I directed all Army chaplains to pray for dry weather. I also published a prayer with a Christmas greeting on the back and sent it to all members of the Command. The prayer was for dry weather for battle.'

General Patton had made progress in his moves towards Thionville, establishing various bridgeheads across the Moselle. Metz had fallen on 22 November but enemy resistance had been fierce. By 4 December, a stretch of the River Saar was in Third Army hands and in some areas it had reached the Siegfried Line. In the Sixth Army Group sector American and French troops struggled on against resolute German opposition in particularly difficult terrain and inclement weather, but by 23 November they had managed to liberate the key city of Strasbourg. In the far south the French First Army broke through to Belfort and reached the Rhine, while holding a line that extended from Mulhouse to the Swiss border. The Germans sought cover in the mountains, thereby retaining a section of Alsace that became known as the Colmar Pocket. From here the Germans would attempt to launch a counteroffensive or at least restrict the Allied freedom of movement. The fact that the Germans placed eight divisions in a 3,000 sq km (1,200 sq mile) area demonstrated how important this region was to them.

The Third Army's 10th Armored Division saw action in France precisely two months after it left America. Within a few weeks it was a veteran battle division with nearly a thousand Purple Hearts earned in that short but furious period of fighting. During those weeks it successfully completed every important objective that it was assigned despite the fact that it was fighting against some of the best German divisions on the Western Front. It was the first division of the Third Army to enter Germany. Tank crewmember Don Nichols survived the hard fighting to take the city of Metz. 'Just before I arrived at the front, the German village of Bethingen had been captured. This was a small action. Its purpose was to give an infantry company its first taste of offensive warfare under conditions that would make a tactical success almost certain.

'When a unit has never experienced active warfare, it is highly important that it should taste success the first time it goes into battle. So, whenever possible, the wise commander plans that first action so carefully and so completely that it is almost sure to succeed. The officer [Colonel William L. Roberts, Combat Command B] who prepared the capture of Bethingen took the trouble to explain it to me in full detail. He worked it out as a highly coordinated operation. There was minute planning of the use of artillery and mortars and smoke to blind the enemy. From the beginning we had superior observation.

'All our men had been well trained for their specific tasks. They had excellent leaders. The entire action [executed by B Company, 20th Armored Infantry Battalion, commanded by Captain "Bud" Billett] went off and through the woods, which bordered the enemy strongpoint. To protect his movement on foot, the four halftracks, partly hidden at the edge of the woods, opened fire on the buildings. In a matter of minutes, all the buildings were on fire and about 50 enemies were killed by the intense fire from the halftracks. Then as Hughes' allotted time for observation of enemy artillery emplacements was rapidly expiring, the tracks directed their fire at the dragon's teeth. The Germans immediately retaliated as Major Madison hoped they would. Within three minutes 88s and mortar fire answered them in quantity. Captain Hughes noted their positions and hurried back to the halftracks with the knowledge that the 10th's own artillery would soon be able to give the jerries some of their own medicine. However, one of the tracks became stuck in the mud and had to be winched out by another and by this time the enemy began to find the range. In the meantime, the other two tracks took off in a big hurry, followed by the third track, which had succeeded in extricating the fourth vehicle. The latter tarried in the area only long enough to hook its dangling cable and it too scurried for cover. However, all four tracks, in their hurry to evade mortar and 88 fire, forgot one important detail. None of them waited for Captain Hughes, who by this time had reached the pre-arranged meeting point. Each track thought the other had picked up the Battalion S-3. And while the latter wondered, "what the hell has happened?" Major Madison reappeared over the horizon in search of his lost comrade. Acting like "old mother hen", the major stood up on his halftrack and watched Hughes duck into an apple orchard. He hesitated briefly, then, probably saying a prayer for the captain, took off again for Nohn. In all probability he would have lost his entire crew had he tried to rescue Hughes, for by this time the Germans zeroed in on the position. Hours later the Captain returned after having successfully dodged both enemy mortar fire and infantry in the woods. This particular expedition was but one of many actions by the crack ack ack men. On many occasions 796th batteries and platoons served as spearheads for Tiger armour and infantry as well as providing anti-aircraft protection and security. The best testimony to their value was in the large number of enemy planes their deadeye gunners bagged during their partnership with the 10th Armored Division.'[56]

The division enjoyed a very brief pause in the days leading up to the German offensive. It remained in a state of high alert until the call came through on 16 December to move north with all haste. There were still problems at SHAEF regarding the way forward at the end of November and the beginning of December 1944.

Montgomery and British Chief of Staff Marshal Alan Brooke remained stridently opposed to Eisenhower's strategy. While Simpson and Hodges were attacking the Ruhr, Patton had managed to penetrate deep into the Saar, while Patch and the French General de Lattre were making significant gains in the Alsace region. They were all on the offensive but there was no mention of any momentous breakthroughs or the availability of reserves. Montgomery made a further request to Eisenhower to dispatch massive numbers of soldiers north to assist in his push to the Ruhr, re-emphasizing that this area was of vital importance to the Reich, and adding that the plains in northern Germany were the terrain that was most feasibly accessible to mobile armoured units. Monty went on to say that, in his considered opinion, if he could go on the offensive there the Germans would have neither the manpower nor the impetus to take him on. It would be the end of the German army. Ike didn't agree and would later be proved right.

CRIME AND THE ARMY

Life on the front lines for the Allies had taken its toll both physically and mentally. Between June 1944 and April 1945, the US army's Criminal Investigation Branch (CBI) handled a total of 7,912 cases. Forty per cent involved misappropriation of US supplies. The rest were cases of violence, rape, murder and manslaughter. Desertion was a serious problem for all the Allied armies in Europe. Private Eddie Slovik, Company G, 109th Infantry Regiment, 28th Infantry Division General, was the only US serviceman to be executed for desertion in World War II. He was strapped to a post in a farmyard at Sainte-Marie-aux-Mines, France, and executed by 12 riflemen who were all members of his regiment. In later years, Slovik's wife petitioned the US government for posthumous clemency for her husband. It was never granted. Aside from Slovik, 101 other US service personnel were executed by military authorities during World War II, all for either rape or murder.

Over 40,000 American and nearly 100,000 British soldiers abandoned their posts during the war and were listed as having deserted. The German army was much tougher on deserters. The Wehrmacht executed some 15,000 soldiers for desertion during World War II. Today, these men are remembered as victims of war. In 1988 a monument bearing the inscription 'Desertion is not reprehensible, war is' was erected to them in Ulm.

The number of German army executions was nothing compared to Russia's record. More than 158,000 Soviet soldiers were summarily executed for abandoning their posts during the war. Others were sent to penal battalions, which was essentially also a death sentence. Unauthorized retreats were not recommended in the Red Army. To prevent this from happening, Stalin ordered the formation of what he aptly named 'blocking detachments'. These units usually had a few machine guns and would be strategically positioned just behind the front line to shoot down any soldiers that attempted to run away. No wonder that Stalin famously observed, 'It takes a very brave man to be a coward in the Red Army.'

CHAPTER FIFTEEN

DOWN TIME

THE PRIMARY GOALS FOR THE Allies in early December 1944 were focused on preparations for an all-out offensive that would bypass the Ardennes to the north and commence in early 1945. Eisenhower wanted to maintain the momentum by keeping pressure on the Germans. He emphasized that the main thrust toward the Rhine would occur in the north, but that there were also sufficient Allied military resources available near the Moselle south of the Ardennes to go forward to the Rhine, bearing in mind that the north would have priority. On the basis of this he gave permission for Patton's Third Army, supported by the Seventh Army, to make preparations for an offensive in the Saar region scheduled to commence on 19 December. At the same time Eisenhower added a cautionary note for his friend General Bradley, saying that he would allow that offensive one week to achieve favourable results.

While detailing its plans, SHAEF clarified its intention to provide sufficient materials and men for the main effort in the north, and that any crossing of the Rhine from the south was to be restricted until the success of operations in the north was assured. Contemporary press releases in early December indicated that, after progressing beyond the

Aachen, Duren, Monschau triangle, Hodges' First Army had commenced driving east. The 5th US Armored Division was spearheading this new offensive, which was launched from the German town of Gey to the east of the dreaded Hürtgen Forest.

Simultaneously, the 414th Infantry Regiment, 104th 'Timberwolf' Division, led by Major General Terry Alleni, attacked Schophoven and Pier on the morning of 10 December. It cleared out all German resistance from the area where fighting had been going on for a week. By 14 December, all assigned objectives had been captured and in a subsequent message to his troops General 'Lightning Joe' Collins stated that he regarded this operation, involving the seizure of Lamersdorf, Inden, Lucherberg, Pier, Merken and Schophoven as one of the finest pieces of work accomplished by any unit of the VII Corps since D-Day.

Southwest of Duren, the US 9th Infantry Division had reached the outskirts of Gurzenich, roughly on the road east to Cologne, and the 83rd Division had opened another main road artery that led east. The Ninth Army, operating on the First Army's left flank, saw some minor action, which had the effect of coordinating its Roer line with that of Hodges' forces. In a move south of Julich the 9th cleared a small enemy pocket in the triangle formed by the River Roer and a tributary stream known as the Inde. Despite largely differing opinions, for some SHAEF commanders the way ahead was crystal clear.

On the basis of this, British and US commanders worked in concert to improve their positions north of the Ardennes. General William Hood Simpson's Ninth Army had reached the River Roer by mid-December, but he was reluctant to orchestrate an actual crossing while the Germans held the dams on the Urft and the Roer rivers to the south. On his right flank General Courtney Hodges' forces had advanced under great duress through the Hürtgen Forest and also reached the Roer. At this juncture General Bradley directed Hodges to launch an attack to seize this objective, commencing on 13 December. This he did, but it would be halted by other events just three days later.

Meanwhile, on 15 December four US divisions held a 143 km (89 mile) front that ran from just below Aachen in Germany, through the Ardennes region and into Luxembourg. The 28th US Infantry Division had been dispatched south to occupy part of this innocuous, quiet sector and in order to rest and re-equip. Its number had been reduced by four-fifths during the terrible battle in the Hürtgen Forest, where whole companies were reduced to just a few men in some of the bitterest fighting endured by any soldiers in World War II.

The same applied to the 4th US Infantry Division, which needed to replenish its seriously depleted ranks down in the Duchy of Luxembourg. One GI of the 4th needed to attend to some pressing, or rather itching, personal hygiene issues. 'I would like to relate something that took place a day or two after we were relieved in the Hürtgen and pulled back to what I recall was an old German training camp,' recalled John E. Kunkel, Company L, 3rd Battalion, 22nd Infantry Regiment. 'A short time after we got there, we were all given a bunk and a grey German army blanket. Well, about midnight it happened, we all started to itch all over. My buddy said he felt something crawling on his neck. I took my pen flashlight out and, sure enough, there they were – body lice. Now the problem was getting rid of the lice. About daylight we found an old kerosene lantern. We poured the kerosene into a steel helmet and with an old dirty sock, we all took a sponge bath. It was hard on the skin, but we got rid of the lice. It was some time until we could take a real bath with good old water. We started to smell to the point we all smelled like Billy goats – it got to where we could not live with one another.'[57]

Meanwhile, Bing Crosby was providing mental sedation by crooning to the GIs in his inimitable fashion, but he had some staunch competition from German-born, husky-voiced Hollywood star Marlene Dietrich, who wowed the GIs wherever she appeared. She had sizzled on screen with the best leading men but Ms Dietrich's most memorable co-star was General George S. Patton. While entertaining the troops during World War II, she ventured to within a mile of the German front lines on the arm of the general, who personally gave her a brace of Colt 45s to see off potential assassins. The Nazi government responded to this affront by putting a seven-figure bounty on the Berlin-born actor's head. She had become a US citizen in 1939, flatly refusing a personal request from Adolf Hitler to return to Germany as the centrepiece of his propaganda campaign. She actively supported the Allied cause throughout the war.

General George S. Patton, commander of the US 3rd Army, with Marlene Dietrich.

AN EXPLOSIVE INNOVATION

Young Jim Cooley wrote a valedictory note to his mother in Oklahoma when he left the United States to sail to Europe with the 106th Infantry Division to participate in World War II: 'You're going to be mighty proud of your son Ma because I'm going to be the first GI to cross the Rhine River.' This turned out to be the case, but it wouldn't be exactly as he had envisaged. He was a member of 423rd Regiment, 106th US Infantry Division, and a few weeks after writing to his mother he would be taken prisoner by the Germans and forced to spend the remaining months of World War II in a Nazi Stalag. But he was indeed one of the first to cross the Rhine, even if it was as a prisoner in a cattle truck. Jim never forgot his time in Europe and would revisit the area with his family in 2000.

During their rest and recuperation period between fighting the violent Battle of Metz and their next combat mission, the 10th Armored Division made history by test-firing the US army's newest secret weapon. For most of World War II, a perennial problem for artillery units had been in predicting precisely where on its trajectory a shell would explode. The best that artillerymen could do when setting a fuse was to estimate how long a shell would be in flight. But in December 1944 the newly-created proximity fuse was unveiled during a secret demonstration.

'While in position near Perl, Germany, the 420th Armored Field Artillery Battalion was selected to organize and perform a demonstration of the new, then secret, VT [variable time] or POZIT fuse. All available Field Officers, particularly Artillerymen of XX Corps, were to attend,' wrote Major Willis D. 'Crit' Crittenberger of HQ Battery, 420th Armoured Field Artillery Battalion. 'The Battalion Commanding Officer and an advance party strong in Survey, Fire Direction and Communications moved out to select a "Demonstration Area" suitable for this mission. The next day, the battalion followed, cutting across the main supply routes of the three divisions in contact and covering the forty-three mile move in four hours. The nearest town on the maps was Marange, France, on the southern edge of XX Corps.

'The Journal entry reads "Departed Perl, Germany at 10:45 on mounted motor march to Marange, France, arriving at 1500. Distance travelled 43.6 miles. Weather cold and rainy. Morale good". An "impact area" of

One of the most admired and respected officers in the US army in World War II. Crit was a career soldier who spent 40 years in the military. A West Point graduate, he fought for his country in three wars. During World War II he lost a brother and later on he lost another brother in Vietnam.

rolling, varied terrain was picked. Shot-up vehicles and farm equipment were placed as identifiable targets in the valley, on the slope, and even on the crest, to best illustrate the standard height of burst of this new fuse.

'Survey and registration took place as others were laying communications for ourselves and to tie in to Corps lines should higher Headquarters need to reach any of the attendees. The usual "demonstration" services were set up; latrines, warming tents, parking areas, hot coffee, mess tents with a hot meal and yes, extra field glasses, a public address system and some folding chairs for the real VIPs. The day of the "shoot," December 11 dawned cold and rainy but happily not foggy. Our preparations for just such a day were both needed and appreciated. The Corps Commander Walton Walker led the list of attendees, dressed for the cold. The firing went well. The targets had been placed to show that the new fuze [sic] would burst the shells uniformly above the target, whether it was on flat ground or on the slope, uphill or down. The hot meal and coffee were big hits too!

'Following the shoot, those interested talked to the Fire Direction and Survey crews and to the gun crews as well. The remainder of the day was spent in "cleaning up the battlefield". The next day, December 12, our "vacation" was over and we marched back to the north boundary of XX Corps in the Merzig-Launstroff area to fire for Task Force Polk, the Corps' Mechanized Cavalry in an economy-of-force role holding a part of the "front".'[58]

On 15 December, everything was quiet in the Ardennes town of Bastogne. The locals had really taken to these fresh-faced young Americans and many lifelong friendships had been established. One resident of Bastogne said: 'We shared everything with the Americans but some of the things they gave us in return were not edible, and a Hershey bar was not real chocolate.'

Major General Troy Middleton had established the VIII Corps headquarters in Bastogne at a former Belgian army base known as the Heintz Barracks, which had been used by the Germans as a recruiting station, among other things, during the occupation. The VIII Corps front wasn't in a particularly good condition. It was held by the 4th Infantry Division, the 28th Infantry Division, the 106th Infantry

Division, the 14th Cavalry Group, consisting of the 18th and 32nd Cavalry Squadrons, and the 9th Armored Division, minus Combat Command B, which was on loan to General Gerow's V Corps. Middleton had an impeccable reputation. He had fought in World War I, had an excellent combat record and was regarded by both Bradley and Patton as one of the best tacticians in the US army. His tactical acumen would soon come in very handy. American Lieutenant Ernest Gessener, of the 28th US Infantry Division, was officially the first American killed in Bastogne when it was liberated on 11 September 1944, but he wouldn't be the last by a long chalk. In early December some GIs of the 28th were still in and around Bastogne.

WAITING FOR THE NAZI RESPONSE

Out on the freezing Schnee Eifel plateau in Germany, John Schaffner, a scout for Battery B, 589th Field Artillery Battalion, 106th Infantry Division, wasn't happy about the location of his unit. He said, 'In a position like this, every member of the gun crew had to stand guard duty at night. This included me and the sergeant. I will tell you, that first night was very nerve wracking. Not knowing very much about the situation or from what direction the enemy might come from, every sound was a cause for concern. Two hours felt like eight. The severe cold made it even more difficult. During this period there was little activity other than a few patrol actions. Few observed missions were fired due to the poor visibility. The battalion did, however, have a substantial unobserved, harassing program that was fired every night. The forward observer adjusted by sound, using high-angle fire, which made it necessary to re-dig the gun pits. Alternate positions were selected and surveyed by the survey officer and his party. There were some reports of enemy activity but nothing, apparently, more than routine truck and troop movements. Headquarters Battery crews reported being fired upon on the 15th and that night an enemy recon plane circled the area for an hour or more. Numerous flares were seen to the flanks of the battalion and an enemy patrol was reported to be in the area. During this period most of my time was spent at various outposts near the battery position. There was nothing to report. At night, watching across the snow-covered fields, one's eyes tended to play tricks. On more than one occasion an outpost guard would fire away at some movement out in front of him, only to find out in the morning that he had "killed" a tree stump or boulder.'[59]

Also out on the Schnee Eifel, Jim Cooley and another GI of the 106th US Infantry Division stamped their feet to stave off the gnawing cold that permeated every sinew. He spoke in hushed tones about Oklahoma and complained about having to pull guard duty at that godforsaken hour. In the distance they could hear the faint rumble of engines but couldn't determine if they were German or Allied vehicles. Jim peered snake-eyed into the murky dense fog, shrugged his shoulders and blew into his cupped hands before saying, 'Sounds like somebody is on the move, buddy.' The other GI inclined his head: 'Is it ours or theirs?' Jim smiled 'Hard to say.'

Allied commanders were still making too many assumptions regarding the state of German forces. On 12 December Omar Bradley had said that, 'It is now certain that attrition is steadily sapping the strength of the German forces on the Western Front and that the crust of defences is thinner, more brittle and more vulnerable than it appears on our G-2 map or to the troops in the line.'[60] Monty mirrored these observations with a few of his own: 'The enemy is at present fighting a defensive campaign on all fronts; his situation is such that he cannot stage major offensive operations. Furthermore, at all costs he has to prevent the war from entering on a mobile phase; he has not the transport or the petrol that would be necessary for mobile operations. The enemy is in a bad way.'[61]

This feeling that the Nazis were backing off filtered down to the troops on the ground. 'December 15 our Battalion Major came to our position inspecting. It just so happened that we had just all shaved up, the tent's contents were in order, our AA guns were cleaned up. He complimented us and said we were the best gun crew he had seen that day,' remembered Albert Honowitz, B Battery, 796th Anti-aircraft Artillery Automatic Weapons Battalion. 'He also let us in on the battle situation at the time. He told us that the 10th Armored tank men were in the far back of the lines practicing manoeuvres for the crossing of the Rhine River, but that most 3rd Army units were back resting up. He said that "the American lines were thinner than they had ever been since D-Day, but that SHAEF doesn't expect the Germans to do anything about it." The Major then parted with the words, "Take it easy fellas, everyone else is."[62]

The pervading mood among most of the Allied units in the ETO was one of calm confidence. They all knew that a fresh offensive was imminent but no one really suspected that the Germans were in a position to take the initiative. While detailing its plans, SHAEF clarified its intention to provide sufficient materials and men for the main effort in the north, and that any crossing of the Rhine from the south was to be restricted until the success of operations in the north was assured.

The purpose of the secondary southern advance was to reduce the pressure on the primary northern attack by engaging as many German forces as possible. To facilitate this plan, massed numbers of troops and armour were concentrated in the Aachen area to ensure rapid movement across the most favourable terrain. Remaining forces were employed to sustain Patton's Third Army in its planned offensive. This focus on the north and south neglected to consider General Troy Middleton's VIII Corps sector in the Ardennes on the right flank of the US First Army. His four divisions were covering areas that far exceeded the prescribed division boundaries, and this would inevitably make them vulnerable. Whereas a division could normally cover a front of roughly 8 km (5 miles), some VIII Corps divisions were dangerously overextended, covering almost 48 km (30 miles).

Above the northern shoulder of the Ardennes not far from Aachen, the US 30th Division was getting some well-earned rest. Its division band that had been assigned to guard duties at Division CP for the duration had discovered some abandoned German instruments and began making music again for the troops. Apart from that there was the excellent USO to provide entertainment from home, and movies were shown three times a day. There was no compulsory training to do, so the soldiers could sleep for as long as they wanted in the separate cubicles that allowed privacy and provided comfort for these battle-hardened but weary foot-sloggers. The regiments took turns to move away from the front line and use the excellent facilities. The hiatus was to be short-lived, though. Ominous rumours about the Nazis amassing forces for a possible massive counteroffensive were in the air, and soon proved to be more than just rumours.

George Schneider HQ Co, 120th Regiment, 30th Infantry Division, wrote: 'As part of the USO troop a guitar player/singer/composer came on stage and sang his most famous composition, "You Are My Sunshine". He was Jimmy Davis, who later became the governor of Louisiana. There was a bit of humor to the incident. Ken Bedford and I laid claim to a farmhouse bedroom. We found a large satin comforter, apple green on one side and pink on the other. Wrapped in this we bedded down for the night. All night we kept itching from some kind of crawling critters running races up and down our backs. In the morning we removed our shirts and long john undershirts and found hundreds of lice lined up in formation in the undershirt ribbings. We got a new set of de-loused clothing. By the middle of December we had reached the banks of the Ruhr River. Upstream the Germans controlled the dams that could be opened to flood our area and bog down a crossing. If we did successfully cross the Ruhr and were allowed to establish a bridgehead, the dams could be opened and we would be at the mercy of the 6th SS-Panzer Army on the other side.'

By early December 1944, frustration among the higher echelons at SHAEF was almost palpable. Triumphalist optimism of victory by Christmas had significantly diminished and the realization of a probable winter stalemate was beginning to manifest itself. They were in effect settling in for the winter months. Despite Allied intelligence officers having received various warnings that a German attack was looming, none of these reports was specific. There was no mention of numbers, commanders or dispositions of German units. Even when the 28th Division inadvertently captured two German prisoners down on the Luxembourg–Germany border no one really believed their claims that a massive German counteroffensive was imminent.

Omar Bradley had gone to great lengths to allay the fears voiced by some of his subordinates and gave his personal assurances that the Germans wouldn't attack during his tour of the Ardennes region. To all intents and purposes he had no valid reason to suspect otherwise, despite vague reports filtering through regarding the massing of Nazi troops and armour along the border between Belgium, Luxembourg and Germany. Growing reports of German units being transferred from the Eastern Front to the west were not greeted with any concerted level of consternation.

Weather reports for the middle of December indicated pressure centres building over the eastern Atlantic, England and Western Europe. A southerly flow existed over the Ardennes region and the air mass was what meteorologists refer to as 'modified cold maritime polar'. With the prolonged airflow from the Atlantic, it was possible to conclude that plenty of moisture was available to support the fog and cloud that continued for several days around this time. As the front over England approached Belgium in mid-December, rain began to fall.

ROCKET ATTACKS

On the afternoon of 16 December 1944, a full house of patrons at the 1,200-seat Rex cinema in the heart of Antwerp was enjoying a showing of *The Plainsman*, starring Gary Cooper and Jean Arthur, when a V-2 rocket scored a direct hit on the movie house.

The bomb, which destroyed ten other buildings, caused 567 military and civilian casualties, with 296 of the dead and 194 of the injured Allied soldiers. This was the single highest death toll from a V-2 rocket attack during the war in Europe. Survivors from the Rex said that the rocket came through the roof and exploded on the front row of the balcony. The rubble and debris was piled 5 m (16 ft) high and it took rescue teams six days to extricate all of the dead.

James Mathieson was a member of an RAF intelligence unit stationed in Belgium, and he remembered that, 'The rocket struck the cinema just at the point in the movie where Gary Cooper had captured an Indian who informed him that General Custer and his troops had been wiped out. That day my CO had decided to allow my friend and me a little free time. I was in a row where only three seats remained attached and I was lying over into space from the balcony. If I had gone down into the pit I would have had no chance. I consider to this day that I have a guardian angel looking after me because I think it was an absolute miracle that I escaped with so little injury.'[63]

Mathieson was taken to a British army hospital in the Belgian town of Duffel (the town that invented the 'Duffel' coat), where he regained conscious-ness a few days later. While recovering he was informed that his unit HQ had taken a direct hit from another V-2 the day after the cinema had been hit and practically everyone within it had been killed outright.

1,100 Belgian citizens and Allied soldiers were enjoying a Saturday matinee when a V2 rocket struck, killing 567 and injuring almost 700. It was the most devastating strike from a V2 in World War II.

Tracking V-2 targets was difficult for the Allies because they were launched from mobile platforms and the missile had a maximum range of roughly 320 km (200 miles). The massive resources devoted to developing the V-2 programme undoubtedly hindered rather than helped the German war effort. The V-2 rocket did succeed in some respects, though. The psychological impact of being targeted by rockets had a significant emotional effect on the morale of the victims.

Using a combination of barrage balloons, fighters and anti-aircraft artillery to destroy a majority of bombs before they reached their target, the British had to some extent learnt to deal with the predecessor V-1 'Buzz bomb'. Fighters such as the Tempest V, Spitfire XIV, and Mustang III were the most successful at eliminating missiles in flight. British radar installations had little difficulty detecting the V-1 while it was cruising at around 640 k/ph (400 mph) over water. First the fighter planes would scramble and get to a higher altitude, and as soon as the bomb was in range the pilot would initiate a dive and fire a rapid burst from his machine guns. This was, however, a precarious undertaking because if the pilot hit the wrong part of the bomb the warhead would explode, showering the fighter with shrapnel and flames. Occasionally, they used another technique called 'tipping', whereupon the pilot would pull alongside the V-1 and bring the wing of his aircraft under the wing of the bomb. This manoeuvre could cause the V-1's gyroscope to dramatically malfunction, miss the intended target by miles and on occasion simply nosedive into the English Channel.

Anti-aircraft guns and barrage balloons provided the final layer of defence. In combination with fighter aircraft they succeeded in bringing down 40 per cent of incoming missiles. Eventually, the British decided to improve and deploy more anti-aircraft batteries to the coastline, to provide the batteries with an unobstructed field of fire over the water. They also introduced proximity fuses in the anti-aircraft batteries that were very effective against these fast-moving flying bombs. By September 1944, the restructured defences destroyed a phenomenal 83 per cent of incoming V-1s.

The V-1 had been a problem but the V-2 was another matter entirely. The Allies could do very little to prevent V-2 attacks. These missiles travelled at such great heights and extreme speeds that shooting them down was nigh on impossible. Failing to prevent the V-2 by any physical means meant that British intelligence was forced to use psychological measures to confound the Germans. By the autumn of 1944 the British intelligence services had successfully detected and turned some German secret agents. At that stage in the war it was far too dangerous for the Luftwaffe to dispatch reconnaissance missions over the British Isles, so it was left to their agents to relay incorrect information concerning the accuracy of the V-2 rockets.

British intelligence leaked the misinformation that most V-2s aimed at London were overshooting the capital by between 15 to 30 km (9 to 18 miles). As a result, Germany modified the rockets' guidance system, causing most of them to land short of the city, often in under-populated areas of Kent. This tactic helped a little, but the most effective method of tackling the V-2 was to strike against its production sites and transportation networks. One statistic revealed that for every V-2 dropped on Britain the average death toll was just two people.

Hitler's WMDs turned out to be little more than another weapon of mass delusion.

EGOS AND ERRORS

The tumultuous autumn of 1944 had highlighted the glaring lack of cohesion between Allied commanders and their men had paid dearly for this. They had taken the fight to within the borders of the Third Reich and, due to incompetent military planning and poor coordination, they had experienced combat in some of the most singularly hostile environments. Allied bombing and low-level strafing attacks on the transportation system in France, Belgium and the Netherlands in the summer and autumn of 1944 inevitably killed many civilians. This was the cost of liberation from the Nazis.

In Belgium, armed resistance units located mainly in the Ardennes region of the country provided invaluable information for the Allies. Elsewhere in Belgium the resistance spent a great deal of time gathering intelligence and relaying it to Allied intelligence services. By 1944, Belgian resistance had the highest number of operable clandestine transmitters. British records indicate that 80 per cent of all the intelligence gathered from Nazi-occupied territories in World War II hailed from Belgium. All Nazi-occupied countries had haters and traitors, and Belgium was no exception. For many it was survival, for others it was cowardice and malice that motivated their actions.

As the fighting breached the borders of the Reich in the autumn of 1944 it is estimated that on average 13,536 German civilians perished every month as their cities were reduced to ashes. But bombing alone could not subdue them. Eventually, Allied ground forces would have to participate in a bitter and protracted fight from village to village and town to town.

Mistakes were made that could have easily been avoided with a nominal amount of tactical acumen. The autumn of 1944 was a time when egos transcended objectives and it was always the men in the field that paid the heaviest price. But even though some reputations were destroyed beyond repair, valuable intrinsic lessons on how not to conduct a military campaign were learned along the way. It would take another six months and many more engagements to bring the war to its inevitable conclusion, but even if the war wasn't over by Christmas it became clear from the end of 1944 that it would all be over someday soon. 'At least the Nazis and their sympathizers were getting what they deserved,' was the general consensus among the liberated. Blame had been allocated and retribution was in many cases brutal.

Collaborators had been discovered in every quarter. Some would eventually escape and some would assume new identities, while others would simply take the consequences. The morality that determines the actions of people is not intrinsic in the people themselves, but in the social environment that surrounds them, and in the right – or wrong – circumstances seemingly 'normal' people can become capable of anything, even pure, unadulterated evil. The moral high ground was frequently obscured. World War II proved that no one is immune to the unbridled temptations of inhumanity. The humanity and inhumanity that occurred during the autumn of 1944 affected and afflicted everyone who was there in some way or another.

CHAPTER SIXTEEN

THOSE WE KNEW

FRANÇOIS SCHAERLAECKEN, WHO WE MET in chapter four and who saw Fernand Wyss and the German Commandant of Breendonck, was my father-in-law. Louis de Pauw was my wife's grandfather. Frank Towers was the president of the 30th Infantry Division and a dear friend. I used to Skype with him regularly. I met and interviewed George Schneider in Maastricht in 2010 and we have remained in contact by email since that first meeting. He wrote a wonderful account of his experiences with the 30th Division in World War II titled *Survivor.*

I interviewed Rudolf von Ribbentrop by telephone 15 years ago and he subsequently sent me the two books he had published about his father, Hitler's foreign minister Joachim von Ribbentrop, who was hanged at Nuremberg.

The fort of Breendonck is roughly 6.5 km (4 miles) from my front door and I have met and interviewed many survivors of that despicable camp over the years. The shadow of Adolf Hitler and his Nazi regime looms large in Flanders. There are some Flemish fascists alive today who want the camp reopened for refugees and other immigrants.

After the war ended, two representatives of the German military authorities in Belgium were tried and convicted. It took six years to convict them and, after the trial, which ended on 9 March 1951, the Brussels court ruled that both were guilty of ordering the deportation of 25,000 Jews but they were not responsible for their subsequent extermination in Auschwitz. Under the Belgian law of remission the sentences of 12 years' imprisonment each were reduced by two-thirds and both men were released within three weeks of conviction.

Former Antwerp mayor Leon Delwaide was another case entirely. After the war Delwaide was in effect forgiven all his evil transgressions. The authorities in Antwerp even named a dock in the harbour after this insidious individual, which was only renamed in 2019. Delwaide was suspended from office but neither arrested nor charged despite the fact that his acquiescence led to the deaths of thousands of Jews. In a radio broadcast and a later TV appearance he defended his actions during the war by falsely insisting that he organized the raids and deportations of thousands of Jews under duress. This was a blatant lie. In 1946 both his and his wife's names appeared on the voting lists for local elections and he was re-elected to office where he served as an Antwerp city councillor for 20 more years before being made a Baron of the Realm. Shortly after that all further investigations into his wartime activities were suspended indefinitely. He died in 1978 and his wife was given the title of Baroness by royal decree.

At the outbreak of World War II, roughly 35,000 Jews resided in Antwerp. Local Belgian police with the assistance of the Nazi authorities rounded up Jews there on three occasions. The mayor of Brussels courageously refused to cooperate with the Nazis. Germans were able to conduct two major and several minor round-ups in Brussels without any support from the local police; they also conducted a round-up in Liège without any assistance from the Belgian law enforcement agencies. The number of registered Jews from Antwerp who fell victim to the Holocaust is disproportionately higher by comparison with those of Brussels. According to calculations, 65 per cent of Antwerp's and 37 per cent of Brussels' total Jewish population were deported.

By the time Antwerp was liberated by Allied troops on 4 September 1944, only about 800 Jews had managed to survive in the city with the help of members of the local population, for the most part devout Catholic individuals and activists of the Communist-dominated resistance. Members of the pre-war Zionist Youth Movements continued their activity in the underground and helped smuggle Jews into Switzerland and Spain during 1942–3. The annihilation of the Jewish community of Antwerp was almost total. Most of the Jews in Antwerp were concentrated in distinct neighbourhoods, and the support received by the Germans from local Flemish anti-Semites was more fervent than in many other places in Western Europe at the time. Moreover, the local Belgian authorities, particularly in Antwerp, apparently displayed no resistance to the Germans and actively enabled these mass deportations. Assistance offered to Antwerp's Jews by the local population was nominally less than in other cities in Belgium.

In 2015 I received two Emmy Awards for my documentary *Searching for Augusta*, the story of Augusta Chiwy, a biracial nurse who volunteered to tend wounded GIs in Bastogne in 1944. Augusta was a great friend and a wonderfully unassuming, courageous human being. It has been seen on Netflix, PBS, Amazon Prime and is available on iTunes. All Belgian TV stations refused, and continue to refuse, to screen the documentary. Augusta was awarded the United States' Humanitarian Certificate, made an honorary member of the 327th Regiment, 101st Airborne Division, and became a Knight of the Order of the Realm in Belgium.

Breendonck SS guard, the Flemish-Belgian Richard De Bodt, was apprehended in 1951 and sentenced to death. This was later commuted to a life sentence with hard labour. He died in 1975 at the age of 66 from complications due to diabetes. A military tribunal sentenced his colleague Fernand Wyss to death on 7 May 1946 for the murder of 16 people and the mistreatment of 167 prisoners. On Saturday, 12 April 1947, he was executed at 6 am with a bullet to the back of the neck.

Although there are few World War II veterans left alive today, over the past 30 years I have been fortunate to interview survivors of that conflict. Many of the interviewees became emotional while relating their experiences, but not all of them. There were some who simply exonerated their actions by exclaiming: 'It was war, what else could you do?'

In every protracted armed conflict there are inevitably war crimes. The determining factor hinges on whether these crimes are also seen as crimes by the military leadership and whether or not the perpetrators are then punished accordingly. Historians and scientists have always discussed the question of how rapidly perfectly normal people can transform into killing machines when the situation is conducive. On the other hand, there were those who demonstrated incredible courage and humanity when faced with the most terrible adversity. The autumn of 1944 was the season of hope and despair when people were at their best and their worst. While generals and politicians argued and haggled people dared to hope and pray for deliverance. World War II has been analysed, romanticized and demonized on so many platforms but these individual stories remain intact, and there will inevitably be many more. Some stories may be consigned to posterity, but they live on in their tellers' children, grandchildren and great grandchildren and the lessons remain omnipresent in some form or another. The autumn of 1944 was the season that determined the outcome of the war and the experiences of those who were there should never be forgotten.

NOTES AND REFERENCES

1   Rudolf von Ribbentrop, interview with author 18 June 2011; additional information from Rudolf von Ribbentrop's *Joachim von Ribbentrop: Mein Vater: Erlebnisse und Erinnerungen*. (Graz, Austria: Arles, 2008).

2   https://www.presidency.ucsb.edu/ws?pid=16515

3   Sur-les-toits-de-paris.eklablog.net/one-two-two-c25181364

4   https://en.wikipedia.org/wiki/Dietrich_von_Choltitz

5   Public records office. Telegram from Churchill.

6   Author interview, September 1997. Name of source withheld by request.

7   Pfc. Carlton H. Stauffer, 13128357, rifleman: Company G., 12 Infantry Regiment, 4th Infantry Division, World War II Unknown Binding – 1996.

8   *Churchill and Roosevelt, Volume 3: The Complete Correspondence*, edited by Warren F. Kimball. Princeton University Press.

9   Author interview, Albert Guyaux. June 1998.

10 http://veterans.heraldtribune.com/2016/06/30/soldier-helped-liberate-luxembourg/_Used with permission.

11 Story provided by Alex Ramael. Culture Service Boom, Antwerp.

12 Author interview, George Schneider. September 2011, Maastricht.

13 Petrus Joannes de Schutter. Interview translated by author from *Ons Volk*, 1948 edition.

14 Translated by author from *Ons Willebroek*, December 1947 edition.

15 Veterans History Project: Public domain: Benjamin Elisberg. http://memory.loc.gov/diglib/vhp/story/loc.natlib.afc2001001.16160/

16 Veterans History Project: Public domain: Claude W. Hoke.
   http://memory.loc.gov/diglib/vhp/story/loc.natlib.afc2001001.16160/

17 Author interview, Louis de Pauw. 1989.

18 *All the Way to Berlin: A Paratrooper at War* by James Megellas,
   p79–80. Presidio Press, 2003.

19 *A Drop Too Many*, by Major General John Frost. Pen and Sword
   Aviation, 2002.

20 https://www.paradata.org.uk/article/operation-market-garden-extract-
   diary-major-charles-panter

21 Author interview. 2009, Oosterbeek, Netherlands.

22 *Airborne Operations in World War II, European Theater*, by Dr. John
   C. Warren, p.146.

23 *The Ghost Army of World War Two: How One Top-Secret Unit
   Deceived the Enemy with Inflatable Tanks, Sound Effects, and Other
   Audacious Fakery* by Rick Beyer and Elizabeth Sayles. Princeton
   Architectural Press, 2015. Used with permission.

24 Christian Pettinger, personal recollections from email to author.

25 Josef Bieburger interviewed by Ludwig Fischer 1986. Used with
   permission.

26 Author interview, August Gövert. September 2011, Nideggen
   Germany.

27 http://contractofficeservices.net/HarleyReynolds.htm

28 Harold Williams,105th Engineer Combat Battalion, interviewed by
   David Hilborn at author's request. October 2012.

29 Excerpt from *The Stanhope B. Mason Papers*, 1942–1947.

30 Kunigunde Holtz, translated from German by author, 1987.

31 Lieutenant Robert G. Botsford quoted in Selected Intelligence
   Reports.

32 Ray Huebner, Clarence Huebner interview, 1 April 1970.
   https://digital.library.unt.edu/ark:/67531/metadc5281/m2/1/high_
   res_d/thesis.pdf

33 *A Tank Gunner's Story*, by Louis Gruntz (self-published). Additional
   items from author interview, December 2013.

34 http://home.scarlet.be/~sh446368/amazing-story-alfred-knaack.html
Alfred Knaak: Used with permission: Scorpio's website.

35 *A Dark and Bloody Ground: The Hürtgen Forest and the Roer River Dams, 1944–1945* by Edward G. Miller. Texas A&M University Press, 1995.

36 http://home.scarlet.be/~sh446368/conversations-j-lawton-collins.html
Used with permission: Scorpio's website.

37 http://home.scarlet.be/~sh446368/recollection-robert-t-bradicich.html
Used with permission: Scorpio's website.

38 Author interview, Hans Herbst. September 2008.

39 *The 893rd Tank Destroyer Battalion* by Lt. Col. Henry C. Kerlin,
https://www.tankdestroyer.net/images/stories/ArticlePDFs2/893rd_Unit_History.pdf

40 http://home.scarlet.be/~sh446368/medal-of-honor-recipients.html
Used with permission:Scorpio's website LEONARD, TURNEY W.

41 http://home.scarlet.be/~sh446368/erinnerungen-hubert-gees.html
Translated from German by author. Used with permission.

42 Author interview, Erwin Kressman. September 2010.

43 Open letter to Scorpio from Robert Westerman. Used with permission.

44 *A Dark and Bloody Ground: The Hürtgen Forest and the Roer River Dams, 1944–1945,* by Edward G. Miller, Texas A&M University Press, 1995.

45 Matthias Hutmacher, author interview. December 2010.

46 *Führer Directives and other Top-Level Directives of the German Armed Forces, 1942–1945,* Washington, 1948.

47 Quoted in *Official History of the Canadian Army in the Second World War: Volume III: The Victory Campaign* by C.P. Stacey. Ottawa, 1966.

48 Allan Notman: http://www.thememoryproject.com/stories/WWII
Used with permission.

49 Bill Davis: http://www.thememoryproject.com/stories/WWII
Used with permission.

50 Les Garnham: http://www.thememoryproject.com/stories/WWII
   Used with permission.

51 https://www.marketgarden.com/2010/UK/veterans/kwiatkowski.html

52 Author research and telephone interview October 2016. Story
   inspired by article: http://www.real-fix.com/relationships/
   ww2-veterans-who-fought-together-are-reunited-by-chance-70-years-
   later/

53 Author research and telephone interview October 2016. Story
   inspired by article: http://www.real-fix.com/relationships/
   ww2-veterans-who-fought-together-are-reunited-by-chance-70-years-
   later/

54 *Hitler: A Chronology of his Life and Time*, second revised edition by
   M. Hauner. Palgrave MacMillan, 1983.

55 Author interview, 2011. Real name withheld.

56 Extract from Don Nichols self-published book *Impact* and
   interviews with 10th Armored Division Historian Mike Collins:
   Used with permission.

57 Author interview, John E. Kunkel. April 2012.

58 Interview Major Willis D. 'Crit' Crittenberger, by Michael Collins.
   Used with permission.

59 *United States Army Combat Forces Journal*, Volume 3. 1952.

60 *United States Army Combat Forces Journal*, Volume 3. 1952.

61 *United States Army Combat Forces Journal*, Volume 3. 1952.

62 Albert Honowitz, interview Mike Collins. Used with permission.

63 James Mathieson. Excerpt translated from Dutch by author. First
   appeared in a July 1945 edition of *Ons Volk.*

INDEX

Aachen 117–20, 122–38

Adams, Richard Francis 43–4

Alanbrooke, Viscount 87, 225

Alleni, Terry 228

Amen, Clark R. 34–5

Antounex, Nicolas 168–9

Antwerp 36–7, 41, 54–5, 60–1, 83, 122, 175–90, 238–9, 244–5

army discipline 226

Arnhem 85–8, 91–101, 103–7, 193–4

Astaire, Fred 141

Baeten, Paul 81

Bastogne 74–6

Baudouin, King 47

Bedell Smith, Walter 87

Belcham, Brigadier 86

Belgium
    Allied advance 76–7, 80, 122, 188–9, 193
    Breendonck prison camp 63–71
    German occupation of 88, 90
    liberation of Antwerp 36–7, 41, 54–5, 60–1, 83, 175–90
    liberation of Bastogne 74–6
    liberation of Brussels 14, 44, 46
    Plomion massacre 35–6
    resistance movement in 55–60, 81–2, 241
    return of monarchy 46–7
    round-up of Jews 244–5
    V-2 attack on 238–9

Bernhard, Prince 47

Bestelbreurtje, Arie 98, 100

Bieburger, Josef 118

Billett, "Bud" 224

Bittrich, General 104

Boehme, William 131

bombing raids 17–18

Borowiec, Andrei 195–6

Botsford, Robert 136

Bouhler, Philipp 219

Bradicich, Bob 158–9

Bradley, Omar
    advance through Germany 71, 72, 227, 228
    difficulties with Patton 40
    on intelligence gathering 207
    view of German strength 235, 237–8

Brandenberger, Erich 119–20, 157

Breendonck prison camp 63–71, 243

Bridge Too Far, A 96

Brooke, Alan 87, 225

Browning, Frederick 'Boy' 105–6

Bruns, General 166

Brussels 14, 44, 46

Bulge, Battle of the 9, 161, 168, 174, 200–1, 214, 222

Caen 18–19, 24, 28

Charest, Albert Salomon 191–2

Cherbourg 50

Chiwy, Augusta 245

Choltitz, Dietrich von 26, 27

Churchill, Winston
    confidence in victory 14
    and Operation Dragoon 44
    view of de Gaulle 29
    view of Montgomery 87–8

Collins, Joe 117, 119, 153, 156–7, 228

Cooley, Jim 231, 235

Corlett, Charles Harrison 124, 152

Corley, Colonel 136

Cota, General 80, 81, 157, 160, 162, 167

Craig, Louis A. 148

Crerar, Henry Duncan Graham 'Harry' 176, 180–1

Crittenberger, Willis D. 'Crit' 231, 232, 233

Crocker, Tallie 31
Crosby, Bing 140–1, 229
Croy, Manford 218

Dailey, Joe 31
Davis, Bill 181–4
Davis, Jimmy 237
De Bodt, Richard 66, 68, 245
De Gaulle, Charles 29, 48, 50
De Guingand, Freddie 93, 96
De Lattre, Jean 225
De Mol, Marcel 59–60
De Pauw, Louis 88, 89–91, 243
De Pauw, Petrus 90–1
Delwaide, Leon 244
Dempsey, Miles 91, 92
Dieppe 14
Dietrich, Marlene 229, 230
Dillard, Marcus 170
Doenitz, Admiral 208

Eastern Front
    Iasi–Kishinev Offensive 15–16
    war crimes in 16–17
    Warsaw uprising 194–200
Eisenhower, Dwight
    accepts Montgomery's strategy 40
    broad front strategy 9, 28
    crossing into Germany 71–2, 227
    difficulties with Patton 39–40
    disagreements over German strength
        225–6
    invasion of Ruhr Valley 122
    liberation of Antwerp 177
    Operation Market Garden 85–6, 87,
        88, 91, 103–4, 106
    style of command 28
    tensions at SHAEF 54
Elisberg, Benjamin 75

France
    Allied troops in 29–31
    control of ports 50–1
    de Gaulle's provisional government 48, 50

liberation of Le Havre 115–16
liberation of Paris 24–6, 29, 31–4
Metz assault 139–45, 222–3
Normandy Campaign 18–19, 20–1, 24
Operation Dragoon 41, 43, 44
treatment of collaborators 40–1
Vichy rule 47–50
Fries, Father 31
Frost, John 100, 101, 104

Gamelin, Maurice 47
Garnham, Les 185–8
Gavin, 'Jumping Jim' 98
Gees, Hubert 165
George VI, King 87–8
Germany
    Allies cross into 71–2, 80–1, 122
    continued advances into 222–6,
        227–8, 236
    fall of Aachen 117–20, 122–38
    Hürtgen Forest 147–74, 200–1
    infrastructure damage 209–10
    military technology 215–19
    Ruhr Valley 122
    Saar 222–6
Gerow, Leonard 81, 153, 157, 162
Gersdorff, Rudolf Christoph Freiherr von
    154–5
Gessener, Ernest 75
Ghost Army 109–15
Goering, Hermann 21, 23, 24–5
Goforth, Major 170–1
Gövert, August 119
Gruntz, Louis 143, 144–5
Guyaux, Albert 46

Hamburg 18
Hanningan, William 98
Hemingway, Ernest 171–2
Henley, Swede 170
Herbst, Hans 160–1
Hess, Grant 111, 114
Himmler, Heinrich 220, 221
Hitler, Adolf

Battle of the Bulge 206, 212, 214
confidence in victory 211–12
defence of Antwerp 175–6, 178
fall of Aachen 126, 127, 129, 132
health problems 212
and Marlene Dietrich 229
orders destruction of Paris 26
Hodges, Courtney 55, 71, 86, 120, 137, 152, 153, 156, 228
Hoekmans, Pharailde Jeanne 69–70
Hoke, Claude W. 77, 80
Holocaust, The 220–1, 244–5
Holtz, Kunigunde 133–4
Honowitz, Albert 235–6
Horrocks, Brian 44, 46, 91
Hoyer-Millar, Captain 100–1
Huebner, Clarence 130–1, 134, 135, 137
Hughes, Captain 224, 225
Hunger Winter 214–15
Hürtgen Forest 147–74, 200–1
Hutmacher, Matthias 172–3

Iasi–Kishinev Offensive 15–16
Italian campaign 15
Jackson, Andrew 200
Jamet, Fabienne 24–6
Jelinek, Ernie 53–4
jet fighters 216–19
Jordan, Chester H. 150–1
Josefson, Hyman 72

Kading, Ken 131
Katyn massacre 197
Kean, William B. 153
Keller, Lieutenant 131
Kerkhoff, Roel 96
Kittel, Heinrich 143, 145
Klinkenberg, Manfred 149
Knaack, Alfred F. 149–50
Knobelsdorff, Otto 140
Koch, Colonel 206
Koch, Oscar W. 14
Kressman, Erwin 165–6
Kunkel, John E. 229

Kwiatkowski, Slawomir 194

Le Havre 115–16
Lee, John C. H. 209
Leigh-Mallory, Leigh 18
Leonard, Turney W. 163–4
Leopold III, King 47
Letchford, Arthur 101, 102
Leyherr, Maximilian 131–2
Lobban, A.S. 216–18
Lovelady, William B. 148
Luxembourg 53–4, 72, 109–15, 120, 122

MacVane, John 31, 34
Maczek, Stanisław 193
Madison, Major 224, 225
Maginot Line 139
Marshall, George C. 177
Mason, Stanhope 129–30
Mathieson, James 238
Megallas, James 'Maggie' 97, 99
Metz 54, 139–45, 222–3
Middleton, Troy 233, 234, 236
Military Government rules 221–2
Model, Walter
    counteroffensive plan 214
    fall of Aachen 129
    Hürtgen Forest 154
    loses Luxembourg 120
    Operation Market Garden 100, 105
    replaced as commander of western theatre 14
Montgomery, Bernard Law
    liberation of Antwerp 175, 176, 177, 179, 180–1
    liberation of Brussels 46
    narrow front strategy 28, 40
    Operation Market Garden 85–8, 91, 92, 93, 96, 101, 103–4, 105, 106
    relationship with Churchill 87–8
    tensions at SHAEF 54, 55
    view of German strength 225–6, 235
Morrell, Theodor 212, 213
Morris, W. H. H. 141

Mountbatten, Lord 106
Mullins, Captain 169
Murphy, Audie 44, 45
Mussolini, Benito 15
Myers, Joseph 218
Myers, Sergeant 150

Netherlands
    Allied advance 189–90, 193, 214
    collaborators in 101–3
    German retreat from 36–7
    Hunger Winter 214–15
    Operation Market Garden 85–8,
        91–101, 103–7, 122, 193–4
    return of monarchy 47
    starvation in 192, 214–15
    transportation of Jews 37
    war crimes in 191
Nichols, Don 224–5
Normandy Campaign
    bombing of Caen 18–19, 24
    casualties from 21, 23
    damage to towns in 24
    German retreat 20–1
Notman, Allan 179–80

Operation Calendar 190
Operation Cobra 28
Operation Dragoon 41, 43, 44
Operation Goodwood 28
Operation Infatuate 189–90
Operation Market Garden 85–8, 91–101,
    103–7, 122, 193–4
Operation Switchback 184–8
Operation Wellhit 170–1

Panter, Charles 100–1
Paris
    Allied troops in 29
    liberation of 31–4
    under German occupation 24–6
Patch, Alexander 225
Patton, George S.
    concerns over Ardennes 222

confidence in victory 14
crossing into Germany 71, 72, 225
and Ghost Army 115
and Marlene Dietrich 229, 230
Metz assault 54, 139, 140, 144, 222–3
Operation Dragoon 43
Operation Market Garden 86, 106
relationship with other generals
    39–40, 55
view of German strength 14
Petacci, Claretta 15
Petain, Phillipe 47, 48
Pettinger, Christian 114–15
Plomion massacre 35–6
Poland 194–200
Pugh, Captain 163, 164

Reitner, Frau 16–17
Renner, Simon 97
Reynolds, Harley 122
Ribbentrop, Joachim von 20, 243
Ribbentrop, Rudolf von 20–1, 243
Riesman, Donald 75
Roberts, William L. 224
Roosevelt, Franklin D. 23, 44
Rowecki, General 194
Rundstedt, Gerd von 14, 107, 126,
    129, 214
Ryan, Cornelius 96

Saar 222–6
Salinger, J.D. 171–2
Schack, August 117
Schaerlaecken, Francois 36, 63, 65, 243
Schaffner, John 234–5
Scheldt, Battle of the 179–88
Schmidt, General 164
Schmitt, Phillip 63, 64, 65, 68
Schneider, George 60–3, 237, 243
Schreiber, Alfred 218
Schwerin, Gerhard Graf von 120, 121,
    125, 127, 129–30, 136
Searching for Augusta 245
Shore, Dinah 141

Siegfried Line 77, 78–9, 80, 81, 118, 119, 124–5, 137
Sikorski, General 194
Silvertop, David 57, 58
Simonds, Guy 180
Simpson, William Hood 228
Slovik, Eddie 226
Sosabowski, Stanisław 105–6, 193
Speer, Albert 210
Stalin, Joseph 15, 197, 226
Stauffer, Carlton 30–1
Stimson, Henry L. 223
Stone, Ed 140–1
Stopczynski, Ted 196
Strong, Kenneth William Dobson 205, 206
Supreme Headquarters Allied Expeditionary Force (SHAEF)
    acknowledgment of set–backs 153
    advance into Germany 227–8, 236
    Battle of the Bulge 209
    confidence in victory 9, 14, 40, 120, 209
    disagreements over German strength 225–6, 237
    intelligence gathering 204–6
    Military Government rules 221–2
    supply deliveries 208
    tensions in 54

Taylor, George A. 136
Todt Organization 14–15
Tournai 14
Towers, Frank 200, 243

ULTRA 204–7
Urquhart, General 97

V–2 rockets 238–41
Vekemans, Robert 56–7, 59
'Vera' 55–6
Vichy France 47–50
Vitchock, John R. 163

Walker, General 143
Walker, Walton 233

Wall, A.E. 216–18
war crimes
    by Allied troops 29–30
    at Breendonck prison camp 63–71, 245
    on Eastern Front 16–17
    Holocaust 220–1, 244–5
    in Italy 191–2
    in Netherlands 191
Warren, John 105
Warsaw 194–200
Westerman, Robert 168–9
Wilck, Gerhard 129, 132, 134, 136
Wildermuth, Eberhard 116
Wilhelmina, Queen 47
Williams, Brigadier 205
Williams, Harold 124
Wyss, Fernand 65–6, 68, 243, 245
Yuill, Charles 140
Zangen, Gustav-Adolf von 87

PICTURE CREDITS

Alex Ramael, Boom Town Hall Culture Secretary: 58, 69

Getty Images: 32, 45, 78, 93, 94, 112, 135, 159, 232

Martin King: 62, 64, 99, 102, 239

National Archives and Records Administration, USA: 172

Public Domain: 19, 25, 27, 42, 49, 61, 67, 70, 89, 121, 123, 128, 155, 161, 167, 187, 198, 213, 230

The Memory Project: 181

United States Army, 10th Armored Division: 142